Scales of the Heart

www.scalesoftheheart.com

Lady Joy Justice

WESTBOW·
PRESS
A DIVISION OF THOMAS NELSON
& ZONDERVAN

Scripture quotations taken from the Holy Bible, New Living Translation, Copyright © 1996, 2004. Used by permission of Tyndale House Publishers, Inc., Wheaton, Illinois 60189. All rights reserved.

Scripture taken from the New King James Version. Copyright © 1979, 1980, 1982 by Thomas Nelson, Inc. Used by permission. All rights reserved.

WestBow Press books may be ordered through booksellers or by contacting:

WestBow Press
A Division of Thomas Nelson & Zondervan
1663 Liberty Drive
Bloomington, IN 47403
www.westbowpress.com
1 (866) 928-1240

ISBN: 978-1-4908-7058-8 (sc)

Library of Congress Control Number: 2015902676

Print information available on the last page.

WestBow Press rev. date: 7/13/2015

Contents

Book Overview

The churches recorded in the New Testament were known for their strengths and others for their weaknesses. The church has been given authority by God, yet the church is not the final authority. Christ himself is the final authority according to Matthew 28:18 which says that Jesus came and told his disciples, "I have been given all authority in heaven and on earth. Therefore, go and make disciples of all the nations, baptizing them in the name of the Father and the Son and the Holy Spirit. Teach these new disciples to obey all the commands I have given you. And be sure of this: I am with you always, even to the end of the age." One of the most prolific deposits into my existence as a believer in Jesus Christ imparted by my spiritual father is not just to know the Word of God, but to know the God behind the Word. Today many call on the name of Jesus knowing his word substantially, but it has been discovered surprisingly that in addition to being familiar with the word of God, they are not familiar with knowing the person of God himself, the God behind the Word, who inspired those recorded in the word, who wrote the word, and those who shall live by the word of God. God's word is extremely vital to the life of the believer, yet God does not desire for us to worship the word as a book, but him as the living word made flesh only. Christians are different from Muslims in the fact that Muslims are the "people of the book". Believers in Christ are not people of the book, but people filled with the very Holy Spirit of God that dwells inside of them, the same spirit that executes the word or the book of God and makes it alive and active. Since the beginning of time in the Garden of Eden good and evil existed in the tree of the knowledge of good and evil, after the fall nothing has changed, good and evil still exists, but instead of existing in a tree it exists in the hearts and nature of human beings. God's scales of justice are always weighing good and evil hearted people with results that deliver in due season. If we anticipate restoring order within the body of Christ it is imperative to understand that godly order starts in the heart of individuals. For true authority from God comes from purity in heart. If the order is not correct in the heart, it surely will not manifest within the church or any other area of one's life. Scales of the Heart is a read that brings the believer back to walking with the God behind the word, that perhaps have drifted into religiosity and it introduces those who only know the word as a book, to the God behind the word. One of God's most interesting actions is that God weighs the hearts of men, every second, every minute, every hour, and every moment of time. The heart is mentioned at least 762 times in the Bible. This book comes from the perspective of a sheep that has been raised in church all of her life. It is not a perspective on changing what the word of God says or any order of the church whatsoever, it is a perspective that God has illuminated to one of his daughter's for the sole destined purpose of health restored in our local church bodies. According to Proverbs 15:11 death and destruction lie open before the Lord, how much more the hearts of humans! One key factor God always considers when dealing with the sons of men is something most church people tend to forget, and that is even the godliest saints are finite, capable of error. How do you represent a perfect God and a perfect Kingdom living in a world born into sin, with a sin nature imparted to you, that must die daily after being born again of the Spirit of God and water as indicated in John 3:5? It is very true that the greatest testimony of Jesus Christ is one's life lived, however this does not mean that there were not mistakes ever present in that life lived. Sadly this has been religiously taught to many, who as a result give up pressing on in Christ as they are being disqualified by mortal men. Christ is the supreme justice for people; the Lord weighs the hearts of men that determine how the scales of justice play out in the lives of people. He that has an ear to hear, let him hear what the Spirit of God is saying to the churches.

Book Dedication

To the greatest teacher of my life, my Lord and Savior Jesus Christ! You are the one who keeps me, carries me, covers me, provides for me, teaches me, walks with me, talks with me, open doors for me, closes doors for me, rescues me from hell, high water, myself, others, favors me, died on a cross for me, was buried for me, rose up from the grave for me, preparing a place for me, and who is interceding for me right now! You are the love of my life. My reasonable portion is that I will praise you and worship you with my life! I have taken what you have conceived in my spiritual womb, and I have formed and composed that which you have called me to do for the healing and health of your bride, the church of Jesus Christ. With the help of your Holy Spirit this baby is now birthed out! After much turmoil in my own soul that you could even, and would even, use a young black lady from the hood who is no high clergy official, for such an assignment, I finally yielded to this assignment with the attitude of Esther; for if I perish, I perish. No, I am not a PK (Preacher's Kid), no, I don't come from a long line of pastors, preachers, teachers, ministers, or lay people (a few far off and between generations ago), however this assignment just didn't seem right for someone like me, so I thought. Nonetheless, I am just a daughter of the most High God El Elyon! Father, thank you, that when you look at me you don't see the flaws and mistakes that others perhaps may see, but you see me as the righteousness of Christ. You saw the best in me! Thank you for the blood of Jesus that washes all my sins away, and makes me white as snow, justifying me before the Father. I believe that you saw this assignment on my life before I was yet born. Despite the wrong turns in life that I have taken, you have always been faithful to my first prayers as a child to never let me wander too far away from you. Thank you for seeing the best in me, and I am forever grateful to you! I am forgetting those things that lie behind and I press on towards the high calling of Jesus Christ. Jehovah Rohi! You are truly the Lord God my shepherd and I love you!

Acknowledgements

I would like to acknowledge those individuals that God uses as instruments in my life for teaching, cultivating, feeding, undergirding, loving and covering me.

To my Bishop and spiritual father. Thank you for introducing me to the greatest man of all, Jesus Christ! I strive to be more like Jesus each and every day of my life, and aim to be like him more than anyone, but I'd be lying if I didn't admit that I picked up your spirit. If we could do a DNA test in the spirit to identify our spiritual parents, you'd absolutely test positive for being my daddy! What a privilege and honor it was as a girl and young lady to tag along and follow you, growing and maturing in my young life, over time I have become more aware of the impartation and mantle that I have been blessed to sit under and glean from since childhood. Looking back, I had no idea what God would do through my testimony, but I remember your teachings in that anytime God wanted to usher in his next work within a generation he always used a woman to do it. What an encouragement, especially in traditional and patriarchal settings where women are not always received well when it comes to addressing leadership. You have made it difficult for me to become accustomed to just any spiritual meal as my spirit has been exposed to an acquired taste early on, and that is the non-adulterated piercing Word of God! You have taught me to know God for myself according to his word and how he reveals himself to me as I am that I am! To know the God behind the word and to be ever so careful in what I agree with, and not to agree with something just because the majority does, but to study the word for myself. You also helped me to get in touch with how I have come to know God which is the wild side of God that is rarely ever discussed or mentioned. Thank you, because of this I have come to know Christ, and not just knowing about him. You have taught me to recognize the Lord and his personality and characteristics throughout the Word of God and in my life, and he is greater than his word as he is the living word himself. Yes he is immutable, but God is the God behind the word. Not only am I a soul saved on your watch, but I am a life changed and a life saved for the glory of God.

First Lady Bishop would certainly be responsible for the influence of "What you see, Is what you get!" You have laid an unshakable foundation for me that I will carry and pass on to everyone I am given the opportunity to do so. You are authentic shepherds! Thank you for starting and continuing Logos Bible Institute where I had the opportunity to learn good sound biblical teaching and doctrine through the Systematic Theology program. I am one of many spiritual fruits that you have borne, and a crown for you in Glory. I have learned so much from just watching you year after year. When the power and anointing of God rests on one's life, you don't necessarily have to walk close to them, even from a distance you will learn more from that person, than walking close with someone where no anointing is there. To my home church family, thank you for teaching me how to praise! You are certainly the tribe of Judah, praise, praise, and more praise! To my spiritual parents, I love you, and thank you for cultivating the little preacher woman in me that I always knew was down there, somewhere. Oh! And Yes Bishop! I am indeed riding that circuit riding horse!

To my spiritual advisor, friends, and prayer partners, thank you for being there for me! You are true examples of resilience and resurrection from the most disheartening of circumstances. You inspire me never to give up on myself no matter what it looks like, no matter the past, and no matter what other's opinions may be. I love and admire your uniqueness and am grateful to glean from your successes and failures knowing that God will use the most **unlikely** of people, such as myself, for destiny and purpose filled assignments for the Kingdom of God. Matthew 13:57, and Jesus said, a prophet is without honor in his own hometown. Prophet J, the way The Lord uses you to overwhelm others with significance in Christ is a blessing to His body! To God be all the Glory! To Mother Evelyn, one thing is for sure, the day after you laid your hands on me, my life has never been the same! To my prayer team! You will never know how much it means to have brothers and sisters in Christ having your back in prayer! To Mama A, what a God sent you are in my life. Thank you for always being there.

To my Apostles, thank you for feeding me good spiritual food, fresh out the slow cooker! I knew the moment I heard you preach that your congregation is benefiting from mighty good spiritual nourishment! You have no idea how your church has been a blessing to me. God bless you and your beautiful family! You all have been nothing but kind and welcoming to me and I appreciate the love of Christ extended. The anointing at this house of God is so thick, it makes one never ever want to go home! The atmosphere is saturated with the aroma of heaven. Thank you for speaking into my life and helping me stay on the narrow path that leads to eternal life. I believe with all my heart that God orchestrated my steps to your local body for the next level of my life in Christ. Dr. B, I am grateful to glean from your seasoned life in Christ as a loving Woman of God. Thank you for never putting me down, always encouraging me to be exactly who God called me to be, and encouraging me to always speak from my heart. I thank God for your mentorship and wise counsel. You both are certainly shepherds of integrity who have been nothing but ever so kind to me, and I appreciate the ongoing love you continue to pour out! I do not believe it was by coincident that I am where I am. I believe it is the exact covering I need in soon to come chapters in my life where God has called me out of my comfortable corner, to share with the world my life and testimony of how amazing God is and has been to me. What a pure house where the glory of God is manifested in every encounter!

To Mom and Dewayne. Thank you both for your ongoing support and wise guidance. I admire your entrepreneurship and class.

To my mother. To your pain, your losses, your grief, your experiences that I have witnessed firsthand. I have no idea how you are still standing with the most beautiful smile I have ever seen in my life! I am still trying to figure out how you remain filled with joy, and are so beautiful on the inside just as well as you are on the outside, with all you have been through, and all the hate and judgments that comes your way. I have watched God take care of you though it all, and one thing I am certain of, is that The Lord really loves you! I wouldn't have another mother in a million years. No matter the ups and the downs, the rights and the wrongs, the things I learned from you, I couldn't have learned them from any other woman on the face of the earth. I love you! Thank you for your support and always making a dollar out of 15 cents! You stretched what we had, and I wanted for nothing. May God bless and keep you always. I love you.

To my father. A man who is not afraid to get his hands dirty! Thank you for taking on the role of my father in life, as my biological father passed away when I was eight years old. You are and will always be my dad! You taught me how to survive, how to press on, how to ride a bike, how to drive a truck, how to fight with my mind, and my fist when I needed to, and how to fire a you know what. One thing is for sure, God certainly used your courage to instill the same in me. I have been able to walk through serious territories of my life without fear because of your overcoming attitude that I witnessed growing up. Even though it began in the physical and the natural, it transferred to the spiritual when it came time for me to do battle in heavenly places. The first car I'd learn to drive was in your Ford Pick-up truck. When I became a supervisor dispatching class A freight haulers, I'd just imagine being with my dad sitting up in his Semi-Tractor trailer cab on the road, and felt reassured during times of difficulty! You are always supportive to me, never failing. If I ever need you, it's only a matter of minutes before you are already half way to where I am. Thank you for all you have done and been to me. I love you. To my brothers and sisters, may God bless and keep you always! To my grandparents, my nieces and nephew, to my aunts, uncles, and many cousins, friends, and church family. May the peace, love, and grace of God be manifested in your lives!

About the Book

Scales of the heart was written for the present and coming generations that will be challenged in a world that is rapidly falling away. If the next generations are raised in churches today that are unhealthy and not looking to heal and recover, then sadly enough their outlook on church and perhaps God may bring our foundations down. For if the foundations are destroyed, what can the righteous do? (Psalm 11:3). The perspective of this book is to give that of a sheep's perspective. Many times we hear perspectives on church affairs from leaders, those with titles, status, and position within the body, which hold high esteem and is certainly reverenced. Nevertheless, it is rare where the voice of a sheep is heard and held in esteem regarding church affairs. Having grown up in church all my life and experiencing the great, the terrible, the exceptional, and the ugly, my soul was burdened with an assignment I believe God has called me to complete and that is writing Scales of the Heart. The intent of the book is to take its place with the remnant of believers who are standing for order and appropriation within the body of Christ, rooted and grounded in love not condemnation. The purpose of the book is to ensure that our foundations remain undestroyed. It's time that the real church, the church within the church: the remnant, began fighting to regain the health and power of the church back as we fight for the faith and for souls to be saved and lives changes so that God may be glorified. It is often assumed that only leaders can drive the church to a point of restoration and health. I agree with leaders being in place to keep watch over our souls and to guide and direct the body of Christ in addition to a grass roots movement of those who do not carry a particular church title other than membership and servant, to join in ensuring our worship places are maintained in integrity. Today, there is good teaching occurring, and the Word of God is absolutely being brought forth, however less and less of it being done in the vein that Christ desired for it to be done in, and that is in love with the right spirit behind the word being brought forth. We need to dig deeper into the issues that are arising and stop living under traditions and works of man that are not enough to advance against the dark forces of this world (Ephesians 6:10-18). Today our foundations are cracked, broken, and abridged by the obvious of divorce, homosexuality, idolatry, ignorance, and rebellion. This is what is primarily recognized across the world. Some other causes of our foundations being chiseled away at may not be as obvious, yet these not so obvious wrongs are severely contributing to the breaking down of the church's foundations. I have never walked in an organization to hear about what that place may be struggling with. Just as individuals, we often praise our positive attributes while at the same time being in denial about some of our weaknesses and things we need to work on, myself included. This could be due to a lack of transparency or this could be due to us not being able to see our blind spots, which we are not aware of until we look in the mirror or another helps us in areas we are not able to see. It's time to address issues that need to be corrected. It is often assumed that if love is extended that people will take advantage of grace resulting in living life with a license to sin. This has definitely occurred and is still happening; however there is another side of the spectrum that is not painted, and that is God's grace and love will motivate one who has had a real experience with Christ to want to get their lives in order after seeing how much Jesus loves them enough to give up His life and shed his blood! Scales of the heart will highlight on some of the obvious but more importantly on the not so obvious. Applying the advice from the book will supersede the mission to restore, repair, and refocus on present denials and blind spots. These swept under the rug situations may not be evident for the new believer, the youth, or the new church member to see, but are ever present, and playing a major factor in why our churches are struggling. It is true that false prophets come to tare down the leaders of the church and in the last days people will be rebellious toward authority speaking evil of dignitaries. Let's make this very clear, that is far from my assignment. I agree with how the format is laid in the Word of God. No, I am not a pastor or have attended to sheep for forty or fifty years, and there are things I'll never be able to empathize with or understand, however my perspective is that of a sheep's perspective, not of a high church official, but a young shepherdess called by God to love, encourage, and lead those he places within my path. Leaders often wear the hat that says we are in ministry to serve the sheep. Therefore, if that is truly the case and if sheep is the focus, why is the sheep sometimes the last to be consulted on the service being received? Jesus often asked those he ministered to, what do you want me to do for you, or what can I do for you? I'm not saying go grasp the perspectives of new believers who have no inclination on being victorious in Christ, but feedback and input from members who desire and have a calling to partner in winning souls, in addition to the established church, those that have been rooted and grounded in Christ for years have much to offer than primarily contributing in many areas other than helps, finances, and faithful attendance. You may be surprise what greatness is sitting among you that hasn't been unleashed at all that could take your ministry to the next level in Christ. One thing I've learned early is that I am not the only person who can usher in the presence of God. Sometimes this can be difficult for some anointed people to accept. God's spirit is not limited to just one person, and because he may use someone you'd never expect to move in and by the spirit of God, you don't have to be threatened. Please don't mistake hearing me say this from one who has it all together, or who has arrived. We are all students of life until we graduate to heaven. I am just imparting some things I believe God has deposited into my spirit. Please don't despise small beginnings, or sleep on the youth because God uses us all. I am not saying that I am just as processed as the believer who has been walking with Christ for forty or fifty years, however I do believe that God has done some awesome things in my life for me to tell of his goodness. We cannot help where we are with our age, therefore if you have been processed over a forty year period, glory be to God for you and your life, however my prayer is that God will hide me behind the cross so that the words that I have to share are not predicated primarily and solely upon my gender, age, and time that I have put in compared to someone who is older. How can you serve someone without knowing the needs and position of that person you are serving? We often hear the perspectives on leadership from leaders and never contemplate that a sheep can contribute or give feedback that will too be of edification in God's house. After all, regardless of position or status we are ALL sheep in the eyes of God, as we those that belong to him are all his children. What a commonality in God's sight. It can be assumed that if you speak up about something that may not be right within the church that you are trying to come against authority, when that is not always the case. However it's just like a relationship. If you refuse to discuss the issues, guess what? They won't be resolved. If only one party in the relationship is able to put out but not receive, there is no mutuality. Many can dish it out, but not take it. An equal flow of communication with distinguished roles brings peace and a healthy atmosphere. If you think each time someone is speaking up it's to discredit authority then it can leave little room for issues to be addressed, and gives the impression that if you even dare to point out a flaw in leadership that you of course are trying to deceive, attack, and dishonor those above you, when that is not always the case. It could also give the impression that you may not care, after all, love listens. Love doesn't always mean you will agree, or that you will implement suggestions, however it does communicate I care, and that you are valued. 1 Samuel 2:7 talks about how the Lord exalts and humbles. The lord gives assignments to those he chooses, and guess what, he doesn't need to stop to check in with the sons of men to see how they feel about the candidate of his choice before doing so, including those in leadership. This assignment on my life has burdened me because I am aware of the opposition that will arise from it, the misunderstandings awaiting me, and the comebacks of those who the book will hit home for, but that's okay. God has prepared me as my favorite song by Daryl Coley states. Some of the not so obvious additions we rarely openly discuss are leaders in the church that have not been processed yet, leaders who sprung up and were appointed overnight (2 Timothy 22), teachers of God's word who have not, and will not study themselves approved (2 Timothy 2:15), ministers who have been through very little and have become the focal point of what a life in Christ is supposed to look like for those who have been through very much, judgmental ministries (Matthew 7:1-5), cliques in the church (1 Corinthians 1:10), works of the flesh claiming to be God inspired and Holy Spirit led, people wanting glory for themselves and not for God (Romans 12:3), a vast number of people who are carrying titles within the church that God did not call, appoint, or anoint, we see how in God's word he called and chose specific people, while simultaneously others who were not called and appointed by God, were trying to convince many that they were God's choice. A great example is in 1 Kings 1 where Adonijah claimed the throne and some where supporting his plans to be the next King after David, however God chose and appointed Solomon in spite of what Adonijah was doing and those supporting him. Other concerns are that the enemy is enslaving people into a bondage that God never had in mind for us to be in at church (2 Corinthians 3:17, John 8:36, and Galatians 5:13-14), hidden rules that are present but not said or recorded, but understood by the notion and mentality of "this is the way we do things around here", people not operating in their God given gifts, but choosing to do what they want instead, people in the wrong ministries that has nothing to do with their calling (this isn't to say that God won't prepare and train you in various helps ministries for your purpose, because he will), everyone believing they are called to lead, teachings that do not exemplify scholarship by examining both sides or several sides of the spectrum to speak to everyone and not just the chosen or select few. More include worshipping the man of God instead of God himself, politics, politics, and more politics, ministers thinking more highly of themselves then they ought to, running the church like a business and centering things around money and not Christ who is the source, and marketing Jesus to make money. No matter how good the message and teaching is within the church, if it is being implemented with all the factors stated above, it is only just that, a good message. The real work of Christ cannot occur until we humble ourselves, come out of denial, position to get healed and healthy, and become re-established and rooted back in love with the right spirit God desires for us to have when presenting his word. Just because one is able to talk about love does not necessarily mean they are operating in love or know what it is. God is love (1 John 4:8). It is not always because people are not willing to follow God's instructions in the bible, or they don't have a desire of the things of God, or they are not filled with God's spirit that keeps them from churches. Sometimes it is what is actually being received at church or a lack thereof when it comes to love and compassion. We often mistake compassion and love for expressing "emotionalism" and in some facets of our walk our emotions must take a back seat, however compassion and love is the very essence of who God is, therefore many times he does care, he expresses compassion often by including the thoughts and desires of his children, just ask Abraham who bargained with God. God gave us emotions, they signal much, and many times they do matter to God, because you matter to God. You may be told your emotions don't matter and in some cases they don't, this is a truth, however God is mindful of man (Psalm 8:4). We are good at identifying counterfeits within the gospel, however it never dawns on us as to why flocks are herding to the counterfeits. The word of God says that the enemy deceives the entire world. What is he using to deceive, something that he knows will for sure bring in the multitudes, and that is the extending and demonstrating of LOVE. The enemy's love of course at the end of the day is no love at all as we know, however it is the bait that's being used to pull in the droves to switch things later for deception. How smart this principle is and why are the real saints of God dormant to allow the enemy to out love our brothers and sisters in Christ with deception in the end. The enemy realizes that no matter how good sound teaching is, a person is not coming to a church where love is absent. Instead they will be led somewhere they feel loved, even if it will cost them their soul, this is sad, but this is what is occurring right now! Walk into a church that is teaching false doctrine and deceiving millions and notice how everyone feels welcomed and loved. Walk into a church that is teaching nothing but God's word where the people are well taught, and of the few members there how none of them or very few of them feel loved and who are not receiving a word to where they are in life. Which place would you rather be planted? Yes I heard the mature saint say, somewhere that will hold me accountable and keep me on the narrow path. I knew you'd say that, this is why this book is written, because it may be hard to see anything other than where you are, instead of where many are falling away and headed to. You may be accustomed to a solid type of preaching where others may not be familiar or un-churched, or have never heard an unknown language, and if thrown at them without love, it may not be received and could be misunderstood for something frightening that will push away instead of drawing near. If we are fishers of men, then we must meet the fish where they are. There are many people on their way to hell because of this deception occurring and you comfortable in your walk doesn't do anything for those who God desires not to perish, and for those just starting out in the faith. God wishes that none should perish (2 Peter 3:9), but the reality is men are perishing daily in spite of God's desire. Take for instance someone who is growing in Christ, struggling and being delivered from sin and bondage, after a while they may find themselves in a congregation where the word may not be as valued, but one thing is for sure they feel loved without measure. So the question becomes, how are we allowing the devil to out love real believers filled with God's spirit whereby love is a fruit of God's spirit? The road we follow as believers is absolutely narrow and few find it, and wide is the gate to damnation according to Matthew 7:13-14, however we should not become so high and mighty where we are allowing the enemy to love more than us. Yes the enemy's love is deception, however real love will cancel that deceptive love out. Yes there are times when it's necessary to operate in "tough love". However according to 1 Corinthians 13 if you have everything else but love, you are nothing. Love is not always extended by the very entity that is to represent Christ better than anything else and that is the church. Yes we know that church is not the building, but it is you and I who are believers within the body of Christ, however when they come to the building which should never be worshipped more than Christ himself, or misunderstood to be the house of the holy spirit, because the temple and house of the holy spirit is the actual believer, the human being that is a child of God. This is not to say that there is not a saturated atmosphere or manifestations of God's presence in a building/your church, but we who have immortal souls in mortal bodies, are the church of God. So hopefully when the world comes into the church hopefully they are experiencing the real building, which is you and I which should be reflecting the love of Jesus Christ more than anything. God first drew us near with loving kindness according to Jeremiah 31:3. He also chastens his children he loves, but always note he first drew us near with loving kindness. Prayerfully people see Jesus in you because you are first loving them and drawing them near with loving kindness and not rebuking them with sorts of correction and chastening. That comes with a relationship. It is difficult to speak into the life of another when there is no relationship established or built and when correction is given in this vein it often is not received well, not due to one not wanting correction all the time. Sometimes people may feel uncomfortable receiving correction from someone they have no relationship with. This is why God does not chasten those who do not belong to him, because there is no relationship established for him to do so. Therefore if you are speaking into the lives of people, make it your goal to build a relationship so that what is being imparted can be received. Now those who just hate to receive correction, that's an issue they have to deal with themselves, however it can be a combination of many things and sometimes we just see it one way instead of several ways it could apply. Leaders have to give an account before God one day about what they preached and taught and that is real and it's understandable, but keep in mind if you fall in this category then you will also give an account on how you loved God's people as well. How do you love God's sheep? Do you define this by rebuking people and chastening them because you love them? If so, prayerfully it is being balanced by gentleness, kindness, meekness, patience, and understanding. It is one thing to have a self-perception that you may be operating in these things, yet in action have a lack of consistency with them. What mode and tone are you ALWAYS in? The consistency of tone demonstrates how loving one is. Do you often see the best in God's sheep? Or are you always noticing the negative? Does the first five to ten minutes of our interaction reflect you pointing out at least five to ten negative things you believe you see in me? This is certainly not the best way to edify. Even God himself drew all his sons and daughters near with loving kindness. There are several issues that are not always openly discussed; however the aforementioned is just an idea to give the reader some insight on topics the book will discuss. Now that the uncomfortable news has been given, here comes the great news! Get ready to be a part of the radical kingdom movement where territory will be snatched back from the enemy. After you read this book, whatever your role is in the Kingdom, please make the choice to take part in dedicating to love people a lot better moving forward, I know I have. We can do this in addition to keeping the standards of God and restoring faith and expectation to the broken who have made mistakes, and that would include us all according to Romans 3:23-24. It's time to depart from all secular, watered down, merchandising, and self-seeking glory ministries, and get ready to see the power of God manifest when we stand for truth and demand health within our local bodies. Yes sometimes tough love has to be carried out by the church, as God carried it out himself, and there are biblical references when the church must rebuke and discipline. There is still time to make repairs and restore the twenty first century church walls according to God's word and pattern, however if the ingredient of the love of Christ is missing then we are in for a rude awakening. Many people talk well of love, having absolutely no idea what it really is. They can describe it, explain it, and quote scriptures about it, however this doesn't mean they are consistent in love perhaps as they may be in other important areas. God said if you have not love, in fact everything else you are doing and saying is a noisy gong or clanging cymbal according to 1 Corinthians 13. One of the greatest blessings of my life is where I originated regarding the house of God. I can firmly say that my spiritual father loves people and goes the distance to pour out the love of Jesus Christ. Many mistake him as an intellectual analytical, yet never really knowing him beyond the surface to see the insatiable assignment to go beyond the norm to show people how much God loves and how much he has gone through to reconcile and love people who were not worthy of him without Christ. His leadership is very pure, and it's seriously rooted in the love of Jesus Christ. The majority of my life I have become accustomed to being very familiar with what pure authority is like. It doesn't always matter where you start out, just as much as where you are going is more important, yet I believe my place of origin has everything to do with the calling and purpose of the assignment God has on my life. When you come from purity and a place that is overwhelming loving, anything that is not rooted the same will stick out like a huge sore thumb. Just as those things of the spirit must be revealed by the spirit and not by flesh and blood, love also has to be revealed to a person for them to totally grasp its meaning. It is evident today that many who name the name of Christ lacks the revelation with their descriptions of love. God must be revealed for one to know who God is as one cannot know God unless God draws him (John 6:44). God is Spirit, and his Spirit must be revealed. God is love and there must also be a revelation of love. He that does not know love, does not know God. Many times love is not received from people, because no revelation of it or God is there. There is a difference between having patience with someone to love you, verses love never being there. It grieves me to hear excellent teaching on spiritual matters when love is nowhere in the picture. Is it possible for a minister to preach on love and sound like the farthest thing from it while preaching it? If you answered yes to this, my point is proven. This book is for believers of the Christian faith primarily. Whether you are a pastor or first lady, preacher, ministry worker or leader, a believer in Christ, a church member, a teacher of God's word or someone looking for the right church home. This book is for you. When we stand before God almighty we won't be standing before him with any titles given to us by mortal men. If you think you will stand before God as Prophet this or Evangelist that, you are in for a very rude awakening. It's an honorable thing now days to walk around advising that you are a shepherd. Hopefully that shepherd hood doesn't model some twenty first century relationships with Christ that are projected, and that is people advising they are walking with Christ yet barely knowing Him. If you are a shepherd how well do you know your sheep? If God almighty cares intimately about his people in every area of their lives, who are you to not want to do the same as you are his representation in being mindful of them just as God is? God not only helps us by leading, guiding, and directing us, but he loves us and his concerned about our entire being. We should also reflect this in our relationships as we are to love one another and to treat others as we would want them to treat us. Yes, the package of the message is delivered like the mail man drops the package off and keeps moving and that's real, yet God does more than deliver packages to his people, he desires to walk and talk with his children and he desires intimate fellowship, being mindful of mortal men, if we are to look like Jesus are we to negate these actions of his after just dropping off the package? I know we as humans are limited in some areas as we are not God, but we can do all things through Christ who strengthens us. In days to come, many people will refuse choosing to make Christ Jesus Lord of their lives not because there is not accurate penetrating teaching, but simply because the church is not doing a good job of digging deep enough into the issues of life, and have moved away from love to instead condemn or is encouraging living life up to the fullest by taking advantage of grace doing whatever one wishes which both are major extremes. This is not to negate the fact that the church will be judged first because it will be according to God's word. It was Mahatma Gandhi who said I was very close to actually becoming a believer in Christ because of the great teaching and revelations, however what held him back was the way he was treated by those who said they were Christians, needless to say love was the last thing he experienced. If we continue to deal with situations on the surface never understanding all the important elements of the fall of man, how God really loves people, and at the same time how God has limits and acts on those limits, how people are free moral agents and their hearts are weighed by God daily, our churches will remain sick, toxic, and unhealthy. Yes the church is indeed a hospital for sick people, but who wants to come to a foul polluted toxic fish bowl to get healed? When you are inside of a dirty fish bowl you don't recognize how unclean it is because you are inside of it. The only way to see it's unhealthy is to step outside the fish bowl and look at it in this perspective. This is what happens at many organizations, the people don't even recognize the filth of the fish bowl they are in, because that's where they live. Any doctor or nurse that would work on another should have hands that are at least clean and sterilized, not necessarily perfect or without flaws, but healthy! The reality that the church is filled with people, and where ever you have people, you will have issues and a mess, as people will be forever imperfect, is acknowledged and a reality, but it is not an excuse to continue unhealthy practices giving the enemy access into our churches where many are falling through the cracks. Prayerfully this book will help with a sought out answer, a better understanding of God's intents from the beginning compared to today's day and age where He is using it all for the good of those who love the Lord, and the called according to his purpose. This book is designed to give insight on the person of God and how he operates and handles situations for His name sake. The goal is to have every believer and local body examine itself, as we are to examine ourselves as individuals in the Lord (2 Corinthians 13:5, Lamentations 3:40). Any areas that could use repentance and open heart surgery for healing and wholeness is highly encouraged for the present and future generations to honor, worship, and praise the Lord freely in our assembling together. There are areas in all of our personal lives that could use repentance and improvement so it is with local church bodies. First, in order to make the first steps, the spirit of pride, arrogance, and self-righteousness must be done away with and replaced with real humility, and an ear to hear what the Spirit of God is saying to the churches. He that hath an ear to hear, let him hear (Mark 4:23, Mark 4:9, Matthew 11:15, Revelation 2:29, Revelation 2:17). Now here is the question that comes, Lady Joy, who in the world are you to tell anyone what they or it should or shouldn't be doing? I'm glad you asked. Wouldn't it make more sense for a high church official to write such a book? Perhaps to man, yes, but God chooses the foolish things in that he will be the only one to receive all the glory. During my meditation time prior to me writing the book, I kept hearing God say "I am tired of my officials interceding glory that belongs to me. No more, no more, no more." God gave me the revelation that he is using the **unlikely** in the last days, the only prerequisite God needs is a pure heart. I am just a young lady who followed a real rare shepherd most of my life and have watched, learned, and gleaned from how to operate an excellent ministry within the body of Christ. I have studied myself approved. I may not have a Doctorate yet in Divinity, however I have learned from awesome spirit filled mentors, teachers, and believers. I intend to follow in my spiritual father's footsteps. He began preaching and teaching before anyone ever licensed him, before a title was given to him, before he received any notoriety or recognition, they had to track him down and tell him, those things were "required" for him to do what God had already trained, equipped, and prepared him to do before any man knew it. He sat in his congregation for years as a brother and saint in the body as a young man who had the gift of preaching from God and no one knew he could even preach. He was just a young man to them trying to learn the things of God, yet did they know in addition to his growing, there was some awesome gifts that God deposited into him. He wasn't given the opportunity really to preach until he stepped out on faith and started his own church. To God be all the glory for my Bishop's life and testimony!

To my Apostle! You are correct. God always makes the man before he makes the ministry. Moses was made before he was sent on assignment as was Joseph. Thank you for speaking life over me and encouraging me to stay faithful in what God is calling me to do without worrying about having all the qualifications. As I walk by faith whatever "qualifications" God sees fit for me, won't help but find me along the way, and even if they don't, to rest in assurance that I followed the voice of the Lord regardless of the many challenges and oppositions that will arise. The deposits you are making in my life has caused me to mature in my walk with Christ, I appreciate you more than you will ever know! God bless you and your loving family!

About the Author

Lady Joy grew up participating in Cheerleading, Student Council, The Newspaper Staff, and DECA (Distributive Educational Clubs of America) where she won local and placed in state competitions. She received the National Career Education and Academic Ambassador Award for DECA her senior year of high school. She also had the opportunity of studying English and Art History abroad in Rome, Florence, Sorrento, Capri, and Rhodes, Italy and Delphi and Athens Greece in addition to several Greek islands. In Europe she had the opportunity to visit several landmarks such as the Sistine Chapel, Vatican, Colosseum, Naples and Pompeii, Trevi Fountain, Forum Pantheon, Apostle Paul's Mamertine prison, Arch of Titus and Constantine, Art of Florence, Acropolis, Oracle of Delphi, Islands of Capri, Crete, Rhodes, and Patmos where John wrote the book of Revelation. She is also a retired cheerleading coach. Currently she is in Ministry School to further cultivate the calling to ministry upon her life. Lady Joy graduated with a Bachelor's Degree in Business and Organizational Communication, a minor in Family Development, and a certification in Parent and Family Education. She was chosen for one of the top ten internships in the United States of America: Northwestern Mutual Financial Network after an extensive competitive process. Lady Joy also completed a three year program earning her certification in Systematic Theology from Logos Bible Institute, whereby she is certified to rightly divide the Word of Truth. She has completed training on every doctrine of the Bible. Upon completing ministry school she aspires to further her education in the area of Divinity, Women's studies, and Biblical Counseling. She desires to walk in her calling to co-lead as a woman to assist the men of God in the body of Christ and equip others with the word of God, in a healthy manner that God would desire for his children rooted and grounded in love, whether that is in a business format, Christian setting, or even starting her own business or ministry. She believes that her place within the home is very vital as a woman as God created women to aide men and co-lead according to Genesis 1:28. God's instruction to both Adam and Eve was to be fruitful and multiply and to subdue, conquer, reign, take dominion over the earth. She believes that God originally intended for men and women to lead together, however in different roles in the uniqueness of how each is created with the man taking the role as the head and covering over the woman and family according to the instructions given by Paul in 1 Corinthians 11:3. She does not agree with the ideology of the patriarchal perspective that the bible was written from and that is "women are nothing but property". Jesus often showed special love to women and had assignments for them just as God did in the beginning before the fall. Lady Joy encourages all women to carry out their home responsibilities, but hopes and prays that they are not afraid of the calling of God within. Especially in these last days, God is certainly using women more so than ever! She understands that this looks different for each woman as it relates to what God is calling her to do. The author is a member of BPW (Business and Professional Women: bpwfoundation.org.) BPW was founded by the War Department of the USA and was one of the original backers of the child labor laws, and among the first of the women's organizations to endorse the Equal Rights Amendment in 1973, BPW has been a leader in passing much of the nation's landmark civil and women's rights legislation including the Women's Business Ownership Act, the Child Care Act of 1991, the Civil Rights Act of 1964, the Equal Pay Act, Title 4, and the Equal Opportunity Act. She is a member of the Godhead International Prayer Ministry. The ministry is composed of New Men in Christ Fellowship, Jesus Women, Youth of Excellence and The Anointed Children of Jesus Women Fellowship. Jesus women are founded on the scripture John 20:18. For Jesus women, have seen the Lord! The Godhead International Prayer ministry appoints one prayer field per country to dedicate and represent that particular country for the ministry and in 2014 her church was the appointed prayer field for The United States of America, where her spiritual leaders oversee the USA for Godhead International. She has experienced the global convocation held in Abuja, Nigeria where she has been challenged even more so to ensure that God remains at the center of her life. She has served in several church ministries such as Intercessory Prayer and Prophetic experiencing the Annual International House of Prayer Movement in Kansas City Missouri, Altar, Nursery, Young Adult Ministry, Teaching Team, and of course her passion: a variety of women's ministries locally and nationally. Lady Joy is primarily called to minister to broken women, in addition to whatever else the Holy Spirit assigns to her for the Kingdom of God. The author has obtained several awards from public speaking and writing competitions, but is more concerned with you learning who she is as a result of the amazing grace of God as she has faced loss, grief, divorce, brokenness and restoration in Jesus Christ. She is transparent with her life that many will see and know that if God did it for her, he can do it for you!

Lady Joy was raised Baptist as a child and later transitioned to a non-denominational church. Here she was provided with a very solid biblical foundation and the love of Jesus Christ. She began walking with The Lord at the age of ten. It wasn't until she went to a youth retreat, where the pastor at that time delivered the Word of God. During her years of adolescents she broke her fellowship with God and tried to conform to the world running from her calling. She finally realized that nothing including herself could keep her from the call and purpose that God has on her life. No matter the hang-ups, wrong choices and mistakes, God has made it clear through miracles, signs, and wonders that no matter which way she turned the call on her life cannot be stopped. The Holy Spirit eventually guided her back to her first love, Jesus Christ at the age of twenty where she rededicate her entire life back to Christ. God began doing a serious work in her. Yes she was saved at an early age but it wasn't until the age of twenty when she became spirit filled and underwent the transformation process of her life. Lady Joy is not someone who desires to hide or cover up her past or mistakes. She is a very transparent authentic believer. She has a passion for hurting people who have no voice in organizational settings. No matter what page of life someone may be on, Lady Joy wants them to know that God has an assignment for you that no eye has seen, no ear has heard, neither has it entered into the heart of man, the things that God has prepared for those that love Him, and you don't have to be fifty or sixty years old for our God to use you, although certain levels of use require a process! She often calls God her page flipper, because often times she has experienced him flipping the pages of her life like a book. She encourages people not to get hung up on the page or chapter of life they may be on because God will certainly flip the page! Through all of her imperfections, one thing is for sure! Lady Joy never stopped loving Jesus! Her number one heart's desire has always been, and still is to please Christ. She ultimately chose Him over everything the devil tried to replace Jesus with in her life, unhealthy relationships, groups, clubs, position, status, popularity, lavish living and much more. She is walking by faith that her latter will be much greater than her past. Today nothing holds her back from her God given assignments, gifts, and talents as she is striving to pour her life out as an offering unto God. She strives to hear well done, good and faithful servant, enter into my joy! (Matthew 25:21-23). Her favorite bible passages are Ecclesiastes chapter 3, as it depicts that there is a time for everything, Hebrews 11, the faith hall of fame, Matthew 5:8 (Blessed are the pure in heart, for they shall see God), Luke 23:34 Father forgive them for they know not what they do, and the tax collectors prayer in Luke 18:9-14, and Matthew 11:25, in that God hides mysteries from the wise and prudent and reveals them to the simple. She has accepted the notion that the devil is a lie, and wants nothing more than for her to keep her mouth closed and conform to any teaching that will label her if she indeed speaks up and out for those without a voice. The enemy thought that broken fellowship with God as a teen, and a disheartening divorce would make her keep her mouth shut when the time came for her to execute this assignment; however he's in for a rude awakening. This has been something she has had to accept over time. Today she is very comfortable with who she is in being different that the crowd. Her favorite songs are He's preparing me by Daryl Coley, Peace Recitation by Juanita Bynum, and Army by Betsy Walker. Soaking in The Lord's presence is one of her favorite delights. Lady Joy is still growing, maturing, and has certainly not obtained it all, or arrived, but she is very wise for her age and has been through a lot. She has a desire to see people set free from bondages of all kinds. She has a preach in her soul and genuinely loves people! She is in high favor and agrees with the word of God, the church, ministry; Godly leadership rooted in love, being under authority that is not abused, and encourages every believer to be an active member of a local congregation. Lady Joy supports education, training, development, and equipping for the God given call in the lives of all God's children. She is in favor of healthy relationships, suffering with perspective, and enjoying life! She is grateful for the many chances that God has extended to her, and how he just won't give up on Lady Joy!

Written by Victoria Michelle-Mother of Lady Joy Justice

A Note from the Author

It is my prayer that Yes! I, a "nobody" with people, but a "somebody" with The Lord can enhance and recover the health of the corporate church, the body of Jesus Christ with a sheep's perspective. If I am talked about so be it, if they slander or ridicule me so be it, nevertheless I know I will be helping that minister, that woman, that child, that first lady, that church member, or new church member who is silently screaming in the middle of a church service for help, but no one notices or even cares to pay attention because everybody is too busy "having church". If the book helps no one in this present generation, which I believe it will, I am certain it will be a great tool for the future generations to understand that history often repeats itself if not corrected. It is my prayer that what the enemy would have typically gotten away with; He won't stand a chance the next time around as the hearts of men are being turned back to the father who is in heaven, that in it's pure state. It's time for open heart surgery! I remember a time where I used to try to meet the mark by doing so very much. Oh how I have learned that all that I am and all that I ever shall be is only, only, only, only, by the grace of God! There is nothing in and of myself that has brought me thus far but the help of the Lord who is with me. My latter will be greater than my past and it's not because of me doing everything right, I cannot take credit for anything, but it is so that no one else can ever get the glory from my life, my testimony, and my victories except the Lord Jesus Christ! If you think your life is in shambles be aware that you are a candidate that God can and will use so that God alone will receive the glory and honor due his name. And they shall say…..it had to have been God alone! It shall come to pass! I also want to strongly stress that what is written in this book does not in any way reflect any leaders or people in my current or home church as I would not be a Holy Spirit filled focused believer in Christ without their leading, guiding, cultivating, planting, and overwhelming love that has never failed. Do not make the mistake of believing that this book is exposing anyone particular, it's not! All of what is written are based off of true testimonies that have impacted several family members and friends of mine in addition to some of my personal testimonies, which several believers can relate to. The purpose is to state what occurred for the intent to bring restoration, health, and resetting in broken areas of the lives of God's servants, including my own. It is my prayer that you don't see me, but that Christ would hide me behind His cross as you read Scales of the Heart, in that you may know me not according to the flesh, but according to the Spirit of God. If my life ended today, I would know in my knower, in the inner most depths of my being, that I followed the Lord's instruction regarding this assignment, and that many believers today will be edified by the book, especially those who are on their way out of darkness into the marvelous light of God. The church of Jesus Christ awaits you to take your place as we celebrate you like the prodigal son in Luke 15! There is a robe, a ring, and sandals for you!

Introduction

I once heard an evangelist make the argument that the best teacher in life is not experience. That the best teacher in life is learning from someone else's experience. For example, if you did drugs and your life fell apart after you began to do drugs, the moral of the story is that "I don't have to do drugs to learn what you learned", I can just learn from listening and looking at what happened to you. Another example of this would be, marrying the wrong person. The moral of the story is that I don't have to go through a divorce to learn the lesson you learned, "I can just listen and look at what happen to you". By all means, the argument is absolutely true in the fact that learning from another person's experience is a good teacher; in fact it's a great teacher! However it's certainly not the **best** teacher. Be careful when you make this teacher your teacher all the time. It can have a tendency to make you look better, smarter and holier by making some else look the opposite. It can make you appear to be the hero of the story, and the person you learned it from to be the fool as if you've never made a mistake. It can disclose one's severe lack of experiences or inability to relate, including the most important experience one could ever have that we shall further discuss (salvation). Therefore, listening and looking at someone else's experience is **not** the best teacher. So what is the best teacher? Experience? Experience is also a good teacher; in fact it's a great teacher! Let's look at the analogy of a jeweler who is around real diamonds all day every day. The jeweler is on vacation in a city where no one knows that he is a jeweler. Someone comes up to him trying to sell a beautiful five carat diamond. The jeweler just laughs because immediately he recognizes that the diamond is no diamond at all, but a counterfeit. The man trying to sell to the jeweler can't figure out why he's not buying it. The jeweler finally gives in and tells him, I've worked at the jewelry store for over forty years and I can spot a counterfeit a mile away. How can he do this? Certainly not by observing or learning from someone else's experience, but because he experienced working with diamonds everyday all day. Experience is a teacher that tends to leave its mark on you and it sticks with you a little closer than learning from another person's experience. But it too, is **not** the best teacher. So which is the **greater** teacher?

As I began to embark upon my life, the good, the bad, and the ugly, I recalled a dream I had at a critical time in my life. In the dream my spiritual father was demonstrating to me in the Spirit how to mantle a big blue horse with a cross on it. He kept telling me don't look to the left, and don't look to the right, but look straight ahead and don't pick up anything fake, but hold fast onto the voice of the Lord, and he kept exaggeratingly yelling as the horse took off with me on it ahead of him "Ride that Horse!" This is the man that God used to usher and birth me into the Kingdom of God, who taught me from a youth like a good father teaches his children, and as a good shepherd teaches his sheep. Jesus, the ultimate teacher who came into my life at the age of ten made all those seeds, along with others many have planted and watered actually grow, blossom, and reproduce. The Holy Spirit began to reveal truths unto me that many so called radical believers today wouldn't dare challenge out of fear, but perfect love casts out fear. After the Holy Spirit did an unexpected work in my Spirit and soul that interrupted my plans and timeline, there was nothing left to do but follow the instructions freely, without worry, or concern. The safety of status quo, pleasing others, and trying to fit in were no longer relevant in my life. Instead my spirit reaches heavenward with the thirst of hearing well done thou good and faithful servant, enter into my joy. The challenge of most of our lives is obeying what God says to do in spite of the push back, opposition, and judgments that will follow. Nevertheless, this assignment was instructed to me by God to go where angels tread to go. What challenge is that you ask? Well, try this on for size....I say try this on for size referring to experience....because in order to try something on, one must experience trying it on.....and not observing only. For example, if you want to know how armor feels on you, there is no way you can know this by hearing about it or observing someone else, you have to try it on for yourself. As I stand in a counter culture position against many popular teachings today to uncover truth which is not attractive or the majority's opinion, I am trusting the Lord as I complete this assignment.

The most important asset that a person has on earth is their relationship with Jesus Christ. Having a relationship with Jesus Christ is by far the last thing on earth that one can ever learn from another person's experience. There are many people today that name the name of Christ and claim to have a relationship with him, but have not experienced Him. Instead they are carrying out a dangerous instruction of merely going by other people's experiences with Jesus. A real believer, those who worship God in spirit and in truth have one fundamental truth, and that truth is that no matter how great of a teacher it is to learn from someone else's experience, you can never in all the earth have a relationship with the son of the living God by listening and looking at someone else's experience. Sorry my friend.....you must EXPERIENCE Jesus for yourself!.....On that day the Lord said: many will come to me saying Lord Lord I prophesied in your name, cast out demons in your name, and performed miracles in your name etc. etc....but I will in return say depart from me you evil worker of iniquity for I never **knew** you. You cannot know someone based off another person's experience, you have to know them from experiencing them yourself. It's easy for someone to say you can learn from someone else's experience in the area of knowing Christ, if they have been operating in their very own relationship with Christ off of the experience of others, and not their own, a dangerous ground to be on. Yet they may have thought it was okay to go by someone else's experiences to apply it to their lives because they may have been taught this in one capacity, however they were left high and dry because they were not taught that there is wisdom to know and operate in what's best.... In order **to know** someone you must experience them....as a man in the bible would sleep with or have sexual relations with a woman it came about not by him looking and listening to someone else know her....but he knew her personally....because he experienced her.....this is the same application regarding the Holy Spirit. It is very easy for someone who does not know Christ nor who is filled with God's spirit, nor has had real life experiences, to miss the fact that beside the greatest asset on earth: which is one's relationship with Jesus Christ, the next greatest asset in this life that will help you like no other is the person of the Holy Spirit, and being filled with this spirit. One could never learn what it is like to be filled with God's spirit merely on the basis of you looking and listening to someone else's experience. No my friend, it is by experiencing the in dwelling filling of the Holy Ghost, that one can truly understand this truth. If there is one thing that my spiritual father has taught me it is certainly to be a scholar, not just for the sake of obtaining information, but to win souls for the glory of God. A scholar dissects both sides of the story, and cannot leave the reader or audience in limbo by just sharing one particular side. So to answer the initial question at hand which is the greater teacher? We shall exceed those expectations! Listening to another person's experiences so that you can learn from their successes and mistakes? Yes it's a great teacher, but definitely **not** the best teacher. Having gone through the experiences yourself? Yes it's certainly a great teacher! However it too is **not** the best teacher. The answer is that the best teacher is Jesus Christ Himself, as He is the one who determines which method to use in your life for the situations at hand. For example in one's lifetime, God may have used experience to teach his beloved child many lessons that perhaps, learning from another person's experience wouldn't have been sufficient, such as knowing him and being filled with his spirit. Perhaps God used "experience" 200 times in one's life before he or she went home to Glory. In retrospect, perhaps God used "learning from another person's experience" 200 times in the same individual's life before he or she went home to Glory. God used both methods in the same individual's life to teach that person what that person needed to learn depending on what it was. Say they had 400 life lessons, and both methods were used at different ages and seasons in the person's life. One was not greater or better than the other, nevertheless one may have been **more important** than the other depending on what was at hand. For example, is salvation at hand? Well of course one will need to personally accept and **experience** Christ for themselves. No matter if a thousand people gave their testimonies to that person so that person could learn from their relationship with God, it is not the same as the individual experiencing and knowing the only begotten son of God. Jesus didn't say know me through other's experiences, he said know me for yourself.

Is making bad choices at hand? Learning from someone else's bad choices or even good choices is a great teacher to guide someone down a better or similar path! Is divorce at hand? Learning from another's experience can be a great teacher depending on those variables that we will discuss through particular parts of the book. If that person could learn from someone else's experiences not to marry the wrong person, that will save them a lifetime of regret and agony, however due to choices, sin, the fall of man, and much more, experiencing a bad marriage and divorce could be the experience it may have taken to get a person to a certain point so that God can use it for their good and his glory. Some may argue that marrying the wrong person or divorce didn't have to happen that it was a mess created. I beg to differ as I have walked a mile in both shoes and have experienced perhaps what the one disagreeing with me has not. This will also be discussed in later chapters. Who is to decide for each person's story? God can and will use both methods to help his children in learning the lessons which are sometimes unique and personal in the lives of those that belong to him. So that's just it. Experience is a great teacher, and so is learning from someone else's experiences, but the best teacher is Jesus and Him being Lord/Adonai of your life choosing which to select. Just for the sake of my thesis did I use these two particular teachers of life.

Scales of the Heart is **NOT** a church or leadership bashing book! In fact, I believe one of the most beautiful, honorable and powerful things on earth is the church of Jesus Christ. I do have the undesirable assignment on my life that involves coming against the spirits of Pharaoh, Haman, Herod, Pharisees and Sadducees, and would have gladly traded it in for another, however God has confirmed too many times. It is a book that is intended to shed light on areas that we have given little attention to. Areas where manipulations and abuse have invaded easily, and areas the devil is having a field day in as no one would dare address because nobody wants to come off as offensive to those in charge who may not accept any suggestions or advice from "nobodies". Church people often walk around on egg shells out of fear that if they disagree with the leader then they will be perceived in a certain way. Amos 3:3 says can two walk together unless they agree? We know the answer to this is no.

This does not mean that you will agree on EVERYTHING to walk together. On the major things yes! Chances are in reality you may not agree on everything, just like in a good marriage where two are walking together and they can sometimes agree to disagree on some things that are not major. This book **IS** specifically written to enhance the Kingdom of God in that the Church is a vital part in God's redemptive work according to the scriptures. Today the church is sick because the saints are sick. (Mark 2:17, Luke 5:31-32) Jesus came for the sick. We often think the sick are people who are embedded in sinful lifestyles but what many fail to realize is that self-righteousness is a high form of sickness, and so is today's worldly churches. Therefore, remember when you reference the punch line that God didn't come to call the righteous but the sick, that means people strung out on drugs, prostitutes on street corners, and murders, etc. but that also includes the self-righteous saint, or a minister that prides themselves on their works, or a someone boasting of serving God in and of themselves and not in the power of the holy spirit. Yes! People actually believe they do God's Word through themselves. We are all to be doers of the Word of God yet every human being at some point in their lives has done something that was not right in God's eyes. When people "arrive" so to speak it's as if they believe they have never done anything contrary to the Word of God. Romans 3:23 says all has fallen short of the glory of God, meaning that some people need to be reminded that yes, they too are included in this group. No one should ever boast about what they have done in regards to their works or deeds in Christ in regards to demonstrating their righteousness, Isaiah 64:6 says that is like putting a filthy rag unto God to show Him how clean one is, when in reality all are in need of the blameless, spotless blood of Jesus Christ. God does not love one more than the other. He loves the stuck up saint that sinners seem to repel, just as much as the carnal believer, the confused struggling homosexual, in addition to alcoholics and drug addicts too. He doesn't love the actions taking place, but he does love them. That is not to say one's fellowship or relationship with God will not be affected if healthy and right living is rejected and refused, it will be. Isaiah 55:8-9 says my ways are higher than your ways and my thoughts are higher than your thoughts. As people we can be immensely critical towards one another not realizing that God sees all about a person when we just see the surface. Be careful who you put your judgments on as if you are God. There is only one judge and he tells you not to condemn or judge anyone before the last day.

Beauty

It became evident to Veronica at a very young age that the way she physically looked made people feel a certain way. Both boys and men always did a double look when they noticed her. Girls and women would roll their eyes, mean mug, or show some kind of dissatisfaction with her the instant she was spotted. She became accustomed to both responses and could immediately discern when one or the other would be communicated. She'd be taken through a series of memories from her adolescence. Often times she would not wear makeup or wear pretty clothes as a teen so that she could fit in with the other girls at school. They seemed to be more responsive to her in this way. Acceptance was more important at that time during her life than anything in the world. She desperately wanted to be included and a part of the friendships she witness daily at school. If she dressed nicely, she'd hear comments made comparing her to a high maintenance diva or that she is certainly a material's girl. Veronica was not either. She could wear a nun's uniform without makeup and still be very striking. Nevertheless, the insults never seemed to cease. When she began attending church services with her mother at a young age she thought church was the most beautiful place she had ever been in her life. Surely she would be accepted at church, so she thought. Veronica had no idea of what "church folks" was, as she solely focused her eyes on Jesus. It wasn't until she began maturing as a young adult that she began to look horizontally at those around her instead of vertically towards heaven. It all became clear to her as she noticed those she thought were some of the sweetest people were issuing more than smiles her way. She was sized up, judged often, and labeled instantly. She decided after experiencing the same encounters repeatedly out in the world that if people had a problem with the way she looked physically at church, they needed to take it up with God. After all she didn't ask to be physically attractive. It was how God fashioned her to be. She learned that church was a hospital for sick people.

Two days after her thirtieth birthday Veronica walked into the crowded church on Sunday morning to greet the upbeat usher that directed her again to a front row seat. She had been visiting a new church for a few months and Pastor Williams had taken notice of the new visitor in his congregation. It was obvious. Veronica was beautiful and everyone there could see it. She often tried to camouflage in the back when she arrived, but as usual the same usher would find her and direct her to the front of the church. Not wanting to be disobedient or resistant, she always gathered her items and moved forward. It's happening again, she thought! Her beauty made her stand out like a sore thumb when she so badly wanted to just blend in. Pastor Williams had become agitated that this new woman that was visiting his church hadn't yet come to speak with him. Who is this woman? Why is she here? Did someone invite her? Is she married? A mother? Divorced? Who she is? She must have trust issues or something. What is she trying to hide? What is she afraid of he thought?

In the past Veronica had been wounded in church settings because of her beauty. She had been a victim of what is defined as "beauty abuse". What in the world is beauty abuse one might ask?

Something that Veronica was all too familiar with. Not just her, but her mother, and her grandmother. She hadn't been going to church for a few months because of some transitions in her life. All her life she was a faithful church member of the same church as far as she could remember. This church visiting thing was not something she was accustomed to, neither was it something she desired for her life, but it seemed to be the ordered steps of her season. Over the years growing up in the same local congregation, she took note of how newcomers within the church were treated and labeled immediately. During that time, she was on one side of the totem pole and could only understand this as a member observing a newcomer. There was a new threshing she had crossed after being released from her home church, headed to a new place she knew not. Crossing this new threshing it gave her understanding on what the other side of that totem pole was like. It was her turn she was taking in life she thought she'd never take and that was to settle as a newcomer in a foreign congregation. She then understood how easy it was to judge someone new to a church without knowing or understanding why they have come to a new place. She was uncomfortable with the way this made her feel. Everything was foreign, from the way service was held, to the praise and worship, the actual building was a lot bigger, and she only knew about two people in the new church compared to where she knew almost every member at her home church.

So many eyes remained glued to her, the faces that were worn on the sleeves of the faithful members who had always been there, knowing every in and out and corner of the congregation as they had marked their territory. What dirt does she have on her that we can pull up? Oh, can't wait to hear this sad story! Why did she have to come to our church? All messages she received as she greeted some of the church members who insisted on discovering this new stranger. This was the third church she had visited after being released from her church home. Her home that she was raised in. The home where her parents took her to church.

This was a maturing process Veronica was encountering and she realized that many people are members of churches because it was the place where they were taken to as a child. It was the family's church. It was a place where you just went because that's all you knew. Not to say that God doesn't use situations such as this, because in many cases it's the exact place where foundations are being established in the lives of believers. The reality many choose not to face is that everyone that is raised within a local body does not always remain in that very same local body until their dying day. Sometimes people do remain at the same church all their lives. There is nothing wrong with either scenario, only when assumptions and labeling is a result of either. It may be God's will for one to remain at a local church all their life, as it may have everything to do with the Lord's agenda, calling, and ministry of that individual. Others, God may call to other places for reasons not known until it's time for the purpose to be revealed. She had witnessed those who remained in the same body labeled as "closed-minded", or limited in their perspectives of ministry. She had also heard those who left churches for whatever reason, whether God was leading them, or if it was their choice, being labeled as disloyal, traitors, and unfaithful.

Veronica was on a journey she knew nothing about as she was being led by God away from the church home she'd always known. Surely she knew church in and out, but more so she had come to know Jesus Christ as her personal lord and savior. She walked with him and talked with him and knew when he was ordering her steps. How did she know when this was occurring? It wasn't always from being Mrs. Perfect. She hadn't always lived an obedient life in Christ as she had fallen away from Christ during her young adulthood. She had come to learn of the Lord's voice by of course moving when the Holy Spirit instructed, being obedient, and confirmations from God, however she also learned from God by being chastened, re-directed, and from failures. Her home church absolutely shaped her faith and kept her near the cross as the word of God was always being poured over her and deposited into her, but it didn't click right then and there. No, she went through a process of purification and sanctification before she heavily began sensing God's presence in her life and his voice and further confirmations.

This was a time in her life where she was to go to a place she knew not. To a place that God had in mind for her to be. A place the Lord was leading her to for her life and ministry. She thought it would be a quick transition, a linear formula of going from here to there, or from point A to point B. Yet she didn't know that the road ahead was going to be a rocky journey that would birth her ministry as her foundation was laid at this point. How uncomfortable it was to leave a place she always knew, to go to a place she didn't know or really want to at first. It wasn't fun being a new face or learning new rules, spoken, or unspoken. Why her she thought? There was such a burden on her life and she experienced the supernatural like ways never before over the past year. She knew without a shadow of a doubt it was the Lord leading her, and she was determined to obey and grasp walking by faith and not by sight.

Her past had a solid record of faithfulness as a church member and she was very mature in the knowledge of God. She knew God for herself, and had experienced being filled with God's spirit on occasions that she could remember. She was faithful to God, church services, and ministry. She certainly wasn't perfect and had trials and tribulations like any young growing saint in the Lord, but she was dedicated, and desired to please God as she had learned the disappointments of trying to please people. Mount Haven seemed to be a place where either God was leading her to in order to settle there or perhaps it was just a stepping stone to her destiny.

By this time, she could care less what people thought. She knew what it was like to be the heart of the church, the faithful, those that showed up and supported everything necessary for the church. She knew what it was like to tithe faithfully and give of her time, talent, and treasure. After a while she became more comfortable in her new surroundings and began coming into a settled rest. Who cared if someone thought she was a new believer who was looking for guidance, or if she was a woman on the run who was hiding secrets. She was neither of those, and she knew how to deal with "church people" by now. People had been talking about her all her life. I guess I'll give them something to talk about she thought as she entered this new chapter of her life fearless. Not careless, but not caring about what would be said, the looks, the rejection, the phoniness and everything else that came along with sick church people who are bound by looking the part and pleasing man.

She was determined to move ahead and not backwards. The instructions she received from the Lord was to take her time with interacting with leadership. She knew the leadership at her home church well, and she didn't want to commit to a local body too quickly as she knew the importance of being spirit led to the right congregation after what she had recently been through. Veronica anticipated meeting the pastor at Mount Haven initially, but later came around to interacting. At this moment in life she just needed to be fed a fresh word of God, as she was always accustomed to growing up. She knew Pastor Williams was curious, but she didn't care. She had a right to come to a public worship service to be fed the word of God without having to pour out the last thirty years of her life. It wasn't that she had intent to dishonor leadership or to be rude, but she just wanted to embrace the assembling together that she was familiar with, and receive the present impartation of what it's like outside of watching the church channel or listening to a sermon on CD or DVD. She knew there was certainly something special that happened in the atmosphere as the people of God

3

joined together that wouldn't occur from media ministry. She was hungry for the right ministry in her life, and just wanted to lift her voice with the saints of God in praise, worship, and prayer.

She didn't desire to be stand offish as many thought her to be. She just desired to be fed the word of God at this broken point in her life without having to go into depths about who she was, where she was from, and why she was there. She had visited a few churches prior and was in serious prayer about the one God would have her to become a member of. She never joined any of the two churches she briefly visited prior because of the recurring issue of beauty abuse. Why had she left her home church? After all, she thought she would always dwell there, live there, and die at the same church she'd grew up at. Boy was she traumatized by letting go of the one place she'd always known as her church home. It was not something she would have ever considered or desire for her life, however after much praying and fasting during a major maturation point in her life, she knew that God was leading her to a land that he would show her. Veronica had grown in hearing the Lord's voice over time, and she had faith that everything would work out in the end.

She was hopeful for this new place she thought to find a home in and she knew the opposition would come as she was used to it at this point in her life, but she was determined to press on. The congregation was just released from another great Sunday sermon when she gathered her belongings and hugged a few people around her. She headed to her car and was at peace as her spirit being was strengthened. She was at peace, but Pastor Williams became irritated…..again. He began labeling her, sizing her story up as if he knew every detail of her life. She knew what he was thinking, and decided that she'd introduce herself that week during their midweek service. It was time, she thought. She was so tired of this strange cycle she'd never had to deal with in the comfort of belonging to the same church all her life. I wouldn't wish this on anyone she thought. It's so much easier to just stay put in the same church all your life. It's more approved and accepted by society.

It was at six pm. Sharp on a Wednesday night when bible study began at Mount Haven. There she is, he thought, the mystery woman who won't speak. He began immediately talking about beauty. "Don't you know that some of the ugliest people on the inside are some of the most beautiful people on the outside? I know a lot of beautiful people who are hideous beasts internally"! His notes were not on beauty, but he was reminded with each glance at Veronica, that he didn't choose a woman with such beauty when he had the chance twenty years ago when he got married. Of course, the first lady was a pretty woman, but he hadn't chose to marry the one he wanted, because according to church folks, that woman who remains nameless was too beautiful to know God. He recalled the voices of many church people ringing in his head. "That woman is too beautiful to take the things of God seriously". At that time Pastor Williams was young, and was filled with fear if he had chosen the woman he felt instant connections with on every level. It seemed to be more approving if he had taken a woman that was not as beautiful as the one he desired. He knew the serious assignment of being called by God and he complied with the advice given to him by spiritual advisors. So he chose a young lady that he was somewhat interested in, which he'd later regret in his own personal closet of prayer before God alone. One thing he realized was that all the people that encouraged and advised him to marry the woman he did, were all dead and gone, by that time he realized years later that he missed his God sent for the people's choice for his life. He was persuaded that the woman he always loved couldn't be God's choice, and that she wouldn't be a good fit to lead God's people. What was ingrained into his mind early on? It was the idea that beauty was to be associated with evil, seductiveness, harlotry, and deception. This is what Pastor Williams was taught as he grew up in a church setting where beautiful women were rejected and labeled. That persona had become a part of him over the years as he stood in his bitterness. He was blind to the fact that he had become what he thought he never would, a labeler. He took a hard look into her eyes from the pulpit and irritation overwhelmed him, he shouted his pitch line looking dead into her face that "Even pretty women go to hell"!

She just laughed inside; for she knew exactly what was happening. She could predict the next few months as she'd been through this before. Even her mother and grandmother experienced similar situations. They were driven out of church settings due to beauty abuse. She declared in her heart, that she wasn't going to let them win this time. She knew the first lady would be all of a sudden led to preach the word of God very soon as the word was just dropped into her spirit all of a sudden on the subject of the seductress strange woman.

Yes, it was a different church, a different generation, but the same story. She was saddened by the fact that the very place people are to come and be edified and encouraged is the same place the devil was having a field day in by all types of manipulations and abuses that no one would ever even dare to address. Veronica had remembered the similar testimonies of her mother and grandmother. She had heard about them, but they never really hit home until now, that she was experiencing the same thing. How many other women had experienced this and no one ever knew she thought? Is it okay for people to just get away with abuse in the church just because they have a title? God will repay as he sees all, but if there was a vessel he'd use to bring awareness to the subject by this time she was the number one volunteer after all she and her family members encountered.

It's funny how people believe that God doesn't see all that is thought, said, and intended. What God views to be more important is not the hundreds of women the first lady greeted after service with a hug, a warm smile, and a word of encouragement. What grabs God's attention is the one haughty look she gave to one beautiful visitor she was to welcome as a foreigner. Situations like this one causes for the heart to be weighed before God Almighty. The lord hates several things as indicated in his word such as divorce, a lying tongue, hands that shed innocent blood, and even haughty eyes. Because one may not posses one of the aforementioned, doesn't mean that there may be areas of repentance in some of the other areas.

When Veronica noticed the look that was given to her, she immediately saw her mother's testimony flash right before her eyes. Her mother Vivian was invited to a private lunch one day by the first lady of her church in Birmingham Alabama approximately thirty years ago. Vivian has issues of being rejected at church because she was also a beautiful lady that was often put down because of her physical appearance. Lunch, Vivian thought, I am finally accepted! She was excited and eager to bond with the first lady. Vivian had always been kind to her as well as all the other women in the congregation, but didn't receive back what she sent out. What a disappointment lunch was. It certainly didn't go how she'd imagined. She was devastated in learning by the time her host was paying for her bill that she had been asked to lunch so a gracious demand for her to leave their church was presented, all at the courtesy provided by first lady Hawkins. Her husband, Pastor Hawkins had been seriously attracted to Vivian, and she was causing too many issues within the congregation of men looking at her, pastor Hawkins included. Vivian had always been appropriate with the pastor and was not at all attracted to him. She was respectful to the first lady and the congregation alike. But it was their church and their rules and their way. There was not a moment within her life that she never forgot how she felt on the way home from that disheartening lunch with her first lady. She left that church as asked, and settled in her heart that she would find a place that would celebrate her instead of tolerating her. A rude awakening settled in as she experienced the same thing as her mother and her future daughter. That started her journey of being the strange beautiful woman who was trying to find a church home, all the while being labeled as a strange wanderer whose motive was to execute the Delilah and Jezebel agenda. As sad as this is, this synonymous message always came from the same source, which is from some offended insecure woman. Being Christ like was important, but not when a beautiful woman showed up in need of a church home. Christ likeness was thrown out of the window and replaced with mission "Get her out of here".

Vivian didn't share these things with her daughter Veronica until it was Veronica's turn. She knew there would be a day where her daughter would experience the same things that she did as well as her mother. The time finally came and she reassured her daughter that she wasn't the first who had been abused in this manner, neither would she be the last. It has been occurring for years, and the story always ends the same. The main lady is overjoyed when Mrs. Pretty leaves her congregation looking for another. Over the years Vivian noticed from her encounters with people of faith that beautiful women were often associated with the devil and evil at church. Sure the beauty of the Lord was referenced, and the beauty of holiness, but she had often heard particular scriptures used in church to down play women who outwardly adorn themselves. No matter how plain she tried to appear attending church, she was still beautiful, and labeled anyway as trying too hard, when the truth was, she didn't have to try at all. It wasn't until God met her where she was in her circumstances and she studied God's word for herself. At this point, Vivian was able to clearly see that God loves people, no matter what they look like physically. She took note that beautiful women didn't start with the devil, they started with God, just like partying didn't start with the devil, partying started with god. Getting high and drunk didn't start with the devil, it too started with god, as one would be high and drunk off of praise, worship, and prayer in the spirit of God. Wise beautiful women didn't start off as adulterous in proverbs; they started with what God created.

The devil imitates. Be careful when you associate a woman who speaks well who dresses well and who is beautiful with the adulterous woman who has persuasive speech because you feel like labeling her that because you expect her to be less than what she is. The adulterous women we read about in proverbs chapter 7 and 30, is nothing but a fake imitation of the real thing that God has made. She has perverted the things placed inside of the real woman of god for evil as assigned by the enemy. Because a woman has intellect, can speak well, and is beautiful doesn't mean that she is an evil woman or adulterous woman to be compared with the evil woman in proverbs. She could be a daughter of the Most High God. I have been in services visiting with family and friends to have someone in the pulpit literally have the audacity to think it is okay to point their finger at me when referencing something evil. I want to make myself very clear. My name is not Delilah, Jezebel, or Bathsheba! It is sad when someone has so much control over things; they literally lose their mind in the fact that they can use their place of position to flat out label someone they don't know. That is not the Spirit of God. This is not to say that there are not women as such who intentionally scheme on evil motives. There certainly are, and that's a reality, however we should not be labeling people in this category, just to shape the perspectives of others to think the same. It is also important to remember that just as there are seducing women, there are also seducing men who have the same characteristics of the adulterous woman and seducing woman, however their motives are pressed upon women. We often talk about harlotry and the Delilah spirit as if it cannot apply to a man operating in this manner. It's sad when someone has to put another down, in order for self to look good. If you are trying to hide the brilliance in another so that you don't look as dull, I'd encourage you to repent before God as the person you are judging may be nothing as you have labeled.

Reacting to Beauty

As predicted, the following Sunday, the congregation at Mount Haven was surprised to be receiving a word of the lord from First Lady Williams. She began by explaining how she just had to get this word of the lord out during this special time and how open the pastor had been about rearranging some things for her to preach the word of God that morning. The agenda was for the pastor to go back to the basics of returning to our first love which is Jesus according to Revelation 2:4. This agenda to re-route as the spirit was guiding the first lady to deliver what she all of a sudden received over the past few months was sporadically surprising to everyone. Veronica thought, okay, here we go, I know exactly what books, chapters, and verses we are about to dive right into. The sermon started off sweet as expected and gradually led down to the bulls eye in which only Veronica knew was about to be hit.

She began immediately by saying she had been receiving serious revelation about a woman in their congregation that needed to leave their church immediately. She needed to go back to where she came from, wherever that was. In a nutshell, the pulpit was used to execute an agenda that reflected a personal conflict of how a pretty visitor was making the main lady feel. It was masked in the agenda of God suddenly depositing a word in her spirit. It was everything of the flesh in the area of jealousy and abuse. Sure, scriptures were used in the word of God, and many truths were stated, however the foul stench of the message was where it was derived from and the intent behind it. The place the message originated from was a place of hatred, and abuse to fire off built up feelings and emotions Mrs. Williams had against Veronica as she just wouldn't leave their church. Mrs. Williams was accustomed to getting whatever she desired and being in a prominent place of control. This situation was one she couldn't control as church is a place open to the public. The best thing she could do was bank on Veronica being uncomfortable from scriptures she'd use to drive her right out of the doors that had welcome spelled out in huge red letters. It never crossed her mind that perhaps that God was leading Veronica there for the lord's purposes. If this did cross her mind, it wasn't convicting enough for ministry to replace abuse. Perhaps if Veronica was less attractive no one would even care or notice her. Then maybe her assignment there would be associated with the plan of the lord and not the agenda of the devil. It is one thing to face opposition as a believer in the world, but to come into the place that is to welcome the saints of God to be driven out didn't settle well with Veronica.

An entire year had passed and every attempt that was made to make Veronica leave the church had failed. First lady Williams was threatened by Veronica's beauty and she just couldn't take it anymore. Every week she'd walk out on the pulpit declaring that the woman in their congregation needed to leave according to what God told her and the woman was disobedient to her instruction from God. Veronica's name was never used in the pulpit. The people just looked around wondering who in the world she is talking about. What awful woman was there irritating the first lady? Mrs. Williams would put on her I'm not bothered face every service, knowing very well she was beyond bothered by the very presence of Veronica. Veronica knew who she was referring to, but she decided this time,

7

no one is making her leave. So every week she kept showing up to the Lord's house, after all Mrs. Williams may have been the first lady, but she didn't own the church. Did the church not belong to God? Could God not send to his house who he wanted? Did God have to check with the leadership before sending whom he pleased to his house for whatever reasons people may never understand? That's exactly what she had experienced. People were acting as if they needed God's permission to do what he wanted to do.

This is certainly not the manner of how every woman of God behaves, in fact there are shepherds who love on all women and men who are sent to their congregation no matter how beautiful or how facially challenged one may be. I am proud to say that I have never experienced such myself, but those in my family certainly have. My woman of God I have been graced to be under is a very high class act who lives her life to the standard of the word of God, and goes out of her way to love on all people! The issue becomes a burden when you are not experiencing what your neighbor is. If someone doesn't speak up for your neighbor or those to come who will experience such cruelties then they won't cease from occurring and the trauma resulting from such will continue. God doesn't like to see people oppressed and abused in any manner and neither should we, and neither should we just allow it as it is gently brushed up under the rug as "nothing big" while yet another child of God is impacted by impurities and insecurities.

Let's take a look at some biblical examples of God's purposes being manifested in how some dignitaries where replaced because of their unwillingness to self will.

We all know what happened to Queen Vashti in the book of Esther. Queen Vashti was replaced because of her unwillingness to comply with leadership. This was the report the people were aware of, however God had other purposes for Vashti to move on. It was a plan that wasn't revealed until the set appointed time God ordained. The plan was to have Esther be the instrument to save many lives! Esther had an assignment to stand in the gap and come against distorted delegated authority within the palace and reign over plight and plot of dirty leadership that planned to annihilate God's people. What some leaders are failing to realize today is that rejection of submitting to the agenda of God will cause for elimination and replacement. Look at Saul and David. Why would God choose Saul to be Israel's king if he knew he would not be pleased with him later? The bible says God was sorry he made Saul King. Here is where we see a sovereign God who chooses to limit his sovereignty to give man free will and choice. The choices Saul made were apparently those that God did not see before hand or he chose not to see as he gave Saul free will. It is a great example of how God chose someone and wanted to bless someone significantly however eventually God changed his destiny after his heart was weighed at a later time. Samuel tells Saul that God has rejected him as King and has found one better than him, one after his own heart. This scenario is not absent in many relationships and circumstances today. Initially it could appear as if someone was going down the right road with God, however behind closed doors another picture may be identified by God almighty who constantly weighs the hearts of men. Just because the heart weighs good in God's perspective one year, doesn't mean the scales have measured the same result the next year. The goal is to keep the heart right before God and be obedient to the Lord's instructions. If the heart doesn't weigh in right, to whom much is given, much is required.

Meanwhile, back at the ranch, Veronica remembered in the past she had tried to appear less attractive so that she wouldn't be a threat to anyone or cause any attention to herself. She wouldn't put on makeup, or wear pretty colors. She would wear flat shoes with the same neutral colors week after week. She'd pull her hair back in a ponytail and would rarely get it done. She wouldn't paint her nails or flash her beautiful smile. She wanted approval and to hear the word of God at church like everyone else without people staring was something she strived for. She was so thirsty to hear the word of God and to be among the people of God that if playing down her beauty was an issue, she'd do that. The problem was, none of that worked. She was still gorgeous even trying not to be. If she would have put on a potato sack she still would have been beautiful. She would receive the famous scripture as did her mother and grandmother repeatedly. 1 Peter 3: 3-4 was thrown at her within churches regularly. That is certainly an important scripture, and should be applied to the lives of all women of God, but it shouldn't be used to beat up someone because of another's insecurities. She wasn't trying to be beautiful; neither did she have to try. It was clear that the way she looked physically made some others feel bad on the inside so they were trying to make her feel bad on the inside. Veronica had done nothing to bother other women within in the churches, and was kind to everyone. It was fine for other women to dress nicely, put on makeup, and present their bests, but if she did it, she was judged as adorning herself outwardly.

She looked back over her life and thanked God that she grew out of that people pleasing stage of her life, where she was trying to fit the mold of being what other people wanted her to be, for their own comfort. Eventually Veronica just gave up on playing Mrs. Camouflage. She dressed up just like all the other women in the congregation as they saw fit to wear their best for the Lord, so would she. She no longer cared if she was hurting someone by the way she appeared outwardly. She was modest and respectful in her attire, but she finally became free in that area after recognizing that nothing she did to downplay the way God created her worked. People were talking about her if she didn't dress nicely, and they were talking about her if she did dress nicely.

This testimony about Veronica is one that many beautiful women face within the church setting and is not typically addressed. It's one of those hidden rules that are unspoken. Pretty women are not always received well in religious settings. Over time other women feel threatened and become jealous, and men that are attracted to them within the church soon replace fondness with bitterness if the woman is not mutually attracted. The other side of beauty abuse is more so projected in the church as it has been passed down to be the only perspective that people ever come to know. And that is that people can be beautiful and be ugly inside. This is a truth. There are people who are very attractive externally, but they are mean and ugly internally. Another truth, that is rarely painted, is that people can be beautiful externally and also be beautiful internally. It's a truth that people can be unattractive physically and be beautiful on the inside. The truth that is not commonly communicated is that a person can be unattractive externally and be unattractive internally as well. Yes, it is true that someone can be just as ugly on the inside as the outside. I am not trying to call someone ugly, as I believe all people are made in the image of God and we all bare his mark on us as created children of God. We don't get all the sides of the truth, only the sides that one is interested in painting, and usually it's for their own agendas. Sharing both sides of a matter has become a passion of mine as I have recognized most people tend to share one side to a matter. Scholars look at all sides of the spectrum, and all truths pertaining to a subject matter which benefit all people as a result.

Beauty and Authority

We often hear about how Abraham didn't have faith in God because when it was time to go down into Egypt he lied about his wife Sarah. He told the Egyptians that she was his sister and not his wife out of fear of what they would do to him in order to get her if he claimed her as his wife. This certainly demonstrates a level of fear that Abraham obtained, yet it also doesn't depict the wisdom in why he intended to lie about this situation. Abraham was a wealthy man who was familiar with how authority worked. Authority and beauty often went hand in hand in those days and even today those in authority still have the insatiable desires of obtaining beautiful objects. It is safe to say that there are some people who have been given authority and power almost have everything they desire at the grasp of their fingertips, however some things money, authority, and power cannot buy, and one of those things is beauty. It is not common for a man who is wealthy to obtain much but perhaps he may not have the one desirable thing his heart so longs for. Often times that is a beautiful woman. We have often read about scandals with those in authority having stepped outside of their marriages in order to entertain a beautiful woman. Sometimes this can be depicted as a woman trying to come between a woman and her husband, but another truth is that some men in authority feel as if they can have whatever they want because of the power and authority given to them, even if that includes a woman that does not belong to him. Just look at what King David did. David thought he arrived in life to get whatever he wanted including another man's wife. Abraham understood that manipulation was no issue at all for the King. He knew that those in authority can manipulate circumstances and situations in order to get whatever their desires were, including his wife Sarah, even if that means killing him. There is nothing new under the sun. The same thing is happening in today's generation. Many beautiful women suffer from this situation. It's not uncommon for a man of God to be attracted to a beautiful woman. The problem comes with what the response is to that attraction. Because a man gets married or a woman gets married doesn't mean that they will never be attracted to another physically attractive person. The issue at hand is what is done with that attraction. There are many cases of this. Let's look at Jackie. Jacqueline, Veronica's grandmother was a very beautiful woman who lived in Birmingham Alabama. She went to a wonderful church where she felt welcome by most, however there was one problem. The pastor's assistant was extremely attracted to Jacqueline. There seemed to be a recurring issue she had noticed with Minister Thomas, who was the pastor's assistant. If any of the men in the congregation ever got close enough to Jacqueline to ask her out, they immediately were recruited by Minister Thomas to serve as his new church intern or assistant. This was a form of manipulation. Jacqueline was not attracted to Minister Thomas as he was three times her age. That didn't stop Minister Thomas from keeping her from someone she may have been interested in, as she desired to be married to a saved man of God within her church. Minister Thomas had made up his mind. "If I can't have her, then no man around here can have her either". Of the two men she actually considered dating within her local church body soon was super glued to

Minister Thomas as his new helper the very moment there was opportunity for Jackie to grow closer to them. He had new assignments for those young men. They were sent out of town sporadically on "sudden ministry assignments" when in fact it was an interference to keep them away from the young woman Minister Thomas was banking on for himself. Now of course one couldn't prove this, and of course it appears as if the out of town ministry assignments should never be questioned because men of God wouldn't be expected to be responsible for such manipulations right? Wrong. This is exactly what occurred with this situation, and many others like it still occurring today. If Minister Thomas was assigned out of town, his new intern had to be right with him, so there would be no chance of them ever moving forward with Jackie in his absence.

It grieved her to know that Minister Thomas would rather have her sit around for the rest of her life with the desire to marry within her church, than to stop manipulating her, and the young men that would pursue her. How loving was this? Isn't he supposed to look like Christ? This was nothing she could prove; neither could the young men that pursued her. But she knew and the young men knew what was really going on behind the façade of remaining ministry minded only. How uncomfortable it would be to bring it up to anyone. The young men wanted so badly to please leadership and submit to authority, knowing all the while that they were being kept from their interest. The call on their lives at that time seemed to be more important than marrying the woman they wanted in Minister Thomas's perspective and advice given. Pleasing the older men in the church was on the throne of their lives, and not the voice of the Lord. They were young and didn't mind being taken advantage of. After all, they were given a place to demonstrate their gifts; some even received monetary rewards, and other accolades that were not worth the controversy. If they moved closer to Jackie, then their finances or benefits were threatened. Discernment was there, but they would never put the "man of God" on blast for having such ill motives. After all they couldn't prove it either, and even if they did mention it, they were certain that some biblical explanation would be given as to why there were sudden changes here, or there, or why they were being turned and tossed in every way, overall, never being able to pursue Jacqueline. Minister Thomas would take them to the side and have long talks with the young men that Jacqueline seemed to have been interested in. He even suggested other young ladies for them to consider marrying at church, but Jacqueline's name was never brought up. The manipulation was hidden behind the importance of having patience in the area of marriage. He'd often refer to biblical scriptures to show them why they should remain single, and not pursue a wife according to Paul's suggestion of remaining single as he was. He'd often reference Adam before the fall, as Adam was in bliss without a mate. Minister Thomas would request the two young men to preach sermons on the importance of singleness during the time it appeared they were getting close to Jackie. Not that this advice wasn't imperative to their marital status. Those principles are important for living a single life with the call of God at hand, but it should not have been used to manipulate or a controlling mechanism by Minister Thomas. If the young men's actions went against what they preached it would be contradictory for the congregation to be in awe of a new marriage union that perhaps would take place secretly. There were times where he'd demand to know the young men's conversations with Jackie. He eventually learned all about her through them, and would wear her favorite colors, play her favorite songs when she was near him, he would change his appearance to anything she positively responded towards. The major issue here is not the importance of singleness being proclaimed, as it is serious to focus as a single, yet when things are being done in a way to manipulate others, it's wrong. There is another side of the spectrum of being single that was never encouraged. God saw it unfit for Adam to be alone before the fall no matter how unaware of

11

his single state he was before Eve was presented to him. A single certainly has time to maximize for the Kingdom of God in ways that married people do not. It is true that God will fulfill a single to keep them focused on the kingdom assignment, but when this picture is being painted to manipulate someone to keep them from their god given spouse it is abuse. This is certainly manipulation when it's being communicated from someone trying to control another person. He wanted those young men to make sure they knew what season they were in, and in his perspective it wasn't the season for marriage. Little did they know, it would never be the season for marriage if that involved Jacqueline. In the past the young men were encouraged to expect their hearts desires including a wonderful wife. What he failed to do was tell them what he really thought and that was "have any woman you want, just not THAT woman, because THAT woman is too much for me to handle seeing you with. Often time's people will encourage you to go for the top, but when the top comes, you will see they didn't mean for you to have THAT house, THAT car, THAT ministry, THAT man, THAT woman, THAT anointing. It's like at first before the blessing came, the friendship was strong, the relationship was tight, but as soon as the blessing becomes a reality, moods begin to change and interaction decreases. If he couldn't have her, he didn't want anyone else to either. He wanted the young men to be just as miserable as he was, because out of it, somehow it felt holy and as if God was pleased with his sufferings in this area. Their season was whatever Minister Thomas said was their season, regardless if it mirrored God's season for their lives or not. If he couldn't have her, he'd rather she left the church, or fall into sin with another while waiting on her God sent spouse, or more so for her to remain single as possible as he sickly perceived an opportunity with her for himself. The minister would often give subliminal messages to Jackie and the young men interested in her centered around controlling their flesh and not being moved by their emotions. These are very serious things that singles should be on alert about especially in regards to sowing and reaping to the spirit as all believers must make a discipline of, but his motive was to keep them from ever marrying when he used these instructions as the authority in their lives. It's true, lasting romances are not built overnight, however everyone doesn't want to be Sarah when it comes to having children, not to say that God's will may be different. Jacob may have worked for Rachel for fourteen years in that day, however seven years in today's time is too long to court anyone. We see how Laban tricked Jacob beyond measure and how he never really released him, Jacob had to take his family and break out, he got the heck out of dodge because Laban became a stronghold that would not allow him to go. That's real, because some people in life outside of marriage, and sometimes within some marriages, you will never be released until you get tired like Jacob and go where God tells you to go. Laban chased after Jacob, but God took care of that terrible spirit as he warned Laban in a dream. God will always confirm when you are supposed to move, and he will make sure anyone coming after you is rightly aligned. Other scriptures such as 1 Corinthians 7: 9 and 28 were never acknowledged, that it is not sin to marry, and that it is better to marry than it is to burn with lust. God gave sex as a gift to married couples. Our sexual drive is built in us by God and before we ever get married it is already activated in our nature. This nature is not of sin and of the devil as many religious people sometimes picture it to be. They were often told if they couldn't master their flesh then they were not like God, when God is the very one who placed the sexual drive inside of human beings. Yes! The response to that drive should be carried out within the boundaries of marriage only and not outside of marriage, however the goal was to make them feel less spiritual or evil if they acknowledged their desire to be with the opposite sex, and if they did acknowledge this quickly they were labeled as being unlike Christ. He'd keep Jacqueline from marrying anyone just so a fantasy of his could be entertained in his mind. Manipulation is manipulation and it is wrong. Just because it occurs by someone who has a title or status of any kind, does not make it right. Minister Thomas was married, but that didn't stop his mind from remaining in denial about keeping young men away from the young lady he desperately hoped became his second wife after Mrs. Thomas one day passed away. Often comments were made jokingly about his agenda of becoming a widow in the presence of Jackie. How sad to even depict this, but how true it is, as this testimony has taken place in several organizations across the world. Nothing is ever done about it as people notice what is going on, but no one speaks up in order to remain safe in the perspectives of others, particularly if it's done by authority who is well respected and honored throughout the areas. It's a sad story that the young man and Jacqueline was never afforded the opportunity to become a couple all because of a man who had distorted his delegated authority to keep them from being together because he was secretly attracted to Jackie. The best strongholds are always the ones where it is difficult to prove. The young men were under Minister Thomas's authority within the church and to disobey him would make it look as if they were not submitted under authority. As crazy as it may sound the scenario is not always minister to intern, it could very well be someone of the same flesh and blood that is manipulating circumstances so that you won't obtain a beautiful woman or wonderful man sent by God all due to someone else's misery. Jealously and greed is not a respecter of persons, it has often belonged to the most respected anointed of persons. We often assume that works of the flesh are always embedded in unhealthy sexual interaction often failing to realize that jealousy, maliciousness, slander, deceit, hypocrisy, bitterness, rage, and anger are also not of God and derive from the flesh according to Ephesians 4:31 and 1 Peter 2:1. People can be in denial about these as they are not as evident to prove, particularly jealousy between women who lie to themselves as if they are not jealous of another but forever demonstrating in their interaction, conduct, and comments that are always displayed to point out the flaws, mistakes, or short comings of another, all to make themselves feel stabilized in their own insecurities. Always remember a leader, teacher, minister, family member or even a spouse may have a wonderful plan for your life. Your goal is to find out what God's plan is for your life and to walk in the steps God orders for you and not man. This does not mean that you cannot heed to wise counsel or get assistance from a seasoned mature saint; it means that what God has for your life may not be revealed for everyone to understand, including those close to us. One thing that King Saul and David shared in common even though they had opposite hearts in God's perspective is the fact that both of them reached a point with their authority and began thinking they could do pretty much whatever they desired. King Saul thought he could deliberately disobey God and still hold the Kingdom by not carrying out the Lord's instructions fully, and David thought because he held the Kingdom in his hands that entitled him to anyone's wife he wanted. Nothing has changed today. I often notice men in authority who believe and think since they hold a particular position and title they can have anything or anyone they so desire. Let's look at the man of God. He has been given authority by God to oversee souls and bring order where it is needed, yet he knows that he is God's representative and that God hears him, however this does not mean that the man is entitled to do whatever he pleases or get whatever he wants, especially when it comes to women that do not belong to him. Mr. Thomas may have subconsciously believed that because he was God's choice for his ministry assignments then he would be okay in other areas of his life. He believed there was no harm in manipulating young men who were submitted to his spiritual leadership. Perhaps he told himself he isn't doing anything wrong, and in fact he is trying to help the young men. After all he would often use the examples of David and Bathsheba and Samson and Delilah to assist him in controlling the young men to stay away from Jackie. These were true testimonies from the bible and there is a wealth of knowledge to learn from these testimonies, yet they should not be used to manipulate and control someone's life. There are several young men who walk behind their leaders with their head hanging low, with a depressed spirit, demonstrating subconsciously how miserable they are from serving one who is controlling their every move, masking it as submission to authority, when in some cases it's just control. This isn't to say that preparing Elisha to take Elijah's position isn't a process that much training and equipping requires, but it is to say this shouldn't be used to deliberately take advantage of one for whatever purposes only God would see fit down to the depths of what others may not be able to see.

We often come to church thinking that everyone is healthy and in their right mind especially if they obtain some type of status. Not ever realizing what sickness is present and what manipulations and abuses are occurring right under the nose of people week in and week out. This is not something pretty or desirable to point out. Who in their right mind would want to shed light in this area? Certainly not me, however I have learned it is better to obey God than to play it safe with men. History has been proven that it will repeat itself if not corrected. God has shown himself in the area of manipulating situations and lives for his glory, this is a different type of manipulation where God causes all things to work out, not the good things only, but all things, that means the good things, the bad things, the ugly things, the shameful things, all of it, to work out for his children who love him and who are called to his purpose. This is not to be associated with the manipulation that derives from man.

Things like this occur in worldly business settings as well. Don't be surprised when the beautiful intern is being placed right outside of the Owner's office or in his main area of supervision. It may not be just because she is good worker. Don't be surprised if things don't go as Mr. Owner expected, when she is all of sudden no longer needed to work there. The spirits of lust and of the flesh strongly dominate secular work settings. You often hear flirtatious comments exchanged by many people, and some are married. There are other instances where an attractive woman is being supervised by another woman that could be treating her harshly in "undercutting" ways solely off the fact that the supervisor is jealous of the beautiful woman she is over in rank. There are times where a male could demonstrate a jealousy as a supervisor over a very attractive man, solely from the root of jealousy. When you walk into an organization and see clearly the goals, values, and mission of the company that is one thing. But to actually learn if they value what is being demonstrated on the walls of their company you have to actually spend time with them to see if things are congruent. The same thing occurs within church. If you are contemplating joining a church, or making any major decision in life, spend time around the group first and notice what is not being said but demonstrated. This will save you heart ache, pain, and disappointment. Trust me; I know this too well from not implementing this principle in my life sooner.

Speaking up and out against such issues regarding authority has always occurred throughout world history and each time it has been perceived as a rebellious act. At times, yes rebellion is involved; however there are other times where it is necessary for many to be freed from a tight grip of controlling, manipulating spirits which Ephesians 6 calls spiritual wickedness in high places. This type of stand can be compared to the fight for the abolition of slavery, civil rights, women's rights, even our own nation the USA being freed from Great Britain. Each year we celebrate Independence Day with all the festive activities and celebrations not always remembering that people fought hard and went against much opposition for liberty. Either everyone suffers from what leaders have imposed or someone has to stand up, be the target, and be the sacrificial lamb to stir up necessary controversy, in order that many don't perish or suffer unnecessary harm. If there is no fight, there is no freedom. If there is no struggle, there is no progression. Do you think the people who rose up against the KKK was labeled as rebellious? What about slaves who tried to reach freedom? Do we label Harriet Tubman as a rebel? That's what she was according to white society, but there was another side they didn't understand, it was her call to cross the line of freedom and take as many people and lead as many people as she could regardless of who labeled her rebellious. Her famous quote after reaching freedom in the north was that I came to freedom and there was no one there to welcome me. Have you ever went through so much to untangle yourself from a destructive life threatening stronghold to finally break free and have no one welcome you? Instead you are still despised? Why is this? It is because of the blind perspectives that have no idea of your story or God paving the way to make you free. For he whom the son sets free is free indeed.

Do you know what it's like to sound the alarm and ring the bell, and cross a threshing that God almighty has helped you get to, to have no one say congrats you made it! Thank God you're free! No, people will look away from you and your victory because they too are bound by the fears of opinions and judgments of others in society themselves, even if that means giving you a pat on the back. It's like when you walk in some organizations. You can sense how much fear is on many people. I am not referencing the fear of the Lord. I am referring to timidity where there is no liberty or freedom in their spirit, not even to worship. They are bound by the looks, opinions, and judgments of church people. You can see this in how they walk, talk, dress, and interact with others, especially depending on who those others may be. It amazes me that people can declare 2 Timothy 1:7 that God has not given us a spirit of fear, but of power, love, and a sound mind, yet walk in fear in many areas of their lives. Particularly in the area of leadership. Leadership in the church should be honored and we should have a reverence for God's leaders. Understanding and respecting authority is certainly something that is missing from today's generation. This is not to say that all young people are disrespectful, because if there is nothing I can't stand more, it's stereotyping. Many things are assumed and said about young people today that reflect a lack of character and much rebellion, not that this isn't the case, but there are some young people believe it or not who are very respectful and who operate how they should. We don't always give them that credit. My point is that it is very critical to understand authority and leadership because it is necessary to be successful and to please God especially in our walks with Jesus as believers and we are called to submit to Godly authority and submit one to another. Even God himself submitted to the authority of his father. It is equally important when dealing with authority to always understand that everyone has not had positive experiences with authority. Sensitivity in this area can be a positive impact to help those that this applies to. In fact many have been impacted traumatically in the area of authority. If you represent God then you represent God's love for people and one thing God hates and that is his people being oppressed, particularly by an authoritative figure where they are crying for help and there seems to be none. I am not referring to a small matter of everyone makes mistakes including those in leadership, I am referencing life changing traumatic events such as a father in the home raping his daughter, or a police officer who is crooked and selling drugs framing and locking up anyone who may appear as a threat, a teacher or supervisor who has intentions on rape, a judge in the court system who is dishonest and accepts bribery for sentencing innocent lives, we won't even touch on pastoral leadership, out of my respect for that office, but just keep in mind everyone preaching the word of God is not pure. As sad as this is to even think about, it is the truth. See we wrestle not against flesh and blood but against spiritual wickedness in high places. The enemy knows that if he can control you he has you! What better way to control you than to get someone who is over you, particularly in some place of authority in your life to give you instructions from that person. It is advised to get wisdom in the multitude of counselors and to seek someone who is experienced, someone older who has been submitted to God for a while, and someone you know to be of wise counsel, yet keep in mind the enemy will use anybody! Including someone you trust, this is why we should seek God in prayer and fasting ourselves in addition to seeking wise counsel.

I have often wondered how a believer could have a real encounter with the living God and be filled with God's spirit that brings a peace and reassurance, to then turn around at the drop of a hat and tremble when the man or woman of God walks in the room. What are they are afraid of? Why are they now on pins and needles when they were not prior? After having seen the face of God and walking and talking with God all day, what human being can get you so out of your hook that the presence of God has been forgotten? I have noticed how people altar their behavior the moment a supervisor walks by, or a police officer rides right by them on the street. I think we should all have reverence, give honor, and respect authority, but I don't believe we should walk in fear being around those who obtain authority. God tells us to fear him only, and that he didn't give us a spirit of fear, but of love, power, and a sound mind.

What is even sadder is when leaders approve of this fear in others because it makes them feel important. Often, when one does not demonstrate this approved fear that the majority expresses, they are despised and misunderstood for not honoring or respecting authority, when in fact that may not be the case at all. Some people are used to others actually worshipping them, and because one may not worship and adore them like perhaps others, there could be a misunderstanding that honor and reverence is not being extended. I believe it is critical to give honor and respect to all people, especially those in leadership, but I will never worship another human being. In fact it is not common to see believers that have eased out of worshipping Christ to worship the one that is lifting Him up, or ease into worshipping a ministry that is to represent Christ more than worshipping Christ himself. Jesus should be the only one on the throne of our lives. This is done in the workplace as well as in the church setting, and other organizations where people desire to be significant. It has been present for centuries. We as believers should be laying our burdens down at the lord's feet and building up those who come into the church doors. This includes those in ministry. In some present day ministries you may as well get a t-shirt that says I'm burned out and maxed out, because that is exactly what is taking place. The enemy desires for people to be so burned out in "ministry" that there is no time to do God's real work. As long as they stay busy running around like a chicken with its head cut off then he is gaining ground. We are so busy today with some things that are nothing but "monkey business". Today one's busyness is associated with their importance. We have adopted the mindset that the busier I am, the more important I must be, when there is nothing biblical about that at all. When sometimes what we really need is a cool drink of water at the well of God, we need to retreat, or rest. Rest today is not something that is encouraged that much. The adult needs at least 9 hours of sleep according to WebMD, and healthfinder.gov. Yes the spirit will strengthen you, but God designed you to go to bed at night and get well rested. Some have the mindset, they will sleep when they die. Yes God has prepared a place for those that belong to him to rest forever in heaven, but my friend, I want to remind you that as long as you are walking on planet earth the Spirit of God is dwelling in an earthen vessel wrapped around in flesh. Whoever believes there will be no struggle in the flesh on earth is crazy. Yes as spirit filled believers we overcome the flesh, but until you come out of the flesh once and for all Paul says there is a war and a struggle that will take place until then. Being filled with the spirit of God daily is a massive help in this area. But I believe people who think they walk perfectly every day with no struggle are delusional.

What does it look like when pressure is involved? Just like in the workplace, when pressure is put on supervisors and managers where do you think it's headed, exactly right down to those underneath. It can be in the area of money, building or keeping reputation, or other coercive practices. If the top is pressured to do a new assignment the pressure is poured out on all, regardless of what the followers feel about it. Because one supports the vision, mission, and church does not mean that everything that is decided by leadership that involves the people's time, money, and efforts are agreed upon. This is not to say that we should not work as a one unit, because two can't walk together unless there is agreement. It is to say that those who do not make the major decisions on moving forward with a new vision or goal are sometimes the main ones paying for the decision that was made, even though they never made it. You just go along with what is presented to you, and if you don't participate in the way it is expected labeling and rejection occurs. When this occurs sometimes at church, the house of God is no longer a place to come and worship corporately and be strengthened leaving in peace, sometimes you can walk out the doors more stressed out and discouraged than that of when you came in, even though we are to edify and encourage. Oh, all the many things to do. There is little time to minister to your family, which we all say is the first ministry. Is it really? How can you be away from your family most of the year when your family is your first ministry? If we are to follow God's order for things is this out of order? There are circumstances that cause for some to commit to an assignment where spouses are separated for a time, but as long as it's that and not merely separating because the marriage isn't working, masking it as a ministry assignment separation. We tend to operate as those things don't happen, just like we operate as if authority everywhere on this earth is pure. It is not. Who spends time with their family anymore? It's typically those who don't have church titles and who are not in every ministry listed. What I am saying is it's not typical to have ordinary families in the congregation where no one holds a title or status within the church and whose marriages and families are a lot stronger and healthier than those at the top. Yes they may not have particular responsibilities and the called life is a different life, but different doesn't mean abandon your family, God supports family as he is a relationship unto himself: Father, Son, and Holy Spirit. This is not to say they don't serve in any form, but they may not be at the church building every day of the week. There are those in ministry whose families and marriages are a living wreck and no one even knows because they have to save face. My heart goes out to you. I have been there myself.

To reflect back on authority I thought it was interesting that freedom has always come as a result of the righteous overthrowing unjust authority. Even with Christ himself, who came to destroy the works of the devil according to 1 John 3:8 who had authority because Adam forfeited it the Garden of Eden. Nothing has changed today. The devil still understands if he can infiltrate a place of authority he is successful. Those who have the call to stand in the gap for people and have assignments to overcome unjust authority, oh my, I am praying for you. This is an area of your life that will be attacked, and if you are not ready for the fight, you already lost! This is something I recognized on my life at a very young age. Anytime I began working for a company or showed up to a place, literally all hell would begin breaking loose and the same result always manifested, someone over me was either fired, demoted, or the company itself shut down, I am talking about breaking news on the front page of the news paper several times. See, if God is going to get anything done in the earth, he is going to use ordinary people like you and like me. When I began to realize this on my life, it grieved me. I prayed and asked God to change my purpose and destiny because this was nothing anyone would ever want to deal with. I knew the labels would come, the misunderstandings, and so forth, but the gifts are without repentance. I'll just say when I truly discovered my God given gifts, it was frightening and I thank God that he sent others to help me understand them. I have accepted at this point, I cannot trade them in for another. And I trust that there must be a reason why God saw fit to impart the gifts he chose to give me, as I pray you will see the same for your life.

As we look on the birthing of our nation the United States of America, it was birthed out of people rising up against an injustice authority system in Great Britain. Where would we be if no one fought against that authority? The Boston tea party was a right rebellious act that birthed this nation to be free from a strong grip! Don't hear me incorrectly. I am not promoting or encouraging people to rise up against authority for the sake of being rebellious. I am pointing out that sometimes there has to be a stand when power is in the hands of the wrong people. Authority in the hands of the wrong person means many suffer due to this. It is commonly known, and not always corrected for business organizations in today's era to partake in unethical business practices. We see manipulation within business, even though there are policies, practices, and laws in place, it still occurs. We see manipulation in marriages and families, various relationships that can include friendships and parenting. Church is a place where everyone comes with a smile on their face, and in their best clothes, seeming to have it all together. It is not a common place to reckon with manipulation however it is one of the places where manipulation is found prominently. Sadly, it is found in ministries and churches regardless of denominations or religious affiliations. When it is done in other settings outside of church, manipulation makes sense and it is more accepted than when it is done within the church. Who wants to disclose any manipulations within the place where we are to honor the man of God, the woman of God, the leaders and ministers? Isn't the reputation of the ministry more important than any little manipulation one is experiencing in it? Who wants to reach for the label that is in big bold black letters reading OUTCAST or TATTLETALE? It is certainly not a desired thing to elaborate on, nevertheless what happens in any setting where someone needs to speak up on behalf of others, and conflict usually follows as a result. But keep in mind that not all trouble and not all conflict is bad. Many times order is a result upon chaos.

Jacqueline didn't belong to any of the men at her church, but some were operating as if she was their property. Did the kingdom of God really matter to them? Perhaps it did, but the struggles of the flesh came out sideways at times. Wouldn't an honorable marriage that demonstrated the love of Christ to others be a great contribution to the body? Not in the eyes of Minister Thomas, who was supposed to be kingdom minded, enhancing holy hook ups within his local church for the betterment of promoting godly marriage should have been his motive. His agenda was more important than the façade he put on. It wasn't until he began verbalizing his motives in his sleep at night when Mrs. Thomas knew what was going on. God revealed it to her right in their marriage bed. She began recording his words during his sleep and played them back after collecting a few months worth. It wasn't until then, that this was exposed and he was the one asked to leave the congregation. Sadly by that time the young man that really loved Jackie married someone else. Mr. Thomas was put on church discipline as he confessed his issue he had over the years. Later he was restored, after getting the help he needed. This is not some book tale for the sake of entertaining readers, this is a true testimony that actually happened, with real people, and was a real mess. No this has not happened to me, and it's not my testimony, but yes it is the testimony of someone very close to me. At the end of the day, Hebrews 4: 13 came alive! Nothing in all creation is hidden from God. Everything is naked and exposed before his eyes, and he is the one to whom we are accountable. It's a tough spot to be exposed to something like this where there is no physical proof, only the discernment and the revelation that God shows you. It's even more difficult to speak up on it in a place where you worship weekly. Especially if you don't obtain a leadership role. How valuable is your voice then? Then the question arises, would anyone even care?

Several women face this, and there is no way any of them would dare to speak up. How could she? Where could should she? To whom would she? Only to the Lord! The Lord sees all things and he knows all things in spite of the uniforms, robes, and titles that people wear in the world and in the church.

Jacqueline had shared this hidden testimony she had carried all her life until she learned that her daughter Vivian, was experiencing the same. When Jackie discovered that Vivian was asked to leave her church too because of her beauty, she wanted her daughter to know she was not alone and that she had been there too. Vivian shared her testimony with her daughter Veronica after learning about how another first lady was ticked off because of a beautiful member or visitor. It's as if they could get away with murder and no one would dare point it out or challenge it.

Veronica was so tired of being beat up about the way God fashioned her face, body, and physical appearance. Why couldn't anyone notice the pure heart that was present inside of her? She often wanted to be seen internally, however the external seemed to be a barrier.

One week Pastor Williams would be so kind to her, only to throw painful remarks out the next week about how beautiful people are not chosen by God. The interaction she received was bitter sweet and she didn't understand why. It was evident that she was affecting him in some type of way. Yes, he was attracted to her, but of course couldn't have her. She would often hear messages about how he's so glad he married Mrs. Williams because she focuses more on the home duties than spending time in the mirror. He'd make remarks that pretty faces don't make meals and maintain a warm home. She couldn't help but think; well do ugly faces make meals and maintain a warm home? The truth of the matter is that a good wife makes meals for her family and maintains a warm home. The face or body is not what's making the home a home, it's the type of woman in that home. That wife may be physically attractive, she may not be physically attractive, but this picture and truth was never painted, only the picture that would appease his irritation of not being able to have Veronica, and his overall marriage decision twenty years ago. The pictures that were painted also appeased Mrs. Williams who often felt better once the comments were made about how wonderful she was. Of course a man should honor his wife and demonstrate verbal and physical affection in public. This is beautiful, but not when it's done to make others feel inferior. Always keep in mind that God weighs the scales of the heart every second of every moment.

Many times it was perceived that it was better to be physically unattractive in the church setting compared to being beautiful. The more attractive, the less holy, the less attractive, the more holy. Beauty quickly became associated with evil. Anytime it was mentioned it was to put down anyone that was physically attractive. It was associated with one that does not know God, or someone who was not modest or virtuous. One day Veronica overheard a mother in the church giving her son some advice as he was trying to choose a wife. The mother said, son, pick a woman who isn't a glamour girl, those pretty girls won't run your bath water or clean your home, they only please they eye. She couldn't believe that a mother would give her son such advice. Veronica thought, could a pretty woman not clean her home and care for her family? If a woman was beautiful did that mean she was good for nothing except to be looked at? Veronica was not a shallow woman. She had integrity and godly character. She was a great cook and homemaker. She had an education and was filled with the spirit of god. Yes she had been through some of life's disheartening circumstances, but she was determined to overcome them all. Veronica was a pleasant humble woman who loved God and people. To hear what was referenced about pretty women troubled her spirit as she believed that no one would ever truly know her for whom she was, and all the good things inside of her because of how she looked externally. One day she screamed out at God. "Why did you make me this way? This is your entire fault! Beauty is a curse!!" Veronica was hurt and abused by what was accepted within church society. No one ever thought to bring an enlightenment and correction to this area as it was a subtle abuse. Every woman wants to be beautiful outwardly no matter how holy she is. It is how God fashioned women to be. Satan was the most beautiful thing God created before his fall from heaven. Lucifer was his name; he was bright, with every shining stone. When he fell from heaven and saw the crown of creation which was Eve, he about lost his mind to see a life giving beautiful creature that reminded him of what God thought about him once upon a time, before he was kicked out of heaven. Woman is the crown of creation, the icing on the cake, the very last thing that God created and she reflects the heart of God, this is why it is not good for man to be alone. Any woman who tells you she is not moved by her outward appearance doesn't know how God created her to be. I am not saying women should invest all their time in their appearance, but I am saying it is okay to realize that God fashioned you as a woman, and that he made you beautiful, to be beautiful absolutely on the inside but as well on the outside. If you read the bible carefully God was highly concerned with how beautiful things appeared on the exterior especially when they represented him. This is a viewpoint that is rarely discussed within churches. Take the tabernacle for example, and the temple for instance, even the attire of the priests. God is a God of beauty, because he is Beautiful. Even God has a beautiful train that fills the temple. Anything of beauty is a reflection of God himself, because beauty comes from God. My point here is that people need to stop making physically attractive people feel bad for looking exactly how God created them to be. Anyone that is attractive or not attractive physically shouldn't be exterior conscious only. Don't put confidence in your flesh and don't focus all your energy and efforts on materials, this is not godly, but it's also not godly to disregard presenting your best before God either as beauty is an attribute of God. It is not godly to try and appear neutral and modest so people will perceive you in a certain light of holiness and god like, when your heart may not reflect the same. I recall in my own life when I meet people for the first time they often associate me as a pretty woman who perhaps may not break a nail, not ever realizing some of the assignments I have had in life they would have never made it through.

Let's examine the suggestion that God does not choose beautiful people for his plans. In fact he does, the exterior is not what draws God. It is the interior. Whether the external is attractive to man or not does not matter with God, but he does use all kind of people, including those who are beautiful. Is this biblical? Yes it is actually. According to 1 Samuel 16:1 The Lord rejected Saul, someone that was physically attractive. Yes God had chosen him prior to be the King of Israel, but due to the condition of Saul's heart this privilege and honor was taken away from him and given to another, which was David. 1 Samuel 1: 6-7 says that when they arrived, Samuel took one look at Eliab and thought, "Surely this is the LORD's anointed!" But the LORD said to Samuel, "Don't judge by his appearance or height, for I have rejected him. The LORD doesn't see things the way you see them. People judge by outward appearance, but the LORD looks at the heart." We see here that there was a physically attractive man that was rejected by God for his selection of the next King of Israel. So it's true God does not judge by the outward appearance. This is an example of God rejecting someone that was not right internally, that just so happened to be attractive externally. There are times where he does choose physically attractive people. If we keep reading we will see what happens next in 1 Samuel 8-12. Then Jesse told his son Abinadab to step forward and walk in front of Samuel. But Samuel said, "This is not the one the LORD has chosen." Next Jesse summoned Shimea, but Samuel said, "Neither is this the one the LORD has chosen." In the same way all seven of Jesse's sons were presented to Samuel. But Samuel said to Jesse, "The LORD has not chosen any of these." Then Samuel asked, "Are these all the sons you have?""There is still the youngest," Jesse replied. "But he's out in the fields watching the sheep and goats.""Send for him at once," Samuel said. "We will not sit down to eat until he arrives." So Jesse sent for him. He was dark and handsome, with beautiful eyes. And the LORD said, "This is the one; anoint him." The word of God clearly indicated that David, whom was God's selection, was a physically attractive man, who was beautiful on the inside as well as the outside. In church you usually hear about the first rejection of Eliab because he was outwardly attractive, however it's not as common to hear that God selected David, and he just so happened to be a handsome man with beautiful eyes.

So when the statement is being made that God doesn't look at the outward appearance, he only looks at the heart, this is not to be taken to mean, that if you are beautiful God will not choose you or use you, because that is not the truth. So if we read the bible and see clearly that God chose beautiful people in some areas as his selection this should clearly indicate that a person with a right heart in God's perspective can be physically attractive, as well as unattractive physically. The point here is we have to stop making it seem like anyone that is beautiful or handsome isn't God's choice. Yes men choose on the basis of these things in addition to materialism, status, position, popularity, etc. but God doesn't. He is no respecter of persons.

Is it true that someone who is unattractive physically could be mean, nasty, and unloving? I believe so. It's easier to believe and accept someone that is attractive physically being mean, nasty, and unloving on the inside because this is the primary picture painted mostly. People tend to gravitate and praise others who obtain physical beauty, however it is a truth that people that are considered unattractive on the outside can be just as unattractive on the inside. Just like God could reject someone with a beautiful face and an ugly heart, he can reject someone that has an unattractive face and an ugly heart, because God doesn't look at the outward appearance.

Let's look at some other people in the bible that God chose and they were beautiful people.

1 Samuel 35: 1-3 says Now Samuel died, and all Israel gathered for his funeral. They buried him at his house in Ramah. Then David moved down to the wilderness of Maon. There was a wealthy man from Maon who owned property near the town of Carmel. He has 3,000 sheet and 1,000 goats, and it was sheep shearing time. This man's name was Nabal, and his wife, Abigail, was a **sensible and beautiful woman**. But Nabal, a descendant of Caleb, was crude and mean in all his dealings. This passage of scripture is so rich because it addresses much. For instance, prior to David arriving in Maon he was already married to woman named Michal. This marriage was an arranged marriage as accustomed in that day and culture David lived in. This was not a woman that David desired for himself, she was a woman that he had earned from his works. Michal's father, Saul had set a trap for David to fail a test in earning his daughter's hand in marriage. Saul believed that David couldn't and wouldn't pass this test. Saul said, "Here's another chance to see him killed by the Philistines"! Saul said this to himself, but to David he said, "Today you have a second chance to become my son in law!" All of this was a trick to get David killed as he was expected to fail the test of bringing Saul back 100 Philistine foreskins as a bride price. (A bride price for the second choice: Michal. Saul was to give his daughter Mereb, but he gave her to another to hurt David). Saul had no idea, that his heart was being

weighed, and the scales of justice was about to deliver. David went out and killed 200 Philistines and brought their foreskins back to Saul. See, the same trap that the enemy will set for you, will be the same trap the enemy will fall in…because God's word does not come back void…..God will expose the hearts of men. Jesus said, these people (religious leaders) honor me with their lips, but their hearts are far from me. That test was designed to kill David. The primary persecutors of Jesus Christ was not the sheep or the people who he was ministering to, it was the elders, the leading priests, and the teachers of religious law according to Mark 8:31. These were highly respected, revered, men with delegated authority which was distorted due to the hardness of hearts. Israel, the chosen people of God rejected the Messiah sent to her due to hearts that were not right. The purpose of light is to bring revelation where there is natural, satanic, and or carnal blindness. They were not able to see Christ as the son of God, their Messiah, because their hearts were not willing. When someone or a group of individuals become a certain way and remain a certain way with no promise of change it is often due to that particular hindering nature becoming ensconced into them. This means whatever the nature is that has been developed it is almost like a snowball affect where the more it travels and the further it grows the larger it gets. Take someone who becomes obese for example, they didn't get obese overnight. It started somewhere and after a while their body weight increased over time. The sad thing is it makes it harder for them to lose the weight without having surgery. The same is with those with a nature that has been so ensconced in them. It becomes more difficult for their hearts to see the revelation of Christ and to accept him. Nothing is too difficult for the Lord, yet it will take a supernatural of God alone to bring light to those described in Mark 8:31. Jesus told even the Pharisees that they erred in not knowing the scriptures. Nevertheless 1 Samuel 18: 28 says When Saul realized that the Lord was with David and how much his daughter Michal loved him, Saul became even more afraid of him, and he remained David's enemy for the rest of his life. The point here is that when people see that the Lord is with you, the fear of the Lord will be upon you and they will be afraid of you. Yes, they will be at peace with you, but their hearts may be even bitterer towards you after realizing that God is with you. Every plan and plot that is made to eliminate you all will ultimately FAIL.

Why would a sensible beautiful woman choose to be with a crude and mean man in all his dealings? Did she choose Nabal? Did Nabal choose her? Was their marriage arranged? We don't know. We do know women didn't have much say over their lives during biblical times, therefore we don't know the initiation of this marriage. The important thing the bible feels it's necessary for us to know is that it's possible to be linked up with someone you won't necessary finish with. The wife that people chose for David was Michal, and if we know how the story ends, we know they didn't finish together. Nabal and Abigail started together, but did they finish together? This principle won't preach well in some avenues, but I do believe you don't always finish with who you started off with. It is ideal, particularly in the area of marriage which we will visit in a later chapter. The point here is that God weighed Michal's heart when she ridiculed David for dancing out of his coat before the Most High God, and she was replaced. God weighed Nabal's heart when he refused to help David and listen to the wife God graced him to have, Abigail, and the scales of justice set it. We can even see this principle with David's request with Nabal. He requested Nabal to help him yet he was basically told no. As a believer I have come to learn that the victory is even sweeter when people have told you no to your requests. It's almost as if God wants to prove to you that he is in ultimate control. Nabal said no David but the yes was with Abigail when she met him with items he requested. When man says no, God sometimes says yes. Not only did David receive tangible items for his journey, but he also received Nabal's wife, Abigail. The scales of the heart will totally change up your destiny. It is a kingdom principle that is rarely studied or projected. God looks at the heart and if major offenses are affecting God's chosen appointed, anointed child, don't be surprised when there is new news that shocks the ears of the public. Can you imagine? Everyone had to have known how unfortunate Abigail was as Nabal was known in Maon, he was a wealthy man. What they didn't see coming, perhaps neither did Abigail herself, was that there was a day that would manifest deliverance for her to assist the next, the chosen, King of Israel.

Abigail was wise, and she appeased David with her words. She was sensible, and brought light in areas David was blinded in. She saved his hands from bloodshed. Intelligence, articulation, and beauty come from God. How is this a contradiction from what Proverbs teach? Let's take a look. The devil never created anything; he just copied what God made. This is why beauty can be seen as evil, and why one that speaks well is considered deceptive, it is because of what the devil has done to God's original intent and creation that mindsets have been set against people that obtain beauty and that are excellent in speech. Proverbs 7:21 says so she seduced him with her pretty speech and enticed him with her flattery. Proverbs 3:5 says for the lips of an immoral woman are as sweet as honey, and her mouth is smoother than oil. Proverbs 6:24 says It will keep you from the immoral woman, from the smooth tongue of a promiscuous woman. Proverbs 2:16 says Wisdom will save you from the immoral woman, from the seductive words of the promiscuous woman. So what is this implying? Is this stating that a beautiful woman that is good with her words is immoral and that she is trying to be deceptive? No, this is not what that means, although this is exactly what is taught to others. The perspective is created that any woman that's good with her words is evil. Is it possible that she could be evil? Yes it is. If so, then what was originally given to her by God has now been tainted by the enemy. The enemy has contaminated what God originally created, which is beauty, articulation, and intelligence. The enemy has twisted and bent what God originally created in a woman to now be used for the perverse purposes for the kingdom of darkness. The point here is that we cannot go around pointing the finger to women saying she's evil, she's a Delilah, she's a Jezebel, she's a smooth talking woman, when there are many women that God selects, ordains, and chooses that are beautiful, who can articulate, and that efficiently and effectively teach and lead others for the purposes of the kingdom of God. We don't get to ascribe and label the woman we choose to because it's the way we want to see her, and how we desire for others to view her as well, because she may be a threat to you. When really the idea of her being a threat to you is embedded in your mind by the enemy. She may not have any intent on being a threat to you, she just might be a human being that desires to come to church and worship with the assembly. She may just want to serve God in ministry and give back. The fact that she is beautiful shouldn't prohibit her from doing so out of the will of her own or the will of others that desire to push her away. Yes! We need to come against the spirit of Jezebel and Delilah nonstop and with authority! But be careful you're not ascribing these spirits to anyone beautiful that may have strong leadership capabilities just because you want to.

It is a truth that women that are not as physically outwardly may tend to be a bit harder on women who are, because there is a reminding pain present that could have stemmed from being rejected or not being selected over someone who was more physically attractive. This is real, but it doesn't give anyone a right to go around putting down beautiful women because of one's life experiences. This is not Godly, and it's not healthy. It's almost as if they have a right to put down a woman that is beautiful because they may not be as physically attractive. I am not sure who approved that lie, but no one has the right to put anyone else down regardless if they are unattractive or attractive.

23

You will hear comments often made, which are true such as beauty is only skin deep, beauty is not everything, beauty tells you nothing about a person's heart. These things are absolutely true, but they should never have the agenda to make themselves look better compared to that of a physically beautiful person. Putting someone down is not always communicated verbally, sometimes it's not what is said, it could be how it was said, or what was not said. Communication comes in many avenues other than it being verbal.

When this type of judgment occurs with women, it sometimes is derived from a jealous root. It pictures the one making the accusations look good, while making an intelligent beautiful woman look bad, and that is not like Christ in any way. It is a form of abuse, especially when it's done from the top. The pulpit should not be used for any purpose one desires, including firing off personal feelings about those within a congregation. If you have done this, you need to repent, and dedicate yourself to love God's people, all of God's people, the smart ones, the dumb ones, the tall ones, the short ones, the ugly ones, the beautiful ones, the one's that seem perfect, and the one's that needed much grace to abound, where much sin once abounded. God looks at our hearts every second of every moment, because out of it flows the issues of life according to Proverbs 4:23. Matthew 15:19 For from the heart come evil thoughts, murder, adultery, all sexual immorality, theft, lying, and slander. These are what defile you. Eating with unwashed hands will never defile you."

How Does God View Beauty?

As we close out of this section on Beauty let's look at some special chosen men of God in the bible that God intentionally arranged to be with women who were outwardly beautiful. Why is this being portrayed? Because in church we sometimes ascribe beauty to satanic intentions when God created Satan and showered him as one of the most beautiful creations that existed, that is before his fall. Therefore we don't recognize as much other creations that God made beautiful such as people because it's assumed that if you point out the beauty in one, arrogance, pride, and evil will spring up as it did with Satan. This is a possibility, but it's not a truth that can be labeled on everything or everyone that obtains physical beauty.

In Genesis we see that the woman God chose for Abraham was beautiful. She was trans-culturally beautiful. What does this mean? This means that she wasn't just beautiful according to a culture or ethnicity, but her physical beauty was seen by all cultures, lands, and peoples. Let's just say, Sarah, was COLD. It didn't matter who thought what about her or her beauty. She was God's choice for the man of God. Did she have issues? Absolutely! Was she broken in areas? Absolutely! What we find in Sarah, Rebekah, and Rachel all had one issue in common. Which we all know were barren women, until destiny matched up with time that is. Yes they may have been ridiculed for a time, but after bringing forth sons that were of destiny their honor was set for generations to come. It wasn't so much that they were barren women, because at the end of their testimony the children that they bore were special at God ordained times. Beauty is often associated with barrenness and it's also done in an abusive way when the intent is to put the woman down because she is beautiful. We know that every mouth raised against them was ultimately silenced. Rebekah received double for her trouble (twins). Rachel may have been viewed as less important compared to Jacob's other wife Leah who bore him more children and at earlier points compared to Rachel, but if you study Genesis 33 you will see it didn't matter how many children Leah bore him, his heart was always set on Rachel. God granted Leah the ability to reproduce because he saw that she was unloved by Jacob. It didn't matter how many children she bore him, his desire was still for Rachel. And the word of God reads in Genesis 33: Then Jacob looked up and saw Esau coming with his 400 men. So he divided the children among Leah, Rachel, and his two servant wives. He put the servant wives and their children at the front, Leah and her children next, and Rachel and Joseph (his soft spot, his heart last). What does this tell you? It tells you that Jacob would rather have his servant wives, which he didn't ask for, Leah, which he also didn't ask for or desire, along with all the children they bore him in front of Rachel and Joseph, if destruction was headed their way. He loved Rachel because she was his choice, and he loved Joseph and Benjamin more than his other children born to him by other women. She had a beautiful figure and a lovely face. Jacob learned just as his father and grandfather, something that God always knew, which is that beauty comforts! I believe this is why God gave the men of God beautiful women, because of the comfort and pleasure that comes from beauty, because beauty comes from God, and

25

in some ways it represents wealth. God created men to be turned on by sight. This does not mean that they should solely go off of sight alone, but it is what it is. Why do you think interior designers make a fortune in earnings? Because they create beautiful atmospheres and environments for people. Beauty comforts! Inward beauty as well as outward. Inward is far more precious than outward beauty Proverbs 30:31 says beauty is fleeting, but a woman who fears the lord will be praised. This is true, yet it doesn't mean that there is something wrong with being beautiful. I often hear women toss this scripture around to make a beautiful woman feel inferior as if she too couldn't have the fear of the Lord instilled in her character. As People want beautiful things in their homes at their jobs and even will choose to drive a particular car that's beautiful, because beauty comforts. I am not saying to invest in beauty, because it surely fades and it's not worth worshipping or putting confidence in it, but it does comfort. When you read the book of Exodus, we see how beautiful God designed the tabernacle, even down to the priests' apparel, he wanted things beautiful. The temple that Solomon built was laid in beauty. The New Jerusalem, the city we call heaven where believers will eternally dwell after this life here on earth is nothing but a reflection of God's beauty. The gates are made of pearls, the streets are made of gold, and the rivers are beautifully crystal clear. So if you have an issue with beauty, you have an issue with God, because it comes from him! The take away is it is not okay to put a physically beautiful person down because that person may make you feel a particular way when they have done nothing to you or because it's socially approved within religious settings. This is done consciously and other times unknowingly. We should make it our goal to get to know people before assuming what they are like despite what they look like externally. If we read 1 Kings 1 we see how David in his old age was comforted by a young beautiful woman who kept him warm and served him, it is because beauty comforts. We live in a world that is sex craved and everything is centered on sex. Sex is beautiful when done in the boundaries of holy matrimony. I find it unbelievable that many believers act as if intimacy and sex and passion all stem from the devil, when God created sex as a gift to husband and wife. This is certainly not the topic of this book, however if you have sexual desires to be intimate with the opposite sex, please don't think you are evil or being like the world, because that is exactly how God created you to be! I encourage you not to awaken love before it's time if you are single and to wait, pray, and fast for the mate God sends to you, and if you are married to get as sexually healthy as you possibly can so you can enjoy the gift in its full dimension that God has given to you. A great read for married couples only is the Gift of Sex by Clifford and Joyce Penner. If you are single a great read for you is I will wait for you by Joshua M. Parker. I encourage you regardless of your marital status to get as healthy as possible dealing with any dysfunctions and issues you need to so that you can be healthy in your mind, body, soul, and spirit for yourself and for your spouse if you are married or desire to be married.

Can the Apple Fall Far from the Tree?

Of course! You've heard the idiom that the apple doesn't fall too far from the tree. This is indicating that the apple which represents the child does not fall far from the tree which represents the parent. This is often said to demonstrate how a child is exactly like their mother or father. Early on it was difficult for me to share about the broken home that I came from, because by no means did I desire to embarrass my family or myself. I have become more comfortable over time sharing about how I was raised. I acknowledge that I was raised by imperfect people who had internal struggles of their own during the time that they were raising me.

I am aware that if I don't share my testimony, then it will not be of use to help others overcome what they are going through, or have experienced alike. Where one comes from definitely does **not** dictate where they are going, but it can give you an idea of how and why they may have started off in life the way that they did. My background **does** give me a better ability to relate to people who have similar stories, and how they too can experience breakthroughs and deliverance from sin, Satan, and self! It's important to share the things you have been though so that you can see how God brought you through, so that you can learn from any mistakes you've made, and of course to help, encourage, and edify someone else who is facing exactly what you've made it through.

I didn't come from a home where my parents were pastors, preachers, or ministers, and that's okay, not all children do. Some children are raised in homes that strictly adhere to Godly principles and a lifestyle that reflects the same. Some children follow in the footsteps of their parents in ministry, and some children don't continue in "the way". Some, it takes them falling away to come full circle in the way they were raised. This is found in Ezekiel 18: 5-32. Suppose a certain man is righteous and does what is just and right. He does not feast in the mountains before Israel's idols or worship them. He does not commit adultery, or have intercourse with a woman during her menstrual period. He is a very merciful creditor, not keeping the items given as security by poor debtors. He does not rob the poor but instead gives food to the hungry and provides clothes for the needy. He grants loans without interest, stays away from injustice, is honest and fair when judging others, and faithfully obeys my decrees and regulations.

Anyone who does these things is just and will surely live, says the sovereign Lord. But suppose that man has a son who grows up to be a robber or murderer and refuses to do what is right. And that son does all the evil things his father would never do. He worships idols on the mountains, commits adultery, oppress the poor and helpless, steals from debtors by refusing to let them redeem their security, worships idols, commits detestable sins, and lends money at excessive interest. Should such a sinful person live? No! He must die and must take full blame. But suppose that sinful son, in turn, has a son who sees his father's wickedness and decides against that kind of life. This son refuses to worship idols on the mountains and does not commit adultery. He does not exploit the poor; but instead is fair to debtors and does not rob them. He gives food to the hungry and provides clothes for the needy. He helps the poor, does not lend money at interest, and obeys all my regulations and decrees. Such a person will not die because of his father's sins: he will surely live. But the father will die for his many sins for being cruel, robbing people, and doing what was clearly wrong among his people. What? You ask. Doesn't the child pay for the parent's sins? No! For if the child does what is just and right and keeps my decrees, that child will surely live.

The person who sins is the one who will die. The child will not be punished for the parent's sins, and the parent will not be punished for the child's sins. Righteous people will be rewarded for their own righteous behavior, and wicked people will be punished for their own wickedness. But if wicked people turn away from all their sins and begin to obey my decrees and do what is right and just, they will surely live and not die. All their past sins will be forgotten, and they will live because of the righteous things they have done. Do you think that I like to see wicked people die? Says the Sovereign Lord. Of course not! I want them to turn from their wicked ways and live. However, if righteous people turn from their righteous behavior and start doing sinful things and act like other sinners, should they be allowed to live? No, of course not! All their righteous acts will be forgotten, and they will die for their sins. Yet you say, The Lord isn't doing what's right! Listen to me, O people of Israel. Am I the one not doing what's right, or is it you?

When righteous people turn from their righteous behavior and start doing sinful things they will die for it. Yes they will die because of their sinful deeds. And if wicked people turn from their wickedness, obey the law and do what is just and right they will save their lives. They will live because they thought it over and decided to turn from their sins. Such people will not die. And yet the people of Israel keep saying the Lord isn't doing what's right. O people of Israel it is you who are not doing what's right, not I. Therefore I will judge each of you, O people of Israel, according to your actions says the sovereign Lord. Repent and turn from your sins. Do not let them destroy you! Put all your rebellion behind you, and find yourselves a new heart and a new spirit. For why should you die, O people of Israel says the sovereign Lord, Turn back and live.

So it is clear to see that it doesn't matter where one comes from, but it does matter what is in the heart of the individual. Cain and Abel came from the same woman: as did Esau and Jacob: the difference between the two: hearts were weighed by God and Jacob weighed out better just like David's heart was better than Saul's in 1 Samuel 15:28.

So just to review from 1 Samuel 2: 12-36: How can evil sons come from a man of God who is saturated in God's word and spirit? God weighs the hearts, and it's each man or woman for themselves, regardless of who your parents, pastor, or spouse may be.

I Thought God Said....

According to Numbers 14:18 which says The Lord is slow to anger and filled with unfailing love, forgiving every kind of sin and rebellion. But he does not excuse the guilty. **He lays the sins of the parents upon their children; the entire family is affected even children in the third and fourth generations.**

Please note that the contradictions you read throughout the book is not an indication that the bible is written incorrectly! I whole heartedly agree with 2 Timothy 3:16 that all scripture is God breathed and inspired, which is absolutely correct! The contradictions that you will read throughout the book will elaborate on the opposing views and instructions that are listed throughout the bible which can conflict with one another. This may be confusing for the reader, particularly the new believer in Christ that's headed to read the Word of God after conversion. It can also create uncertainty for the sinner who reads God's word. We know that things of God cannot be revealed to anyone unless they are revealed by and through the Spirit of God. This is not related to 1 Corinthians 2:10. We know that people are not to approach and read the sacred word of God like we read any other literature or reading material, but my point is very basic relating to just reading opposite information on the same subject with confusion as a result. The mature saint may not struggle in this area and that's expected, however there are many people who may need more elaboration on God's word and according to 2 Timothy 2:15 we are to rightly divide the word of truth, therefore it's expected for it to be taught correctly by those who are called by God to preach it and teach it.

For example, what we just addressed with parents and their children. In one area of the bible God says he will repay the sins of the parents to their children even to the third and fourth generation. Some scholars argue that this is generational; others argue that during the times this was written, it was not common to have a household composed of three to four generations living in that same house hold together, and the sins of the parents affects the third and fourth generation because they are all living within the same house hold, just as in 1 Corinthians 7:14, where one sanctifies their entire household regardless of who is living there. This idea suggests that as one could sanctify a household, one can bring the opposite as well such as a curse to those in the household in the Old Testament. The New testament involves the Holy Spirit being sent to believers to help them in their walk, thus the believing spouse we see in 1 Corinthians 7, has the ability to sanctify their home, however in the Old Testament the Holy Spirit was not sent to permanently indwell the believer, thus one in the same camp or home would affect all that is in the same home or camp. The second study is rarely ever discussed or shared, and it is assumed that the writer was indicating generational affects in relation to time instead of the family all living under the same roof. This came from the idea of one sinning in the camp, if one sinned in the camp of Israel in the Old Testament they had to be removed from the camp by either being put away for a certain time, by death, or escaping to the city of refuge as we see in Numbers 35:6 and Numbers 35:28.

Needless to say, **whatever was indicated**, regardless of how the sins were imputed to the children in this passage, Numbers 14:18 says that the children will suffer because of the parents. In another area God says that he won't cause the children to suffer from their parents' sin as we just read in Ezekiel 18:5-32. By no means am I questioning God as he is always right. The point of me asking is because as I have gotten to know God personally for myself. I understand how relational God is. God is interested in walking and talking with his children. If we have questions about his word, I encourage you to go to God in prayer about it so that he can reveal it to you. If you are not mature in your walk, seek out Godly counsel from a trusted Spiritual Advisor, Pastor, or teacher of God's word that has studied them self approved. Today if you ask a question about what the word of God says you may not be well received, or labeled as trying to twist or adulterate the word of God, when that is not always the case. When Abraham had questioned God about saving his nephew Lot in Sodom and Gomorrah, did God reprimand him for asking him questions about the very thing God said? No he didn't, he interacted with him relationally. What about Moses? God told Moses exactly what he wanted him to do and how he wanted him to do it. Did Moses just say okay, no problem? He did not. As ideal as that may sound and would have been, that was not the case. It is imperative to obey God without question for the assignments that he has on our lives. My point is in relation to our personal relationship with God. God is so intimate and he desires to interact with you. He is waiting for you to come to him and talk with him and walk with him. You will be amazed to see that the God who is Holy and shouldn't be approached just any kind of way, is the same God that talks back to you in your prayer time, throughout the day, even in your sleep. You will be in awe at how he answers your prayers specifically for you. This is what I love about God. There are many people that try and tell you what your personal relationship should look like with God. We all must abide by the commandments that uniform a real believer's walk with God, however the way we get in touch with God and commune with him may be different than another person.

My encouragement to you is that if you do have a question about what the word of God says, if you are not getting any answers from man, because man expects you to just "do it", which that may be the case, however I can reassure you that there is a loving God that welcomes you with open arms to anything you may be confused about or need guidance on. We see that Moses did obey the Lord, he had some anger issues, but God could handle and was bigger than Moses' questions and appeals when he was being instructed to stand before Pharaoh and deliver the children out of Egypt. God was also patient with Abraham who interacted with the First Voice, which is God, who revealed the plan he had for Sodom and Gomorrah. As communication and interaction continued between God and Abraham, the result was Lot being saved. What if Abraham would have said, okay God, do what you said you're going to do in Sodom and Gomorrah whether Lot is there or not, out of fear that He is not able to question God. Abraham knew God. He didn't just know about God. When you know about God it is easy to say what you should or shouldn't be doing according to the word. When you know God, you realize he is greater than his word. His word will never come back void and it will accomplish what it was set out to do. That does not limit God in being sovereign. Yes God can do what he wants to do, when he wants to do it. Yes he gives us free will, therefore he chooses to limit his sovereignty so that he can interact and work with us due to the gift he has given us of free will. The point I am making is that the plan of God was communicated to Abraham, and Abraham didn't take it as it was. He went before God and they had a situation changing conversation. Just as Hezekiah did regarding the time he was supposed to die in the book of 2 Kings 20, and Isaiah 38:5.

It is true, we should trust God and not always be in question about what he is saying, however, I believe that the story about Abraham interacting with Lot was written for more than just watching Lot get rescued. As I believe the record of Hezekiah was written, not only so that we can see how fifteen more years was added to his life, but to understand that God does not shy back when we come to him with our plea even if it is opposite of what he has already declared. That makes God relational. That makes him what the word says he indeed is, and that is love. Religion says, do what I tell you to do because I said it. Love says do what I tell you to do because I know what's best for you, and I will interact with you and be in relationship, extending free will to you. Love says I will work everything out for your good, the good, the bad, and the ugly if you are the called of the Lord's, it will work out according to his purpose. This is not to say go and make any decisions you want as a believer because you know that God will work it out for your good. This is saying if God be for you, then who can be against you? No one! I believe God wants us to see that we, as spiritual sons and daughters can come to him in prayer about situations that have already been declared by God and intercede and pray for those being affected. You will be amazed at how God hears you, he desires for you to come to him in faith knowing he is there according to Hebrews 11.

Can God say at one time he will do something and later, say he won't? Depending on what it is, I believe the word of God has many examples proving that he does. We all have heard the saying that goes: if God said it that settles it! Looking at what we discussed he said a few things in one area and in other areas of the Bible he is saying something totally different. So in an essence God said a number of things to Abraham and Hezekiah, and that didn't settle it. He is in ultimate control and what God says is the final say, however that final say may be different than what he initially said. This is primarily true when it comes to his people.

When it comes to God's children, he is passionate and what he initially intended may not be final because he loves to love us, and be in relationship with us. I am not pointing this out to indicate that God is bipolar or unsure. I am pointing this out because God doesn't work or think like we as humans work or think. God looks at the heart of a person and that heart is being weighed. The heart along with intercession can touch God in such a way that he takes whatever he has said and may do the exact opposite of what he originally said because of a change in heart or persistence in prayer, or just because he is sovereign and can do whatever he wants to do without having to check in with anyone, or to get anyone's permission before he does it. Yes, in many situations he chooses to limit his sovereignty as stated before, however when God has determined a thing according to Joseph in Genesis 41:32, nothing will deter it. So be encouraged if you've made mistakes or have fallen short of qualifying for what man says you should, when God has determined a matter, it is coming to pass. Stand still and see the sovereign salvation of the Lord!

We see this all throughout the Bible when God just shows up and does what he wants to. My friend, if religious leaders thought Jesus was being rebellious for bucking against their authority; don't be surprised when you're labeled too. For example, one of the commandments of God says to keep the Sabbath holy and don't do any work on the Sabbath. Clearly in Mark 3 and Luke 13 Jesus does something that the first voice which is God's voice, instructs us to do, and that is to keep the Sabbath holy, there should not be any work done on it. How can the same God that instructed this, be the same God that broke this rule? The Pharisees wanted to trap Jesus by showing he wasn't keeping the law as he proclaimed to be the son of God, God which gave the law. Notice the one who broke the rule, it was God himself. In Matthew 12 we read about how the Disciples of Christ were hungry and began breaking off heads of grain to eat them. When Jesus was confronted by religious leaders about why his disciples were breaking the law, he referred to an old testament even of David who broke the law of eating the sacred loaves of bread that only the priests could eat. Jesus tells them that there is one greater than the temple. The one greater is him. God is greater than the church, the law, and the bible itself. He is Lord over it and just as the word will endure forever he will endure forever being Lord over all. We see Jesus doing the exact opposite of what was instructed in the law, why? It had everything to do with his love relationship for the one that needed to be rescued, even if it was on the Sabbath. God will break a rule for one that he loves to keep them from danger. God will put aside even himself for his child that he loves, even in the face of what religious people thing should happened. This example is knowing God personally and not solely knowing about God. One thing you can trace in the New Testament is the satanic pattern of religious people holding anyone to their past of breaking a rule or law. One thing Jesus was familiar with was passion. Not the kind of passion that rots the bones in Proverbs 14:30, but the fire burning passion to go the distance for those he loves. Often we witness lukewarm walks with Christ in our modern day generation that does not exuberate passion. Wherever this kind of passion is present it may be difficult to do business as usual. The same is evident today. Have you ever experienced a traumatic past where the door has been shut and you moved on with your life, to later find the exact people who should be encouraging you hindering you by pulling you back to your past? This is a predictable attack of the enemy. It is the only thing he has on you. To bring up a fault, mistake, wrong, or law that you have broken to keep you from moving forward. The intent is to make you feel bad by condemning you with the word of God, all the while with the efforts to make them look better. It is sad thing when this is done by the world, however when it's believer to believer that grieves the heart of God. Have you ever experienced someone trying to say bad things about you, only to make them look better, so that others won't find you so appealing? This is a form of sickness, and I encourage you to pray for anyone persecuting you in this way, that God will reveal to them their significance so that they don't have to downplay yours. The law was given to reveal men their sins according to Galatians 3:19. 2 Corinthians 3:6 says He has enabled us to be ministers of his new covenant. This is a covenant not of written laws, but of the Spirit. The old written covenant ends in death; but under the new covenant, the Spirit gives life. The religious leaders would have rather saw the sick remain sick on the Sabbath than a child of God healed or saved on the Sabbath. What a terrible heart. That's why God is God and religious people are just that, religious. Don't' let religious people keep you from your healing and deliverance, because they will if you let them. God is love! So the point is proven. God does declare what he has said and he means it, at the same time, he is weighing each situation, and the heart weighs out unexpected results many times. The rules were made for the heart, not the heart for the rules. I encourage you to obey all of God's instructions and listen well according to what he has told us to do and not do in His word. Do not think I am telling you to disregard what the Lord said, I am not. I am simply confirming Isaiah 29:13 and Matthew 15:8, and that is people can honor the Lord with their lips and in several other ways, but what God is interested in is a heart that is close to him.

So God says one thing, however depending on the heart the first voice may say the exact opposite. Does this mean that there is someone else talking if God changes his mind? No, it doesn't. It means that the same God, who said one thing, may change his mind and say another depending on the situation. God's character does not change, but it's proven in the word of God that he often changes the plan on account of one's heart and the situation, and by all means if that is what God wants to do, then who can question God?

The more you get to KNOW God and not just about him and what he tells you to do, you will see that God gives you instructions so that you will have access to holy fellowship with him and remain in relationship with him. God's personality is demonstrated by His works and the various things he has done. God loves his people, and he is not letting anything such as a rule come in between his love for you. This was proven with the crucifixion itself. Jesus being fully God put aside all of his deity (all of his divine status, quality, or nature) to come to his footstool, the earth, being born of a woman who never had intercourse with a man at his conception, survived the death sentence of Herod, taught at the age of twelve when old leaders were astonished that he could even relate and understand, heal the sick, raise the dead, even on a Sabbath, pay his tax money from the mouth of a fish, walk on water, quiet the storming seas and wind, transfigure on a high mountain, where others could see him in glory, die on a cross, rise again after being buried for days, descend down into hell and redeem those that belonged to him before the foundation of the world declaring his triumphant victory over death, reappear to over thousands on earth after his physical body was not found on the third day, commission his disciples to go into all the world in Matthew 28:19, doing greater works than him according to John 14:12! If you think his bending the rules stopped there, I'd beg to differ. God is manipulating situations all the time as He is God for those who love him and keep his commandments.

Above anything else, I have learned more about what I am motivated by, and that is the authentic love of Jesus the Christ! Nothing motivates me more! Not works or deeds, not money, status, position, etc. All of those are great. We should aim to serve in ministry and give our lives back to Christ. I am simply saying that nothing motivates me more than the LOVE of Jesus. You can always tell when love is not the motivator behind a ministry. God is love, and he commands us to love him more than anything, and to love others as we would ourselves. When you do this, everything you need in this natural life will be provided for after loving God, and others, and seeking his kingdom first! That includes any healings, deliverances, answered prayers, everything! This doesn't mean the journey will not be difficult. Life is full of trials and tribulations, but the Lord delivers his people from them all. I am a witness that if you love God with all that you are and maintain a pure heart before him and walk in his ways, God will open doors for you that no man can shut, and he will shut doors for you that no man can reopen! Where God has put a period, stand firm when the enemy tries to use man that will come back around to you, trying to put a comma, where God has put a period!

God is not man; therefore He is beyond figuring out. This is why it is imperative that we TRUST him. How can we trust a God whose indecisive you ask? I can assure you that God is not indecisive. I'll prove to you that He is decisive based upon two things, His name or Himself, and based upon how your heart weighs out during the check in of the scales. Just like we stand on scales to determine our weight, God has an invisible scale that he uses daily with people that he uses to weigh the heart. There are numerous scriptures throughout the Word of God that deal with the heart. From the beginning the heart was involved. God's heart and love for people was so major that he took time to create a place for humans to dwell (earth), he was so generous and giving to the people he created that he gave them time, days, seasons, food, work at that time wasn't non-pleasure able.

God himself had a heart to risk an interruption within the triune Godhead, where the son would have to leave the Father and the Holy Spirit forsaking his deity and all that they were experiencing to come to earth in flesh and blood, as a full man being fully God at the same time, all **for the sake to save those whom he foreknew and predestined according to Romans 8:29.** Who did he foreknow? Those who decided to believe that Jesus is the son of God and that God raised Jesus from the dead IN THEIR HEARTS by faith according to Romans 10:9. Those that love God by keeping his commandments, and fully repenting when falling short of those commandments, not out of habituation, but out of being an imperfect human being that fell, but got back up and got back on track following God's instructions.

How do we know which is true? The answer is not either or, but it is both. Sometimes we believe that things have to be black or white, and in some cases they do. For example, God desires for you to be hot or cold and not lukewarm. Either you are saved or you are not saved. Either you love brownie Sundays or you don't. Either you are born in America or you were not. There is no in between on many things when it comes to God; however there are many gray areas that we may not understand when it comes to God, especially when he has caused something drastic to benefit his child. When that child of God does not fit the black and white spectrum that many will associate them with according to their perspective, it can bring confusion. Although confusion may be present, it doesn't stop God from blessing his child regardless of whoever may have a problem with it. God is a mystery and he is beyond figuring out. Godly wisdom, the word of God, prayer, Godly spiritual advising, and spiritual revelation will give you **the discernment to know the difference** and when and how to apply the scriptures especially when fasting!

The point of the matter is this. James Cleveland said that God sits up high and he looks down low! This is true, yet at the same time, the same God that sits up high and looks down low is right in our midst, holding together every molecule in your being according to Colossians 1:17. God is present in outer space and at the same time he is sweeping closely throughout the earth looking and weighing hearts every moment of every day! God holds the world in his hands and yet he lives inside of clay pots such as you and me as believers that are made in flesh. That's why God desires for us to have a pure heart **so that we may see him**. Can you have a relationship with someone that you are not able to see? Yes! I am not referring to physical sight, I am referring to faith! Do you have to see China to know that it's there? Do you have to actually see the corals at the bottom of the sea to believe that they exist? No, you don't have to see them and you know that they are there. The same is true with God. Whether one believes that God exists or not, does not stop the fact that he is truly there! Praise be to Jehovah Shammah!

Is it possible not to have a pure heart and still see God? Only a pure heart will allow you to see God. God has said that those with a pure heart are blessed according to Matthew 5:8, and the result of someone with a pure heart is that they will see the Lord! Notice the scripture didn't say that you'd be able to serve in ministry, teach, preach or carry out projects. It says that if you're heart is pure then you will see God. Just because someone may be in position of status, power, and responsibility doesn't mean their heart is pure. Godly authority comes from purity, having a pure heart.

Adam and Eve had a pure heart in the Garden of Eden before the fall, and they walked with God in the cool of the day, in addition they talked to God. They saw God. There is much activity going on today that are noble and honorable things to help enhance one's natural and spiritual life, however I always ask, are they seeing God as a result of a pure heart? You can have the greatest lesson in the world, but operate in a bad spirit. One of the purposes of Scales of the Heart is to remind myself and my brothers and sisters in Christ to line up our spirit and heart with what we are preaching, and prayerfully that is the love of Jesus Christ. God weighs the heart and those with a pure heart usually come to the highest points of authority. There is the other side, where the enemy has infiltrated one of his ministers to the top; therefore you must use discernment and prayer when interacting with believers and ministers you have just met. The devil's master craft is deception. Just as God has an order, the enemy imitates everything God has set up. What does this mean? Don't think everyone in a position of authority has been placed there by God. It is not your goal to go around trying to figure out who is real and who's fake. That will automatically manifest itself throughout and over time.

Impure Authority

Let's take the time and look at Exodus 1: 15-21. This is a passage of scripture that points out clearly what I am referring to. There are times when you will have to obey God over man if man's instruction is opposite of what God has told you. This is a hard pill to swallow. It may be perceived as being rebellious or bucking authority, when that is far from the truth, however I have the heart of Shiphrah and Puah and fully understand when it's time to either obey God out of fear for his instruction, verses obeying a man in one of the highest earthly forms of authority. Romans 13 instructs us all to submit to all earthly authority, yet if you read Exodus and other areas of the Bible you will see a situation weighed out where obeying God's voice who was the Supreme authority was valued more by God than submitting to an authority placed in the earth, because it was impure. We are to follow leaders, as they follow Christ, not simply because they obtain an office of authority. Starting from Exodus 1:15, the scripture reads: Then Pharaoh, the king of Egypt, gave this order to the Hebrew midwives, Shiprah and Puah: When you help the Hebrew women as they give birth, watch as they deliver. If the baby is a boy, kill him; if it is a girl, let her live. But because the midwives feared God, they refused to obey the king's orders. They allowed the boys to live too. So the king of Egypt called for the midwives. Why have you done this? He demanded. Why have you allowed the boys to live? The Hebrew women are not like the Egyptian women, the midwives replied. They are more vigorous and have their babies so quickly that we cannot get there in time. So God was good to the midwives, and the Israelites continued to multiply, growing more powerful. And because the midwives feared God, he gave them families of their own. These Hebrew midwives had more heart and courage than some of our well known modern day believers of the faith who won't take a stand against the same destructive spirits. Why won't they take a stand? Pride, arrogance, lack of courage, maybe their pockets are being filled with money from the very one's they won't confront, which is very common today. What a stand to take! I give them a standing ovation and a round of applause! Why? Because they disobeyed leadership? No! Because they were able to recognize that God is Supreme and regardless of a man's position and authority that has been given him, it is better to obey God rather than man regardless of the consequences. Rationality would have said, we have no choice let's kill these baby boys, but the inner man or woman says God is right, and he has our back, so their safety was in their obedience. I once heard a pastor say that the only difference between one that God sets up to bless continuously, verses the one that keeps missing the boat and living in lack, is that one of them followed "the instructions". However I beg to argue that there was a piece missing from his point, and that is that God is not the only one who gives instruction. The devil gives instructions too. The thing that must be discerned is whose instructions you are following. We clearly see Pharaoh was giving plenty of instructions. Was he the King? Yes! Was he in charge? Yes! Did he have authority? Absolutely! But there was one thing that needed to be recognized, THE DEVIL WAS USING HIM! There is a spirit of fear that has been set up as a stronghold in the church where people are afraid to say anything about what they are seeing and experiencing because no one wants to be labeled rebellious. The church has a particular order set forth by god in his word, yet if there is no order in the hearts of men to be pure, then how do we expect the order of the church to rightly come to pass? Order starts in the heart. This is why one can be involved in the order of the church yet things are out of whack. It could be a reflection of the heart. Order is essential and important, but there are operations run by those whose hearts have not been circumcised and who have not had a heart transplant from God, therefore if this is the case, whatever order is in attempt to be set, it won't be effective positively if the heart is not right. This is an issue that must be discussed! Why? Ephesians 6:10-18 tells us to put on the full armor of God. Against what and who? One another? No! Our warfare is not against each other. It is against spiritual wickedness in where? In HIGH PLACES. Don't be a fool to think that some of those high places are not in the present day churches that have fallen away from foundational truths. I appreciate leaders today such as Apostle Parker whose assignment is to confront the high places of spiritual wickedness in a perverse generation in need of order, protocol, and pure authority to liberate the believer in right standing with God. Some of the greatest demonic principalities that we are at war with are those the enemy has used to start and maintain ministries that are deceptively pulling people away from the way, the truth, and the life. Hebrews 2:1 says so we must listen very carefully to the truth we have heard, or we may drift away from it. What is happening today? Many are being led astray as they are drifting far and far away from the way, the truth, and the life. Isaiah 3:12, Isaiah 9:16 and Jeremiah 23:1, all say very clearly how the people will be led astray. And that is by leaders. The word of God instructs us to honor and revere leadership and those in authority, yet it is very important to also note Ephesians 6:10-12. There are those in high places that represent good and there are those in high places that represent this scripture. It was a burden in my spirit to know that both good and evil authorities both have the same uniform on, they both look the same outwardly, as having goodness ascribed to them in many areas, yet the word of God clearly states that some of those who are wearing the same uniform are not what they profess and are indeed leading people away. It is not the uniform that one wears but it is what is behind the uniform that God sees and weighs.

It is unfortunate that the pulpit has been used to project whatever one desires in addition to teaching the word of God, such as painting pictures that flow out of personal issues and insecurities to make one look better than another, or it could be used to manipulate situations out of control issues. This is not something fun to admit or put out there, but it's not as if this is new to people or people are not aware that this hasn't or isn't being done. If one speaks up about this truth, it can be taken as one bucking authority or not in alignment with order, as that is not always the case. In fact, if someone doesn't speak up or bring things like this to light, do you know how many people suffer because of silence? The fear of the Lord is necessary! But no one should be fearing anything but the Lord, including someone that is operating in manipulation and controlling measures as they believe they are the head rooster in the hen house. Religious spirits always produce bondage, but where the spirit of the lord is there is liberty. Can you imagine Jesus being around the multitudes and the atmosphere is so liberating, until religious leaders showed up. Have you ever been in an atmosphere that was liberating and peaceful until certain presences and spirits arrived? Did you notice a total atmosphere change? If an atmosphere is much more liberating and pure when certain individuals are absent then he or she that is a discerner of spirits should pray about the situation that whatever hindering forces or impurities present that are keeping God's people from liberation need to be addressed by God. Some things it may be better and much wiser to take vertical directly to the

Father to take note of so that He can do what only He can do. Ecclesiastes 3:7 says there is a time to keep silence and there is a time to speak. Just because one sees something that is not right operating doesn't always mean that the person needs to bring up the matter to others. Sometimes, it's best just to pray about it; however there is another side of truth to this, which is, there are times when one sees something that is not right and God calls you to be the one to speak on the issue. It's easy to adhere to the advice given by men to leave it alone, put it in God's hands, let it work itself out, but if you know that you have a call on your life to speak up at the appointed time on the matter, I pray that you will obey God. There is a time to be silent and there is a time to speak up and out. When you do speak out, cry loud and spare not (Isaiah 58:1). There is a time for peace, and there is a time for war when it's time to fight! When God does a work in the earth he uses people to carry it out. Everyone may not understand your assignment and may give you opposing advice according to what God has called you to carry out. Your assignment is not for everyone to understand. The beautiful side of Godly authority is that it produces boundaries for the body of Christ to operate in and provides protection and liberty, when it's PURE. This kind of authority produces effective results against the forces of darkness because it's not tainted. Could you imagine if we didn't have police officers, a military for our nation, teachers, or fathers? Our world would be flipped upside down and chaotic if there were no authority in place. Therefore, we need authority, but just not any kind, the authority that mirrors Luke 22:25, which is that of a servant shepherd. The world has leaders; the kingdom of God should have Shepherds who lead. The world has its kingdom set up based on hierarchy which believers are not to operate as such, but we are to model the kingdom of heaven. The world's kingship and the kingdom's kingship are different. Which one are you modeling? All leaders are not Shepherds, but all Shepherds are leaders. One may ask how can I know this for sure? Well, after having my soul watched over by an authentic shepherd most of my life, when I was released from my home church it greatly disturbed me when I was contemplating joining another ministry long-term, that the shepherd of the house was rarely there and that greatly disturbed me. Remember that Scales of the Heart is coming from a Sheep's Perspective. If you don't care about a sheep's perspective, then keep in mind, people don't care how much you know, until they know how much you care! I had a conversation with a young man who started his own ministry because of an issue that many young ministers face. He felt as if his gifts and anointing was being used by those over him to build their ministry up, when he didn't feel that he was truly cared for. Many young people have felt this way as to why they have left from under authority. The young man told me it wasn't that he didn't want to be under someone's authority, because he really did, however he was frightened by how constricted things were that did not free him and his gifting; instead it was almost like the enemy designed the system to ensure that they would remain dormant and held down tightly. My heart went out to him because now he has been damaged in such a way he cannot even receive the authority of God somewhere else to keep him safe. There are many who feel the same. Then there are those who are so embedded under authority that they don't even have an idea of who they are in Christ. They follow and mimic the personality of the person they are submitted under, never coming into who God called them to be. They don't always have the courage or strength to stand firm on matters of their own lives because there is no discernment to determine the thin line of being submitted and serving, yet fully being aware that God has some personal things in store for their lives as well, in addition to remaining submitted and serving.

There are many times where no one should have to question leadership and should be able to follow instructions without understanding or explanation as this is how God desires order to be within the church as he has set up authority for the good of the people, nevertheless there are times that cause for someone to stand or speak up to leadership. Then we have the example of Christ who said he only does those things the father tells him and those things that pleases the father. We are not to assume that every authoritative figure is as trusting as the Father whom Christ could trust. As stated before it would be ideal and great to accept a notion, believe it, and walk in it, however there are many scripture references where we see how some were actually rejected by God, for example King Saul. He had so many opportunities to get things right and he still chose to do his own will. Pharaoh and Saul were alike in the fact that they would keep making promises to leave the people of God alone and yet we see how they only repented in afflicting situations or when caught or called out, yet it was always just a matter of time before they reverted back to their old nature with their impure motives. As many times as David spared King Saul's life, Saul still wanted and tried to kill David regardless of how many times it appeared he had peace with him. No matter how many times Moses prayed to God for the Egyptians to be relieved of the plagues Pharaoh always went back to holding the children of Israel in slavery. Some spirits you just cannot play with. Potiphar's wife was in a place of authority with Joseph and she was instructing him to do something he should not do, which was to sleep with her while her husband was away in Genesis 39. When someone is demonstrating this type of wayward stubbornness, do not waste your time. God always has to be the determining factor to showing them that he is in control and that he is greater and stronger! We can sometimes operate in a way like there is no present day Haman's, Harrods, Pharaoh's, or modern day Pharisees and Sadducees, when in fact there are. When no one stands up or speaks up to them, there are many people who suffer great harm. How does the enemy gain territory with wickedness in high places? It starts from the top. Yes, there are some leaders that are precisely put in certain places of authority for no reason other than to infiltrate a demonic satanic spirit that will get away with murder just because of the status and position they hold, that could be in a business, club or social group and even within the body of Christ. They have become respected in some aspect or another to have reached their level and position, even though many, especially the ones that have appointed them are blind to the fact that they were not called by God, but by another source. There are many cases where a servant of God started off pure with all the right motives and something happened along the way to harden or cloud their heart years later. A good reputation was built from their former heart, but no one ever notices how the person has changed along the course of life's tests and trials. This is the purpose of Scales of the Heart. Just because I may have a good heart today, doesn't mean I will tomorrow, and since God is always watching my heart to weight it, I must stay on the winning scale. Everyone with a collar on does not belong to God. In fact Christ himself warned us that there would be wolves in sheep's clothing. He tells us that he sends us as sheep among wolves. This doesn't mean you may not experience loss, grief, or damage, but our discernment will make all the difference in the world. David was a good shepherd. He said when a lion or bear came after one of his sheep, he blocked the attack and fought it off and killed it. The same is with Christ. Those shepherds that represent Christ are like this, they will go the distance to make sure their sheep are not torn and killed. A present Shepherd equates to safe sheep. No one man or woman can do it alone. Those who are called to Shepherd should do it together and cover all ground, especially for those who must be absent on various assignments. God calls an overseer to tend to the flock and be a shepherd not a worldly King, this is not to say that we are not a royal priesthood, but it is to say that there are many servants that God calls to shepherd God's flock operating as if they are a King modeling the world's standard of hierarchy instead of the Kingdom example of leading Christ demonstrated for us. Our Lord's kingdom is not of this world according to John 18:36. Pilate responded to Christ out of fear in John 18 according to the ranking of hierarchy set up by the world, yet Christ responds to him out of reassurance that he doesn't need to be threatened by his authority or anyone else's because he had authority. When you get the revelation of authority you will be at peace in submitting to anyone's authority you are under because you too have authority and their authority can never demote yours if Christ gave it to you.

If Isaiah 9:16 says that the leaders will lead God's sheep astray, who do you think he will use to gather them back up? Don't be surprised if the remnant he is choosing (the house within the house, the real church, within the church) are ordinary people who are not popular or important among the majority, who are not identified with man as a "leader". This is not to say God won't use the leader, because he often times he does, but not always. God hides things and people that he uses so no one even knows what's going on. The one on the stage may not have the grand assignment from God, it may be the little old lady or man in the back row, wearing jeans and T-shirt with a hat on, or a youth that others assume is not contributing just yet to the Kingdom in a major way. God will often use the very one who no one expects, because if he uses the one everybody expects to be used, then he can't get any glory out of that.

God is a God who camouflages. That is why the enemy mocks God. The enemy is deceptive because he understands that camouflage works! The enemy knows the anointing when he sees the servant of God, but that devil can't figure out all the details of God's plan because God has a way of hiding things and people until it's time for them to become fully known. Let's look at Joseph, yes he was in the pit, in Potiphar's house, in the prison, being processed, but more so, God was hiding Joseph. It's a beautiful thing when God hides you for a work where God will be the one who will eventually pull back the curtain at an assigned time so the world will see what He's done! What about Esther? Esther was an orphan, hidden in her cousin's residence, and hidden in the palace when she was summoned initially. She was positioned, and when it came time for the King to cross her path, the favor of the Lord busted the scales! She was an orphan, a Jew, the very nationality leadership was trying to annihilate. She was the least likely candidate to be in the palace as Queen at that particular time. Is God funny or what? The point is, take a low seat in the temple, until the Lord calls you up. Everyone you see sitting on the front row in the assembly has not been called up by God.

Haman was a leader who had influence and power. He had an agenda given to him from the devil to destroy God's people. Had not Mordecai, Esther, and many other Jews put in a plight to come against this demonic infiltrated leadership many lives would have been lost. This is the type of thing that God sees and knows is happening behind closed doors. Haman was preparing to have Mordecai a righteous man hanged near his property because of his unwillingness to bow to him. Mordecai stood tall and strong against Haman regardless of his position. In the end, the same trap that the enemy set for Mordecai is the same trap that Haman fell in himself. The same gallows that was prepared for the death of Mordecai was the same trap that Haman was hanged on after he was exposed for the devil that he was. This is the one of the main purposes of Scales of the Heart. It is not to come against good leadership; it is to expose the bad leadership that we are in denial about in this present age. No one wants to be labeled a Haman I'm sure. But they are out here. Working and deceiving God's people. The word of God is being used against God's people who will dare to speak up. They are often being bullied into silence. They will often be labeled as rebels who buck authority, when in actuality God may have an assignment for them to be a modern day Mordecai, Esther, Nehemiah, Paul, Peter, Joshua, Caleb, Anna, Mary, or Lydia. Haman was a leader and he had power and authority, and it crushes my heart to know there are people who have yet to be born that will grow up in churches where fear will be instilled into them by these modern Herods and Hamans. I am not talking about the fear of the Lord; I am referring to fear of interacting with leaders, with what will happen with their lives as the enemy has his ministers positioned. The enemy's ministers will be waiting for them to come in to churches for help and healing, only to receive a bondage God never had in mind that was orchestrated by Satan. God is certainly greater and he is in ultimate control. But we are in a battle every day! A spiritual battle for the souls of people is still at hand. One thing that will always be relevant is a burning hell that awaits those who reject Christ as Lord and savior. It is real and the battle ground that has become so common where people rarely ever notice anymore is that within the church. It has become so easy for the enemy to infiltrate his angels of darkness in churches as the great falling away has begun in our times. The last days are certainly here on earth. There is a work to be done in every area. This is the particular area that I know God has called me to. The enemy has run so many people out of God's house, now it's time to see the devil on the run out of God's house where it was never designed for him to occupy.

I see people so nervous in church. I am not talking about the nervousness that a sinner has when entering Holy Ground, or about the back sliding believer that the Holy Spirit is convicting. I am talking about ministers, and the core people of the church, who walk around on egg shells, timid to even open their mouths and talk. It's like everyone is so nervous and bound in being themselves. Where the spirit of the Lord is there is freedom. God never intended for you to go to his house to serve, worship, praise, fellowship, and to be fed, to be shaking in fear the entire time your there. God wants you at peace, and free, when you come before him. You cannot even worship God in spirit and in truth if you are so afraid of being in the building because of the people that are there. This is exactly what the enemy wants. The enemy wants people to be afraid of God, of leaders, of church so that their lives can be controlled indirectly. It is possible to obtain the fear of the lord and have reverence for leadership and honor those put in authority which is beautiful without walking in fear of them. God didn't give us a spirit of fear, but of love, power, and a sound mind according to 2 Timothy 1:7.

This is a major reason why people stop going to church. Everyone doesn't shy away from church because they don't want to be accountable to authority, even though some do. Some people have been so traumatized by those in churches and don't desire to live under subtle abuse that does occur. There has been hurt, or misused delegated authority and no one can even question it, or speak up. The enemy has choked the voices of those being hurt by this stronghold so they don't even have the place to speak up and be heard. It brings me to tears to know that there are more and more of the enemy's ministers being placed over the body of Christ in these last and evil days than people that God has called and chosen. I am no different than anyone else that is to submit and align with godly authority, to honor and revere, but it is difficult when there is a call on your life to pull back the veil on infiltrating spirits in a way that's not common or desired. I understand why Jeremiah was the weeping prophet. Who in the world would want his assignment? Who would want Jonah's assignment? Isaiah? Esther's? Paul's? Yes they end well but there was so much opposition and warfare for them that brought a real denying of self and crucifixion as Jesus himself. Who would want Jesus' assignment? Living for Christ and taking the call full speed ahead, putting our hands to the plow without looking back testifies that we are overcomers. Even when it looks like we are not overcoming, God knows how the story ends. Stand tall in the Lord no matter what it looks like because in the end we win! There is a purpose to your pain!

Let's look at the three wise men in Matthew 2:1-12. After meeting with Herod in search of the Messiah that was born to save the people, Herod instructed the three wise men to notify him once they found the child. Won't the devil have you do his dirty work? Sounds right to me, the person that you may be looking at that shows up or is on assignment may not be the real demonic force at hand. The Jezebel spirit or the controlling agent behind the evil plans and intentions is rarely seen, their representatives are the ones usually seen. The real force behind the evil is somewhere passing out "instructions". Nevertheless the three wise men were not called wise for nothing. God warned them in a dream not to go back to Herod, and they were obedient. They were not even aware that their instruction came from someone evil, until divine revelation occurred. They had to be warned in a dream by God for their steps to be ordered. Never question God when he orders your steps, he knows what's best even when we cannot see. The three wise men listened to God, and not the leader they had just met and dined with prior to finding the child they were looking for and that was Jesus Christ.

The leader is a gift to the people, and a good leader is like oil being poured on Aaron's head, running down to the beard and running down to the body. A bad leader is curse to the people, and my heart grieves for those that are under a demonic realm and don't even know it. How can you know if you're under a demonic realm? There are many little things that you can pay close attention to that don't seem to impact as much but in reality they do. One tip I can give is that you are surrounded by darkness. If you are worshipping anywhere and the only light in the room is artificial electrical light. Yes you can be the light shinning in dark places as believers and we often are, but there is nothing like natural light that invokes a setting, particularly that on a Sunday Morning for worship. When churches don't have windows for God's natural light to come forth, in my opinion I'd wonder if it's being shut out for a reason. When you look at some of the Jehovah's Witness halls one thing is for sure, there are not a lot of windows for natural light to come in. It may seem that the setting is dark just for the lights, camera, and action, but here could be another reason that is never acknowledged or considered. Any prayer rooms or side areas where natural light is being forbidden, where windows are boarded or blacked out are dead give aways that light is not welcomed. This may be all new to you, as you may be a new believer in Christ. My prayer for you is not to be afraid as God is greater and stronger than any demonic realm or principality, however don't think that witchcraft is something in scary movies or books, it's in the word of God and it's real. You must be careful where and with whom you are worshipping, and how and what you listen to and allow to be deposited into your spirit.

Again we see that the word of God indicates that God's sheep will be led astray by who? By leaders. Therefore if God's leaders will lead people astray, as much as we are to honor, revere, and submit to leadership, I'd be concerned if we are ignoring what God is clearly advising, and that is there are some leaders that will lead people astray and away. Therefore, it is not good for God's people to follow such leaders. Regardless of the labeling that will occur, opposition, or rejection, the uncovering of present day Pharaoh's and Haman's need to be acknowledged and confirmed as we have generations behind us. Paul before he was converted on the Damascus road was an example of a leader who thought he was doing God's will, but he was actually leading the people away and astray and murdering believers for what he thought was right. See, sometimes we can be fighting for the wrong things and don't even know it. If the foundations are destroyed, what can the righteous do? We see that when the foundations are destroyed the righteous can do nothing. The word indicates that the leaders will lead astray God's people. Does this have anything to do with the foundations being destroyed? Yes the people are compromising, falling away, and being deceived, but that is not the only way the foundations are being destroyed. Highlighted within the book are areas where the leadership that can contribute to the foundations being destroyed. This of course for me is an uncomfortable position to be in. Why? Well, I'm sure it's the question you all want to know, who am I? Who do I think I am? What have I led? Precisely, God will use the least likely of candidates to follow through on unordinary assignments. God usually hides things and uncovers them at appointed times, such as the wealth of the wicked that is laid up or covered up for the righteous at a special time. Don't be surprised when those within the church who no one really knows or acknowledges are given grand kingdom assignments by God to carry out his work. They may not be seen in the same light as those with notoriety, however that's precisely the hiding and disguise God desires so they will be in a sense "out of the way". Where do you think spies originated from? God will send his spies places where no one will ever have thought or known the reason for the appearance. He will use those least likely to be discovered. It could be someone with circumstances that scream; of course God isn't using me, look at my life. That could be just the thing God uses to keep eyes and ears away from individuals as such.

I pray that Jesus would hide me behind the cross so that you would see past my gender, my age, or ethnicity, and my socioeconomic status, if possible, for some that will always be a barrier, yet Christ tells us to know one another after the Spirit. I don't believe that God was referring to all leaders when he said my leaders will lead them astray. I believe that God had a certain group in mind when he was referring to "the leaders" leading sheep astray. The enemy has been passing down accepted notions and mindsets in the lives of corrupt teaching that certain things are supposed to be taught and accepted, for example, slavery, certain projections with marriage and divorce, and areas of authority.

There are many great pure hearted leaders today, but I'd be lying if I said they all are this way. They all are not this way. So what do we do? Yes your church may be okay, but what about the church where people are being led astray? Do you care about them? Since the church was established after the ascension of Christ, demonic forces have been infiltrating the church even with the "early church", so how much more do you think it's infiltrated today? We walk around as if everyone is there for the right reasons. As if the major infiltrates can't be sitting in the front row, or be over a ministry, or on staff, or have all kinds of access to much. Keep in mind of the great falling away that the word of God talks about, how the church is falling away, and in the last days many are being lead away from traditional churches in exchange for a lukewarm gospel of compromise and a license to sin. When strongholds are set in place to keep people from speaking up and out on major issues, what do we do about this? The church is looking more and more like the world in many ways. Yet it shouldn't be a surprise to you, as it should be an indication that the end times are here. As sin levels increase and many believers fall away, there will be much impact on the lives of believers, and God will ensure that those belonging to him will not be destroyed. The greater the falling away, the greater the impact on believers will be, at work, at church, at home in families and marriages, and so forth. Know that because the enemy is going to be busy with the great falling away, God will be busy rescuing his people to the degree necessary for those who are subject to impact due to the great falling away. Some things you go through in life have nothing to do with you, more so than it does with the times you live in. He will prepare you for the time you were destined to complete your Kingdom Assignment. People who were raised in different generations may not get you, but that's okay, God is known to do a different work according to 1 Kings 19. As the world's organizations maintain a human resource system and open door policy to ensure that no one is being manipulated, this practice is not found as much in modern day churches. If we are going to adopt the world's ways in the church and if nothing is being done to stop it, then why not adapt this principle to clearly regulate manipulations of every kind? You might think I'm crazy for even suggesting something like this. Perhaps your church already has something like this set up, perhaps it's not being utilized if so. God has given me a vision of the church in its future state, and the way things are going with quick promotions of leaders that are barely processed, it appears that it will be more of a dwelling place for Satan and his ministers' more so than in any other time period in history. We have to stand, and fight for those who are not even born yet who will be headed to the house of God to be healed, whole, loved, and ministered to, but instead receive the results of an operation whereby nobody fought to keep the faith! (A great new read by Bishop Joey Johnson: Fighting for the Faith). This book will help you learn what to fight for and what not to waste your time with. What will God's people face in churches fifty years from now? A hundred years from now? Will anyone even care? Yes we are going to pray and shut the demonic down, but what practical things are we going to set in place to a world that is falling away and will continue to fall away according to scripture. When the Human Resource Department fails within a company the next step is to take the matter to the Better Business Bureau? Why is there a better business bureau? So that those within the area are able to utilize this resource of knowing what organizations are up to par on demonstrating what they are portraying!

It also gives others a chance to voice their experiences so that the area will be aware of positive and negative reports that could also affect others and their business choices. Why not have a board or group of people that mirrors a Human Resource Department where anyone can come and invest into filing a grievance or issue that has happened. This would be beneficial for the people who don't necessary have a position or title or status within the church. There may be something similar to this already within your church. As you join a new church you are usually encouraged to ask your questions with leadership. My question is, is it possible for someone in leadership to be an angel of light, or one of the enemy's ministers? We all know the answer to this question. Of course. No ministry wants to think that anyone in their leadership is evil, or being used by the enemy. So therefore everyone walks around as if everyone in leadership is working for God. If we know this is not always the case, then what are we doing about infiltrating spirits that get a hold to positions such as this?

Is it possible for a devil to be over the prayer ministry? Has this ever occurred before? Some of the most respected "anointed" men of God who are to be leading God's people have been known to put serious demons over important ministries. How can this be? Wouldn't the man of God above anyone else have the discernment to see who he's putting over a ministry? You'd think so, however with today's set ups, you'd wonder. Usually the heart of the church is the prayer ministry. Is it possible for a pure hearted, mature man of God to place an infiltrating spirit over prayer? You say, of course not, shouldn't he have discernment? Well, my friend, these are the days we are living in. People are joining churches left and right and have no idea of who they are interacting with. This is not to alarm fear with anyone who has joined a church, but it should challenge you to learn your word as much as possible, as the word of God is filled with scriptures about being careful. The word of God says in Matthew 7:15 Beware of false prophets who come disguised as harmless sheep but are really vicious wolves. Jesus said in Matthew 10:6 that I send you as sheep among wolves. If this is stated, then we shouldn't be walking around as if everyone is a tender hearted sheep or shepherd. Ephesians 6:18 says be on alert always!

Why would I even dare to write about this subject matter? Who would want to face the warfare dealing with such a topic? Who wants to disturb the peace? Who wants an assignment to come up against demonic authority and leadership? Do you know what the processing looks like for one with such a call? I understand why Moses didn't want the assignment of challenging the greatest leader of the land. Yes he would have to disobey that ungodly demonic leadership and be labeled a traitor but there were many people who needed to be freed. Those that were currently living and generations to follow that were not even born yet. The work was great and the opposition was great, but God was greater! My friend, God has a way of using you after bringing you and your reputation to a standstill next to nothing so that he will get the message across. It is no longer about who I am, or what you think about me, or what you will say about me, my reputation is dead. When God takes a believer through a process like Moses to no longer care about their reputation a boldness comes on the believer that others will mistake for arrogance when it comes to executing the assignment God has called them to do. You will always be advised over and over by those who are threatened by your gifting or acknowledge the Spirit of God in you, that it's not about you. If God has done a work in the believer to go and get the assignment done at particular levels, usually by that time, they are well aware that it is not about them, at this point, they could care less about being confirmed, or wanting to take God's glory. It no longer becomes an opportunity to impress others or show off, it is a matter of confidently projecting what God has assigned you, regardless of the haters who will be upset because you had the boldness of God to do it without timidity. I am writing about this because there has been so much damage done to people, and it grieves me to even think that those who are not even born yet to be saved and attend church and ministries later in the years to come that will be affected by the same old issues that we fail to address. History repeats itself if not corrected.

Yes we should be following God's outline of how the church should be set up. I am not saying we should go and do our own thing outside of the word of God, I am saying that it's a scary thing to be in a place where you have no voice and no one knows what has happened to you or what you are going through in relation to leadership. So why not leave and go somewhere else? That does not solve anything. There is no perfect church anywhere. The grass is not always greener on the other side. We often say the grass isn't greener on the other side, however when you think about this, in some situations the grass is much greener on the other side. If your job is asking you to make bricks without straw, guess what, there is greener grass somewhere else. In the area of marriage, we often hear the statement, it may not have been God's will for you to get married, but it is his will for you to stay married. I beg to argue that it depends on the specific situation one is in. If someone is being oppressed in a life threatening way, I believe God will deliver his child from a tare that is oppressing his child. God's will for Israel was to live holy, and we see what happened to Israel. God's will for Israel changed several times, yet her destiny was fulfilled in the end and still being fulfilled today. This goes back to really looking at both sides of the spectrum depending on the situation at hand. If someone is being physically abused by a spouse, man or woman, guess what, I will probably be the only one to tell you this. If you seek help for years and there is no change, and you have gone through all the counseling and deliverance ministry possible and that person is still abusing you, there is greener grass on the other side, if it be God's will for your life. That is something you have to take to God yourself. We all who name the name of Christ should go to church regularly, and have a desire to go to church in the pattern that God set forth and instructed. There are many reasons why people decide to quit church and stop coming. When you are not able to relate to something like this, it's easy for you to just give your opinion or suggestion, however when this hits home for some, it gets real. No one who truly loves Jesus wants to stay at home on a Sunday instead of joining together with the saints for worship and fellowship. We know the enemy desires for us to be against one another and he of course uses the conflict and issues to keep people away, so we shouldn't add insult to injury by helping the enemy out. Is church a place where people come on Sunday freely to worship God without anxiety, fear, or tension? Or is it a place we add to our weekly list where we go in to receive more stress and more anxiety about the million things that have to be done, not to mention all the issues going on that no one will discuss, but is affecting everyone. Who wants to go somewhere like that every week, multiple times a week? We have to do a better job at laying our burdens down. There are some churches where there is so much work to be done it's as if you are working a shift on a Sunday morning. Our labor is not in vain and we do work for the kingdom, but there are so many ministers and leaders who are not being ministered to because of falling into the trappings of being a busy body. Perhaps they didn't sign up to be a busy body but it's what they have become with the intent of doing work for the kingdom. So instead of going to lay your burdens down, you went to pick some more up to what you already had. Psalm 55:22 says Cast your cares on the Lord and he will sustain you, he will never let the righteous fall. Yes we have to serve and serving takes work, however lets be sure we are working Monday-Saturday in the world not just on Sunday morning for set times as if we have a show to run. Church should not be approached with the mentality "it's show time"! You often hear things like never give up and don't back up from challenges. This is certainly true in that we should persevere to overcome, yet there are times where one may need to back up or give up. For instance, if the challenge is you going to a job where chemicals have been expose to you every day for the past ten years, and you now have lung cancer, and you don't smoke. That may be a good time to back up from the challenge of working in that environment that may be a good time to throw in the towel. Throwing in the towel is perceived primarily in one way, that there is a loss. However there are times, depending on the situation and the variables involved, that throwing in the towel means there is something to gain. This person may have been encouraged to stay on their job for those ten years and to overcome the obstacle, however one must decide with God's leading how to proceed further as listening to others can be beneficial many times, especially people who obtain wisdom, yet it also can deter you and derail you from your destiny. Another saying we hear, is that you never leave your family. I am not sure where this came from as Jesus Christ made it clear that those he calls family are those that do the will of his father in heaven. When Jesus was teaching he was interrupted by someone advising him that his mother and brother were looking for him, yet he answered that those who do the will of his father in heaven are his family. This is found in Matthew 20:50. Jesus also says in Matthew 10:34 That he did not come to bring peace on earth but a sword to divide and turn a man against his father, a daughter against her mother, a daughter in law against her mother-in-law, and a man's enemies will be that in his own household. Sadly the truth is that this is seen in the area of marriage. There are couples where one is a believer and one is one that God predestined before the foundation of the world would reject his son no matter how much their spouse sanctifies their home. Yes, the enemy would desire for them to be divided, yet in reality they may have already been divided from before the foundation of the world. The enemy aims for separation; however Jesus also separates the wheat from the tares. Jesus also told one of his disciples who said that he was going to go and bury his father first before following Jesus, to let the dead bury their own. In 1 Corinthians 5:11, it is written that we are not even to eat with someone who professes to be a believer in Christ, one who is mature, but is engaging in unrighteous activity. This scripture is not indicating that we should not interact with the "lost" or those who are not saved, or the newly converted, because we are. This scripture is for those that know God's Word and are fully aware of the things of God; yet still choose to partake in ongoing sin. The Word says you are not even supposed to eat with them? This could be your own flesh and blood. Are you a doer of the entire Word? Or just the parts you like? The matters of the heart could be involved if this is your child. If your child is not living the Word of God knowing better, the Word calls for action on your part. It gets real!

It may be easy to reprimand another that you are not closely linked to, but when it becomes your brother or your sister, or your parent, you may have another story. I'm not saying we are to give up on people at all! We are not, yet if we are to follow the order of God and be conscientious of what we stand for, then don't lighten up when it's your folks.

What Are We Doing About It?

Are we just going to let the enemy have his way? It's easy to say, my church is good, we don't need that, but what if another one does? Who stands up for those people? We are not to adopt the world's system of doing things, but Human Resources within the church is a suggestion with where we are today and where we are headed. Think what it will be like fifty years from now if the Lord delays his coming. What will the church be like? Will the enemy's ministers outweigh the righteous leaders? What can we do now to stop it, other than just pray? It's true, no one wants to deal with all the complaints that will show up from such a system in the church, but think about the benefit that will be available to enhance the freedom of those who wish to continue not forsaking the gathering together due to knowing that their voice counts. We are fighting the good fight of faith. If we are going to fight for something, why not fight for the bride of Christ to stay as pure and guarded as possible, even if that means extra work in the area of issues being organized when reported. The church is becoming more and more like the world over the years. What are we to do? Why wouldn't the enemy want to take over churches and control them for himself? Is that possible? If the foundations are destroyed what can the righteous do? So what if the power is placed in the wrong hands, then what? Is that possible? Yes, it has happened, is happening, and will continue happening if we don't do something. If you are not among this type of ministry regularly then it may be easy to bypass or dismiss going to the depths of standing in the gap this way as you don't fully understand experientially what is occurring from actually witnessing this deception first hand, however if you are familiar with being among this kind of ministry then you understand my heart for those being led astray ignorantly, and how far the enemy has advanced to pull the wool over the eyes of God's people. God is greater! And I am excited to see what God will do regarding this area, yet he will use you and I to get the job done!

We all know that there are laws in place that state businesses are not to practice discrimination against race, ethnicity, gender, and age, however even though they are laws, we know discrimination happens all the time. We know that saying you are a believer and living your life to reflect that are two different things. In human resources there are policies in place so that retaliation is reprimanded, however that doesn't mean that retaliation never occurs after complaints have been made. We all know the Human Resource Department where the manager is buddies with the person over HR, so there is no use in reporting your issue to the person you're reporting's friend. Yes this can be a sticky situation, however with it in place it brings awareness that one cannot just operate in any type of way within the church as a leader just because you are a leader. Perhaps having an HR system in the church is a stupid idea. Nevertheless we need to be generating ideas on what we will be leaving generations that are right behind us. The enemy has infiltrated ministries so tough, what are we doing to make sure they do not take over what God never saw fit for them to have? Loyalty is defined as a strong feeling of support or allegiance. It has been said that if you are loyal then you go along with the program no matter what it looks like, if you agree with it or not. I beg to differ. What if the situation calls for you to be loyal to a demon or infiltrating spirit, or to an operation that is hurting people? What do I do? Remain "loyal" and keep silent and go with the flow? Or do I break out and sound the alarm and receive the rejection that's headed my way on account of not keeping man's definition of loyalty. Situations vary, and the one size fits all answers are not a solution to the idiosyncrasies of life. In essence going with the flow in some situations regardless of how you feel about it is necessary, but it depends on what the issue is. There are many people who have the characteristic of being "faithful" according to what is seen on the outside, however God is the one who determines who's loyal and who is not. For example, I know a couple that has been married over fifty years. They were faithful to remaining in the marriage. However both the husband and the wife had children outside of the marriage overtime. How faithful is that? How loyal is that. Is it true you can wear the t-shirt that says faithful because you have years in, however actually not be faithful or loyal? Absolutely! They may have been loyal to a contract, but the not to the covenant that was made. Saying I do and doing I do is two different things. Saying and agreeing to be accountable within your marriage is one thing, but actually following through with the accountability action steps is another. Even if one has been faithful to their spouse for years of marriage without ever having stepped outside of it, that does not mean they have been faithful to God in every area of their lives. For example, a woman is faithful to her husband for forty years, however over that time she lies, steals, and backslides in other areas of her life. Does this means that she is faithful to God only because she has remained married to the same person all of her life? I would say no. Let's look at Pharaoh in Exodus who agreed to let the people go a number of times when the aftermath hit of his decision to keep them enslaved. He kept wavering back and forth about letting them go. It was only after a plague struck that he wanted to comply, but it was just a matter of time before the real Pharaoh resumed in heart and deed. This happens a lot in marriages. Ecclesiastes 4:12 says a cord of three strands is not easily broken. In many marriages in the Christian faith there are usually two strands apparent, one being Christ and the other being either the husband or the wife and not them both. The enemy recognizes the strand that is not attached to Christ and the other spouse is the exact strand where he desires to gain entry to divide. Ecclesiastes 4:12 doesn't say a cord of three strands cannot be broken, it says it's not EASILY broken. It's not always said, but a covenant is made to last and not end, yet a covenant can be broken by one who that offends the covenant. God knows this from experience as his covenant was broken repeatedly by Israel. The same forgiving, compassionate, merciful God is the same God who kicked Satan out of heaven before the beginning in Genesis and who threw Israel into captivity. You often hear things that are stated such as "If you are really saved and filled with the Holy Spirit then everything around you should be saved too". There is some truth to this as you will be a light and impact those around you, however no one can force anything on someone as God desires voluntary freewill for our choosing him. When Christ was hanging on the cross there was a man to his left, and another to his right. He told one of the criminals that today, you will be with me in paradise but not the other. This is an example of how the Son of God himself was around someone who was not going to be in paradise with him. There were many religious leaders Christ was around while here on earth as he was filled with God's spirit without measure. There are many who did not get saved that were around Christ and there may be many around you, a spirit filled believer who chooses to reject Christ, even if you are really saved. To have someone think anything other than this is putting a pressure on one that was never intended by God. Many ideas as such have been transferred down throughout generations and the results from strongholds as such bring fear, which the enemy knows, and it keeps people in a bondage instead of liberation. Truth is you could be as close to one as Jesus was to Judas Iscariot, and there still may not be a transformation.

It is true that the faithful are the heart of the church. The heart of your ministry will be more faithful in their absence then some people you look at very often who are physically present yet spiritually absent. The heart of the church or your ministry will go with them if there is a need to depart, but because they may not be a part of your flock any longer, doesn't remove their standing as the heart of the ministry. Some people are faithful to church services and not to regular prayer meetings. Some people are faithful to church events but not when it comes to serving or tithing. Everyone who leaves a ministry is not leaving because they are not faithful. God may have a faithful work for them to do and your ministry may have been a building block or stepping stone for his plan for their lives. We need to stop labeling people and thinking we know why everyone shows up to our ministries. We don't know. Trust that God will be God and manifest the purpose in their lives.

Trust that God knows all and sees all and he has a way of taking care of things. In the book of Genesis, Joseph had a pure heart and was really the leader of the Land. He had enough influence and impact over the first in command which was Pharaoh, he may as well been number one, in God's eye sight he was number one, but for the people to them, Joseph was number two. In many instances in life you may seem to be number two or three with man, but in God's eye sight you may be number one. I am sure women that you have been reminded by men that the man is the head over the woman. This is beautiful. Beautiful you ask. Absolutely! It is because as many times as we get this reminder I often notice that the other truth of the matter is not present with it. What truth is that? The truth is that the man is over the woman according to God's design. The other part of this same design is that in relation to marriage, the man's relationship with Almighty God is predicated on how he is treating, interacting, and considering the woman he is over according to 1 Peter 3:7. (Talk about an HR policy divinely set up by God, maybe it is biblical to have an HR set up in the divine institutions of God after all☺)You'd be surprised that there are husbands walking around truly believing that God hears them and their prayers regardless of how insensitive they have been to their wives. Do you know how major that is? If God sees the man as the head and covering and the wife is able to bypass the man and use the "open door policy" with God's divine Human Resource hook up then maybe the church should adapt the same. It's tough to be in a spot where you need to cry out for justice and there is no one to cry out to. Yes we can cry out to God, but when you have one hundred, one thousand, ten thousand people to flock, we may need a department. God says that if you don't love your wife he doesn't even want to hear what you have to say. What a dangerous position to be in. So ladies, I think we got off easy on that one. God loves women and wives and he does not play about them! Not even the man he placed over us has the last say in the matters of the heart. God has been known to show up for women whose husband's go about doing things their own way, just look at Abigail in 1 Samuel 25. Look at Sarah in Genesis, after Abraham lied, just like his son Isaac lied about his wife Rebekah being their sister and not their wife. Abraham was right in a sense that Sarah was his half-sister, but to deny she was his wife was dishonest.

So ladies don't be upset that authority has been placed over us as a result of the fall, I think it's the better position to be in. Women have a way of getting in touch with God more sensitively than men in my perspective. Before the fall we were equal in status with Adam leading in a different role, however because of the fall, man has been put over woman. To whom much is given, much is required. Now that Jesus has died on the cross the roles of husband and wife are very crucial, but

God says that in the last days he will pour out his spirit on all flesh according to Acts 2:17 and Joel 2:28. That includes women. Jesus says anyone that has faith in me will do what I have been doing, and he will do greater works than these in John 14:12. Did the scripture say all men who have faith in Jesus? No. It said anyone. That means, women, children, black, white, pretty, ugly, fat, skinny, married, divorced, diseased, anyone! Myles Monroe pinpoints women are called to lead by God in his famous read which is one of my favorites called The Power and Purpose of a Woman. He elaborates on abuse being inevitable when the purpose of something is not known. If a man doesn't know the purpose of a woman, it's possible he may abuse her and vice versa. If God's people and even the world don't know the purpose of the church, then what do you think will happen? Abuse is ahead. If you know your car runs on gasoline but you put water in the tank instead, you have failed to recognize the purpose of the vehicle and it has now been abused. This is exactly what is going on with the church today. The church was not created to become more like the world, but to call the world in to be transformed into the likeness of Christ. If leadership is not understood according to how God designed it to be, then it will be easy for leaders to lead the people astray and for the foundations to be ruined. This is what is occurring. Abuse in the church. As we are so busy having church we are missing what God has to say. We are missing God showing up because of familiarly within churches. He that hath an ear to hear, hear what the spirit has to say to the churches.

Ladies do you know that God will shut some things down just for you? I call it operation shut down! When Jonah was on the ship headed to Tarshish, the storm came because one man was on the boat. The enemy called a census for all men to return to their birth place as to why Joseph and Mary headed to Bethlehem because one child was expected to come. When Sarah was taken into Abimelech's palace (The King), God closed all the wombs of the women of the King's house, why? Because of one woman, Sarah! Abraham put her in a bad spot, and when her earthly husband failed her, God had to come and perform operation shut down! If you think Operation Shut down ended there, you may want to look back over your life. I have my own testimonies where I seen God at work with operation shut down in my own life in many areas. The point is, sometimes no one will show up for you, but God. He won't send an angel or man; He will show up for you himself!

Review and Rewind

Matters of the heart are essential! Because a great sermon is preached, and the power of the Holy Spirit is manifested, that does not mean that you've seen God or that your heart is pure. It could mean that you're well learned, that you are just religious, dogmatic in beliefs, strong in discipline, faithful to your schedule, calling, and the people, you could even be one of integrity. All of these things are great and expected from every believer, whether you are a leader or just a believer positioned with a kingdom assignment from the Lord. Nevertheless good preaching, teaching, and the accolades are not a guarantee that you have SEEN HIM and that your HEART is pure. We have all read what the world will look like in the last days. I believe it is due to a lack of purity in many areas of the believer. The enemy has come into our lives violently and forcefully having impacted our purity and foundations. This is one of the contributions in these last days of our foundations being chiseled away at. Who has a pure heart anymore? Is that even important? What's important today is the number in your bank account, the title that's given by a man; the building one goes to worship at, the reputation that is being built by man, and many other things that have absolutely nothing to do with how God sees people.

Can you rightly divide the word of truth without a pure heart? I believe it can be done. Many are doing it well. Can you preach the greatest sermon of the century and still not have a pure heart? I believe so. Can you have popularity and notoriety, status, position, power, and wealth and still be missing a pure heart? Yes! Can you cast out devils and speak in tongues and still not have a pure heart? You better believe it! This is the sole purpose that I have written this book. So many things are held in high esteem today such as your tithes and offerings, your faithfulness, your vigor and passion for the gospel in relation to serving in ministry, your life's track record and so forth, which are all things that should be held at high esteem naming the name of Christ, **yet we are not concerned as much today of believers having a pure heart and ensuring that we are demonstrating the LOVE of Jesus with one another.** It may be mentioned from time to time, but not as much as other things that are being discussed.

The very thing that will lead souls to salvation and the very thing that God tells you to guard, the very thing that is weighed consistently on God's scales are not your sins, mistakes, hang ups, or past, **but it is your heart.** This is why God says in Ezekiel 18 that **he will not** repay the sins of the father to the third and fourth generations because each man is responsible for their own salvation which is worked out in fear and trembling according to Philippians 2:12. Your salvation must be operated within the heart that becomes circumcised. When someone is converted what happens? They are given a new heart, a heart of flesh for their heart of stone. What is a heart of stone? Jeremiah 24:7 says we need a new heart given to us by God. God will give us a new heart! The tongue is powerful and life and death are in it, but what rolls up off of the tongue comes from the heart, which would make the heart all the more powerful, this is why God clearly instructs us about keeping our heart right in his word, because he knows that what's in a man's heart will overflow out of the mouth. A heart of stone is the hard heart you received when you were born into a sin sick world, as you were given a sinful nature by Adam and Eve as they fell in the beginning of time in the Garden of Eden. When you become saved, your heart begins to change according to God's expectations, evaluations, and His word. Your heart becomes circumcised. This is not something anyone can physically see, but God can see if you're heart is circumcised or not. You know you've been circumcised in heart when there are changes that become evident in your life. Those areas include but are not limited to, what you say out of your mouth, for out of the heart the mouth speaks, what your actions look like continuously, what your thoughts are like, for as a man thinketh so is he, and what places, people, and things you hang around and surround yourself with. One of the hardest things after conversion and or being filled with the Spirit of God down the line of your life is saying goodbye to people you are so used to hanging with.

This could be family members, best friends, familiar places and more. Your friends may not have had your experience, however you are still responsible before God in getting your life in order no matter who you're connected to. Even if they are not in agreement with the new life you desire to live in Christ. Ultimately you have to stand before God and give an account of your life. Why did Jesus say do not hinder the children from coming to me? Why did he say you cannot even enter the Kingdom of heaven unless you are like that of a child? Children are innocent, and their hearts are pure before learned behavior contributes to their being. You are not able to see God unless you have a pure heart. There are many avenues that business is being conducted today within ministries. What about the avenue of having a pure heart? This has become irrelevant in the twenty first century life as a believer. Yes we are living in the last days, yes we have to stay on the straight narrow path, yes we have to remain in the remnant of real believers, but does that mean we are to stop showing people the love of Christ consistently? How are we commissioning people within the gospel to do all types of assignments having yet checked to see if their heart is pure? Just because someone has on a collar, church robe, a title, a parking space, and so forth does not mean that their heart is pure. Many who obtain these, I hope and pray the heart is pure, but I know it's not one hundred percent. A pure heart is powerful and it weighs in God's direction and favor.

There are women who come into the church half-dressed because they have not received a new mind yet, however their heart may be in better condition than Perfect Patty sitting on the front row covered with an altar shawl. God sees it all. It is essential to cover yourself ladies as you go into church, as it is for men to also dress appropriately as we want to honor the house of God and ourselves as the Lord calls us to, however we need to worry more about what someone has in their heart than what they have on their body or lack thereof. My point is that it is sad if someone in ministry is running to cover up the new girl who comes into church with an altar cover, when that ministry worker may need the same prayer shawl she is ministering with to cover any impurities in her own heart. We often assume that those who are put in leadership positions are without flaws. They experience the same temptations, trials, and struggles that any believer does! I am sure it has to be difficult for them as their entire lives are under a microscope. The thin line is where you are projecting to the public a lifestyle that mirrors Christ as a great witness; however the rigidity can overstep the necessity to become out of the box for the gospel. For example, many people who came to Jesus were not people who had it all together, they were desperate for a miracle and embarrassment was the last thing they were worried about. They were not worried about looking the part, as they understood that they needed Jesus and for Him to move on their behalf. The desperate people in the Bible were real examples. Great enough examples that they are recorded in God's Word. Today you have some church people that act the way they do because they can't imagine being embarrassed, a laughing stock, or talked about, yet that is the very thing the Word says wins souls, by the foolishness of preachers. I am not saying go grab shame and things that don't look good for the gospel; however I am saying that when you have died to your reputation you are humble enough to look whatever way you need to for Christ and the gospel. Even if you are a young divorced woman trying to enhance God's body. Embarrassment is something I am past, I've bought the t-shirt, the hat, and the mug. John the Baptist could care less about being embarrassed or talked about, as he paved the way for Christ. Usually when someone has passed this stage of dying for the faith, they are fully aware that their gift from God is not about them, you don't have to keep reminding them. By the time one has faced life threatening and near death situations, still amazed to be living, the last thing they'd think about is glorifying themselves. In fact, sometimes these things are the very thing that breeds a boldness to go forth where angels tread to go. You can always tell when a believer doesn't believe that Romans 3:23 doesn't applies to them. It's almost like they sort of think it applies, not fully understanding that their works is as filthy rag unto God when it comes to one presenting their righteousness and justification by their own works. Therefore if anyone should sit down from proclaiming the gospel, that would be every born of natural and of spiritual non corruptible seed. The closer you get to the light, the more dirt you should see on yourself. You will be motivated to remove the log from your own eye before commenting on the speck in your neighbors (Matthew 7:3-5). I know the closer I really came to Christ, the more wrong I saw about myself more than anyone.

The enemy is just waiting to hold all their mistakes and flaws against them in attempt to discrediting the gospel that they stand for and preach. This is why it is essential to make sure you don't have pastoritis. What is pastoritis? This is when the pastor becomes the idol of worship. Many church members don't even realize they have pastoritis. When the pastor is on vacation or visiting another church, when the numbers dwindle for service that Sunday or Wednesday for Bible study, it's a high indication that those who chose not to show up because someone other than the pastor is preaching or teaching indeed have pastoritis. Jesus did not call us to worship a leader, only Him. He said do not have any other gods before him. I don't believe people intend on worshipping their pastor, I believe it seeps into their spirit overtime after wanting to be significant, wanting to be recognized, and wanting to be in full support of the ministry. Somewhere along the way they lose sight of Jesus and replace the throne of the lives with their pastor.

This book is not purposed to only expose areas we all need to work better in, however it is to commend those who are in leadership that have been able to maintain integrity and who are loving and feeding God's people consistently and carefully, through the help of the Holy Spirit. I'd like to thank those leaders who speak up on behalf of the people instead of operating in "group think". What is "group think"? Group Think is defined as: when everyone agrees with everyone else just to keep the peace and stay away from conflict or confrontation. This happens a lot within the church. Everyone sees the issue at hand, but instead of confrontation and speaking up, everyone is silent because no one wants to disturb the peace or be the problem starter. Do you know how many people suffer on behalf of your silence and unwillingness to carry out your calling of leading? Leading means you do what's in the best interest for the people not yourself. This may look different in many ways according to what the situation may be. Sometimes you have to rock the boat.

Transformation Varies

We are often surprised that a stern anointed Godly man can have children who are rebellious in every way doing the exact opposite of how he raised them in the fear and admonition of the Lord. It can be a barrier for those looking on the outside in, wondering how can this man be so powerful in God, yet his family may not reflect what he has preached for years. Carefully reading and studying the bible will clearly answer this. God holds each person to their own accountability regardless of who their parents are, or who they are married to, or what ministry they belong to. Yes! There may be sanctification and a covering when you are married to an unbeliever or living with rebellious children, however salvation is not guaranteed, neither is their own actions justified by being "blessed by association". What does it mean to be "blessed by association"? Many people receive titles, position, and status through being "blessed by association". Let's take a look at Abraham and Lot. Lot was Abraham's nephew. When Lot was in trouble in Sodom and Gomorrah, he ended up being saved by the Angels of the Lord, not because of anything on Lot's behalf, but because he was connected to Abraham. Abraham interceded for Lot and because of this he was saved from destruction. What about Lot's family, they too were blessed by association. Most of them were able to escape the destruction of Sodom and Gomorrah because they were associated with Lot, who was associated with Abraham, who was certainly, associated with God. Lot's wife looked back after being instructed by God not to look back and was turned into a pillar of salt.

I believe in the body of Christ today we often look at one's anointing and wonder where it comes from. For example you can look at a well-known minister of the gospel such as Benny Hinn and immediately wonder who was his mentor? Where did God train him, who imparted what to Benny? All of this can be important depending on what the focus may be. I know without a shadow of a doubt where many of my blessings early on came from relating to being blessed by association. No doubt am I a believer and am entitled to the promises of God as his child, however there is no way that being raised in the circumstances I was raised in, and making some poor decisions throughout my life early on, that I should be standing where I am today. I believe that God certainly had his hand on me, but I also know that it has a great deal to do with the particular spiritual covering that was over my life. The mantle of the people who were over me spiritually played a major role in this principle becoming manifest in my life. Today I am certainly blessed by the association of my Apostles that God has ordered my steps to, for his purposes, and for my life to have an expected end (Jeremiah 29:11).

Overtime I have listened to ministers in the gospel spend a great deal of time giving patronage to where they come from, and who's anointing they came from under. There is definitely some significance to this, although this can be done in ways almost to worship the person and not God whom it all comes from according to James 1:17. I am grateful for my home church, but I wouldn't be honest if I didn't share what God has said to me. "It does not matter if the anointing and mantle came from someone highly respected in the gospel, a power house of in the gospel, someone who's

55

lived a full life of integrity, or even a stray dog walking by me off the street, **I'm just glad that it got on me**, however, and through whomever it happened doesn't make a difference, yet I aim to honor those it did. To god be all the glory! How many of you know that in his presence there is no flesh that can glory? I am glad to be saved in Christ and to carry the anointing he saw fit for me to have. God can use anything and anyone, if God can use a rod in the hands of Moses, a sling shot in the hands of David, or a donkey's mouth with Balaam, I am certain he can use anyone or anything. It is essential to honor where you come from, but we should not worship people, places, and things. Set up an altar or a stone of remembrance and honor, give respect and honor, and turn your worship to God almighty, because it all is ultimately coming from him.

Let's examine some areas in the Word that may appear to be contradictory as we studied earlier, where in one are it mentions one thing, and in another area, it mentions something that appears to be opposite. After having many conversations with new believers, I kept getting the same questions in regards to being saved at different times and ages in people's lives.

There are several scriptures in the New Testament that state that if you know God you will obey him. I whole heartedly agree, but I also would like to acknowledge where some may be at with their age and development which can be a factor in their obeying him even if they do know him.

For example if Christopher gets saved at seven, he knows God and he loves God, but he may not be mature enough in his mind, emotions and will to really put into practice all of God's laws as he is a child. Christopher may have accepted Christ at an early age and knows God and loves God. Christopher may even know scripture however during his teen years, he may fall away from the faith due to what comes naturally with being born into sin as he may not be filled with God's Spirit yet, relating to maturing in every area of his life. Yes he was born again, but now he is being more exposed to a sin present world during his adolescents. Sadly if Christopher is not in the right environments and atmospheres where Christ is the center, his relationship with God will be affected.

Does God still love Christopher? Yes! Will their fellowship be the same? No! He will find it difficult to hear God's voice and living through and by the Holy Spirit. If Christopher falls away from the faith because of a particular season of life does this mean he does know God? I don't believe so, I believe that his disobedience and sin nature is being fed and he will need to rededicate his life back to Christ, the sooner the better. Prayerfully he will rededicate his life before he begins sowing too far ahead in the flesh imbedded in immaturity, ignorance, and lawlessness. His rededication could be a result of a revelation from God, self-inflicted experiences, having an experience and being filled with the Holy Spirit, there are a number of things that can lead Christopher back to God's original plan for his life, and it looks different for everyone, the Holy Spirit is the source of true rededication regardless of why it's taking place. It would be nice to pick the one that sounds the best, but in life that does not always happen.

The same is true for adults. Christopher was 7 years old when he gave his life to Christ and became saved by grace. People are being saved at all different ages in life. Not everyone gets saved at an early age. Sometimes you are looking at a man in his fifties who has just become saved, and he is being told by a minister of the gospel that he doesn't love God because his entire life shows you are not obeying God's commandments. Little does this supposedly mature saint fail to realize is that this fifty something year old man is Christopher in the spirit! The age of accountability is different for all people. There is not a law in the bible that says when everyone turns sixteen they have reached the age of accountability for their faith and life. The age of accountability is different for each person. It depends on where someone is in relation to receiving and walking with Christ. Isaiah 61 clearly demonstrates why Christ came and how we are to operate in the earth representing him. If a man is blind how can you beat him up because he is blind? This is what we do. We don't really know the moment a believer becomes mature and is no longer blind anymore. Yes if people are doing things in the wrong manner it will certainly have affect on the order that God set, and God is able to handle them and the situations involved. There are times in the bible where people needed to be stoned, cut off, or executed based on the wrong teachings and examples set forth, and at the same time Christ came and died for those who are sick because blindness will cause people to do things they have no idea what they are really doing regarding their impact. We cannot always say, well if you just follow wisdom, or if you would just do right. Perhaps that person does not know wisdom or to do right. Not because they choose to disregard wisdom, but perhaps it was how they were raised or not being in environments and atmospheres where wisdom was taught and demonstrated. The fatherless generation is dangerous to the order of God and what should be implemented in the earth as blindness and ignorance is real. Yes it is possible to come out of that but what about everything before the point of revelation and change? See God uses it all to work out for the good for those who love him. At the same time Psalm 27:10 clearly depicts God being the father to those whose natural parents have forsaken them. Psalm 51:5 is where David says he was brought forth in sin and in sin did his own mother conceive him. Perhaps this is why his father Jesse did not present him to Samuel as a selection to be anointed as King. There must be parts to this testimony that are not found at all in the bible. Yet I find it interesting that the very man God chose who had a heart after God's own naturally originated from a sinful situation. The unholy situation did not stop God from noticing his pure heart before God that outweighed hands down his natural circumstances. This reminds me of the tax collector in Luke 18. One who was not holy made contact with God because out of the pureness of his heart he repented and found the ear and attention of God who heard his prayer and acknowledged him over the religious Pharisee who thought he was holy because of the works he had done or not done, yet his heart was a foul stench before Christ. Each day you put both feet on the ground and stand out of the bed is another chance to accept Jesus, rededicate your life and get it right! Shame on you if you are procrastinating coming to God for salvation or rededicating your life because you think you have many days ahead to make that decision. That is not what I am encouraging. I am saying don't let another day go by without lining your life up with salvation and the word of God if this applies to you.

People are in various stages within their journeys in life. It is easy for us to look at someone and label them not knowing where they come from or their history, and because their history does not mirror ours, it sometimes can create a barrier to our understandings of where they may be. They may not have been raised like you; they may have a different educational, cultural, or sociological background than you as well. Don't let your differences separate you because that is what usually happens, yes even in the church.

Christopher breaking his fellowship with God does not excuse his behavior because by all means he will reap the consequences of what he's sown regardless if he's saved or not. I do believe there is a difference when you belong to God and how those consequences will play in the very end of your life having been worked for your good. This is not to encourage you to do whatever lawlessness or rebellion you desire with the mindset that God will work it out. This means line your life up with the word of God through the power of the Holy Spirit and don't live intentionally sinning.

This example of Christopher's life is also not to be compared to a serious reality of someone rejecting Christ for fifty years. This too is a reality. After having been exposed to the gospel, good teaching, good preaching, and opportunities to get one's life in order, yet they still choose to reject God over time, every time, there is a serious issue at hand, it must be addressed as soon as possible. **There is a difference and you must know and discern both when ministering to someone.** It could take you investing time spent with them to really discern correctly in addition to spiritual revelation from God. To make an accurate evaluation of someone it takes time, because you have to get to know them, other instances depending on your spiritual gifts and level of discernment, you may sense it immediately, especially if you have prior experience with the same familiar spirit. God gives us all spiritual gifts according to 1 Peter 4:10. We did not get to pick our spiritual gifts out of the hat. One may be upset because another has the gift they were hoping to operate in, but that's just the way it is. I encourage you to learn exactly what your spiritual gift is. There are many assessments that strive to advise you of what your spiritual gifts are, however I believe that God himself will reveal it to you over time and confirm it. When he does, learn all you can about it so that you can operate in the gift God has given you to the glory of God. God revealed to me that my main spiritual gift is the discernment of spirits. This is a gift I would have gladly traded in for another one; however we don't get to choose. There is a lot to face and deal with this particular gift and it's not always fun. If someone is not pleased with your gift or doesn't want to believe you have the gift you know God revealed unto you, it's not your job to prove yourself to anyone that you are correct in knowing your gifting. Hearken to the voice of the Lord and carry out any assignments he has commissioned you for. It may sound weird, crazy, and you may lose your popularity and favor with men, however you will be pleasing God living by faith and according to 1 Peter 5: 10. He himself will confirm, restore, establish, and strengthen you according to the scripture.

There may be a pronouncement of generational curses on your family due to the sins of ancestors long ago, and they indeed may affect you just because they were passed down to you, however God is a heart weigher. Therefore if you inherited a generational bondage or curse, but prove to God with your actions and your life that your heart is good according to the word of God, then the scale that your heart is being weighed on just broke those generational curses off, along with your continued obedience in Christ with his grace and mercy that you don't take advantage of. So even though in Numbers 14:18 he says he will repay the parent's children, the same first voice and the same God that said he would make you pay, changes his mind about you and says the exact opposite in Ezekiel: 18. Therefore what God says first is important, however if he changes his mind, it doesn't change the voice that said it, it simply means that the first declaration of what God said is now altered according to him being a God of the Present (**The great I am**), who interacts with people in the present tense for relationship.

Love is the essence of who God is. After teaching and preaching on the word of God and explaining what the scriptures mean, it is imperative to remember the very essence of God through it all. The essence of God is that he is LOVE. Many scholars have argued that God does not have emotions and that he is not like people whose emotions are tied to their humanistic features. It is true that his ways are higher than ours, and his thoughts are higher than ours, and that God is completely spirit unlike us, however he is passionate just like we are made in his image to be. Love is passionate. Why did God create us in his image? Humans are made to be sexual beings. Does God have sex? That's a contradiction right there. Of course God does not have intercourse like a man and woman does, but he does know what it's like to be intimate with another, for example with his Son who is Jesus, and the Holy Spirit, and even with you and I as believers.

It is believed that with circumcision with a males' penis the intent was so that of course the male can be marked having been identified with belonging to God before Jesus came and died on the cross for the finished work, but Studies have shown that this was also a gift to the man, that anytime he entered into his wife he'd experience a paradise that was to take him back to the Garden of Eden where the full pleasure of walking with God fully without the presence of sin was experienced. Could this be a reason why we live in such as sex crazed society. We give so much credit to the enemy; of course it's the enemy trying to ruin the destiny and course of people if he can get them sexually bound to someone that has nothing to do with their destiny, especially at early ages. Sex is a gift from God. It's not just for procreation. It feels great, it is spiritual, and it takes you out of this world's elements! Why wouldn't anyone want to enjoy sex? Yes there are many sexual dysfunctions and emotional and spiritual issues we will address in a later section, however living in a world such as ours, the spiritual pleasure of escaping this world's pressures and presence of evil it is a gift to do so in the bounds of marriage. Is this stated anywhere in the Bible? No it is not? Am I forcing you to adopt the results from studies? No I am not. This is my book and assignment from God, and if you choose not to continue reading it because there was something listed in my book that is not found in God's word, then by all means do as you wish, however I believe that studies and research, and rationality can assist in helping lead others to Christ. These things are not always used to deceive people or come away from Christ, sometimes they can be used to lead people closer to Christ. The Apostle Paul said to become all things to all men that we may win some. If you are the type of believer that believes that rationality is only a barrier to the spirit of God then I am praying for you. Rationality can also be used to persuade those to come to Christ. Yes the Spirit has to reveal, yes they have to choose, however according to 1 Corinthians 1:21 and 1 Corinthians 9: 19-23 it gives the example of being flexible with a variety of avenues to win souls. Why would God even give a woman a clitoris for her to enjoy sex if the sole purpose was for her to have sex just to reproduce? It is medically proven that the clitoris has no other use or purpose on the female but for her to experience pleasure during sexual intercourse. What does that mean? It means women, that God created you to enjoy sexual intercourse with your husband. I believe that sexual intercourse is to be experienced only in marriage according to the word of God. I also believe that people desire to have sex prematurely because of the pleasure it brings which gratifies the flesh as we know, but also gives you the high and spiritual mystery that God intended. Spiritually it gives us as humans a sense of what the Garden of Eden was like before the fall, and what eternity was like before we were ever born into flesh. Sex is spiritual! It is heaven on the earth. Sexual intercourse during marriage is for procreation and carrying out God's command to be fruitful and multiply, however it is also a gift from God that is a mystery in the spiritual oneness that is experienced. It is full of pleasure and more importantly for this topic it is full of passion. This is a good example of the purpose of sex not being one or the other, but both, for procreation, and pleasure.

The Scales Never Lie

Of course we know that after Christ died on the cross there is no longer a need to be physically circumcised, but the believer is to be circumcised in heart. This is also the essence of Scales of the Heart. A heart is in big trouble if it belongs to a believer but it's not circumcised. Can you be a believer without a circumcised heart? You can say you are, but you're not until you've received a new heart that has been circumcised.

So yet again! Why is God always saying things throughout the bible that he will do, then turning around changing his mind a few moments later? I beg to argue, that it is because of who he is and his greatest attribute, characteristic, and essence and that is love. Yes God is holy, he is powerful, mighty, strong, all knowing, omnipresent and so much more, but love outweighs immensely everything else. That is the only way a Holy God that cannot be approached just any kind of way would ever come close to us who's righteous deeds are like a filthy rag before him according to Isaiah 64:6. God who is Holy, broke all laws to come save and redeem us to himself because of what? Because he knew you would be faithful in ministry, tithe every Sunday, graduate from minister's school, found a ministry, write a book, etc, etc. Absolutely not! He came and saved us because according to John 3:16, which you may think is played out, but it's still the cream of the crop scripture in the bible and that is Because God so LOVED the world that he gave, (he compromised, he gave in to his holiness, he put aside himself, he broke the rules) his only begotten son that whosoever will believe in Him shall not perish, but have eternal life. The scripture says whosoever….it does not say males only, or those who go to church, it says whosoever, that is young, old, black, white, Jewish, Russian, fat, skinny, tall, short, woman or man, you will have eternal life according to what the scripture says and you will **NOT** perish! In John 10:28 Jesus said I give them eternal life and they shall never perish, no one can snatch them from my hand! That means just that, no one can snatch you from the hand of Jesus! The devil will have you thinking that something or someone can snatch you from the Lord's hand, but the scripture says that whosoever believes on the Lord Jesus will not perish but have eternal life.

This does not mean that your fellowship or your walk with God can't be affected depending on your actions, and your heart which is able to change. According to what we read earlier in Ezekiel 18, we saw where people were righteous in God's sight, and then turned to do evil. This means if you have a bad heart, then there is a possibility that you can have a new heart, and if you have a righteous heart, the goal is to keep it righteous and don't allow it to be evil, because that too is a possibility.

What happens when our experiences catches up to our knowledge? Let's look at Saul before he was converted on the Damascus road.

Saul was a knowledge filled man, he knew much, and operated from what he believed was truth and correct. He had passion, and zeal, and he was full of fight! However he was filled with the wrong fight. The enemy knows if he can take all of what God has put down inside of you and turn it so that you are using all of it towards something wrong, he wins, yes you are full of knowledge, fight, passion, and zeal, however if poured into the wrong direction many will be negatively affected. He was killing Christians by the droves. He was there when Stephen was being stoned, and encouraged by many of who were also following the wrong way. Yes Paul lacked the Spirit of God and conversion, however God allowed the origin of his knowledge to be used for the assignment that God had coming to Paul. Paul thought he had learned what he learned in regards to opposing Christianity, but Paul had no idea that he was learning what he was learning in the Sanhedrin Council to later build Christianity, and not to destroy it. Won't God blow your mind with things you never imagined? God knew that knowledge and the filling of the Holy Spirit was both important! One is more important than the other and that is the Holy Spirit. Therefore if you notice someone with one, don't sleep on them as if the greater is not coming, and don't judge them as if you already know if they have God's Spirit or not. This area may be similar but not the same as all people are different. God gave Paul the lesser of the two first as he did Moses. First he gave him the knowledge that he would need knowing that when the time came for Paul to be filled with the Holy Spirit of God, Paul would be unstoppable! Isn't that just like God? Surprise, surprise! Let's look at Moses! Moses was raised in the palace of Egypt learning and equipping for something as he thought he would be in the leadership of Egypt in some capacity later in life, however the knowledge and wisdom he learned there was purposed for him to combat the same empire he was preparing to be a part of. He was to lead the Israelites out of Egypt and that's what he did. Moses was equipped in the mind with wisdom and knowledge first, then came the desert experience, then came the Midian life experience, then came the burning bush experience (note no one told Moses about a burning bush…he EXPERIENCED it firsthand himself)…God knew that once the Spirit of God was in the midst of them in addition to the knowledge and wisdom Moses already acquired he would be molded just right to go before Pharaoh and complete his assignment. I'd like to liken this to what I often hear comparisons to. Sometimes I'll hear a believer discuss how God does not like stuck up church people who are self-righteous. How God loves the broken, confused sinner that just can't seem to get it right. In Luke 5:32: I came not to call the righteous, but sinners to repentance. Here God is saying that he came for the sick. What we often fail to realize that self-righteousness and arrogance is a form of sickness. So if we leave no stones unturned and examine both sides of the spectrum it is clear to see that God also came for those imbedded in a mindset of self-righteousness because that too is a severe sickness. So God came for the down and out sinner, but guess what he also came for the stuck up church member. God loves them both! Honestly, there could be more use with using a stuck up church member like the Apostle Paul before his conversion, than someone who has just been converted and has no knowledge at all, depending on the assignment. God knew all Saul needed was a Damascus road EXPERIENCE and all Moses needed was a burning bush EXPERIENCE. Once truth and revelation was brought along with a heart circumcision, they would be fierce and unstoppable for God's work. God can take Mr. or Mrs. Stuck up, because all they need is a good healing from their sickness, and they will be very impactful for the Kingdom. That is not to say that a new convert that was wrapped in sin would not be useful to God, trust me, I am a living witness to the fact that God takes the least likely candidate and prepares them for the journey! However, Saul was also the least likely candidate that God chose to embark a great Christian awakening. Once the experience caught up to the knowledge that Saul already had, he would be ready! So just like we don't disqualify a downright sinner from God's work in the future, don't disqualify those you see that are a hot self righteous mess. He uses it all.

Speaking of disqualifying candidates, let's look at the women God specifically chose for great men of God. They all had issues at hand to bring, whether that was legal, moral, or just a complexity that no man of God would dream to deal with.

The four mentioned women are listed in the Chronology of Jesus Christ: Tamar, Ruth, Bathsheba, and Mary, please note that 3 of them all had a husband prior to meeting destiny and one was deemed just nuts!

Let's start with Ruth….Boaz was an older man that was living his life in his routine when Ruth just showed up out of the blue. Perhaps Boaz had a young lady in mind to marry that was in his town and perhaps there was already a relationship with someone else. We don't know. We do know if that was the case, her name is not in history it is Ruth's. Yes the woman that lost her husband to death, clung to a woman who had nothing, and said goodbye to everything she once knew including her own flesh and blood sister Orpah, she traveled with little, being a young woman herself with no husband or children, she settled in a foreign land with people who only heard about her and her story. Yes this woman is the woman God chose for the "man of the town". How does this foreign woman qualify for Boaz? Shouldn't other candidates have more pull than Ruth? After all they knew all about Boaz, his likes, his dislikes, they had watched him, supported him, perhaps brought him food, caught his eye. Regardless of all of that it was in God's plans for Boaz to take Ruth…whether he wanted to or not. God gave Boaz the interest and desire for Ruth that was supernatural. It is just like God to demonstrate the opposition with the "close relative" who by the law had more of a right to Ruth, yet instead what was ordained took place. In spite of what was politically, socially, and religiously correct, God's agenda overcame all of that, and Ruth became Boaz's wife.

What about Tamar? God had seen what was being done with Tamar. Leave it up to a man she would be a widow in a far off city waiting for the rest of her life for a promise to be fulfilled. It didn't matter how much Onan didn't want to honor his brother by taking Tamar as his wife to produce offspring on behalf of his brother, or how Judah: a good man, didn't want to give his other son Shelah to Tamar. Regardless of the shame and loss Tamar experienced, it was in God's plan that Judah be the one to fulfill Tamar's promise.

What about Mary the mother of Jesus. It didn't matter if Joseph was afraid to take her as his wife, or how he was arranging his plan of putting her away secretly….it was in God's plan that he take the woman everybody else deemed crazy for saying she was pregnant by the Holy Spirit.

Let's look at Bathsheba (Oh Lord please help us here), could she have been God's choice selection to be the mother of the next King of Israel after David? How could she be when she was married to Uriah? Why would God arrange this in his plans? Perhaps God saw that even good men sin including David. He knew David would sin, even though he sinned which he shouldn't have, but did, perhaps God chose the woman that he would sin with. It is more easy to just believe that Oh God used their mess, and after the consequence was paid of them losing the child conceived in iniquity, then it was aligned right for them to conceive again after marrying and doing things the right way, even though it originated in sin. God does not always need to tell us what he is doing or why he is doing it. God had a way of teaching David, it does not matter if you are King or not, you still must abide by the same rules and commandment as the people you are reigning over. With that lesson, along with generations of consequences from David's sin, a King was born, a child that God loved according to 2 Samuel 12:24. How could God love this child but hate what David did. It can certainly be studied, however God is sovereign and he can do what he wants to do when and how he wants to do it. It is just like God hates divorce, yet loves those who have experienced divorce who are his children.

Of course we can't forget about Gomer. It didn't matter if Hosea didn't want to take a prostitute as his wife or not. Why would any man of God want to take a prostitute? It was in God's plans.

Did Salmon take Rahab because he planned to? He took her because God set a desire in his heart for her to be taken. Where is this said in the Bible? Do you not see the chronology of David? In the beginning was the Word of God. So let it be written so let it be done. And it was done, regardless of Salmon's expectation or perhaps plans.

Let's look at Mary Magdalene: delivered and healed from evil spirits was the first person commissioned to spread the Gospel of Jesus Christ, where were all the men? Why were they not at the tomb? What about the disciple that Jesus loved? Why was he not there!?

Every woman who was a virgin before marriage and who has been married to the same man all of their lives should be applauded and honored! That is the way God intends it, but face another truth, the truth that he also handpicks those that have been broken and beaten by life to usher in the next man or people of God through the wombs of these women also. Never make the assumption that because a woman's testimony is not traditional according to man's ideal of what it should be, that God isn't and cannot user her. In fact, both types of women have been proven throughout the bible for great Kingdom use. Isn't it interesting that the four women in the Genealogy of Jesus is composed of yes a woman that was a virgin who remained married to the same man all of her life, yet three others who were opposite in their own idiosyncrasies of issues? I hate to break the news to you men of God waiting for your bride to arrive in freshly tight packed bubble wrap without flaw, wrinkle, or baggage, but God could be preparing your wife for you and the assignments for you both in ways you would have never expected and through circumstances you may deem undesirable. Jesus didn't come the way religious people expected. You may be expecting your wife or husband to come only a certain way, but they may be coming in a totally different dimension than what you were never planning and hoping for. Jesus was born in a manger not the Taj Mahal. Ruth came with nothing but the favor of God. She didn't stroll into town as a rich lady with all her hand maidens assisting her. She was assisting a woman that had nothing herself. Abigail went with David and no, he was not her first and neither was she his first. So if a man or woman is not feeling you because of your history too bad because it can certainly be their lost, stop sleeping on people because of their past, when they could be your answered prayer.

Yes you have free will to choose, but the man of God always seems to choose what lines up with God's plans, if you don't believe me, just read your bible. I have seen how men are afraid to death to take a woman with issues before the people, yet knowing in his heart she is the one! He can't explain it or understand it, yet after walking by faith like the 3 Hebrew boys that walked into blazing fire, Jesus showed up! All was more than okay, and they were respected by all! And the King's decree was written Daniel 3: 29: Therefore, I make this decree: If any people whatever their race or nation or language, speak a word against the God of Shadrach, Meshach, and Abednego, they will be torn limb from limb, and their houses will be turned into heaps of rubble. There is no other god who can rescue like this! (Which still implies today in many instances including that of being tied to a tare or goat, or a person with the heart of Pharaoh). God will rescue you as he judges what's best for your life.

What about the woman at the well? We all assume she had 5 husbands because that was her choice. Many fail to see her position in the time she lived in. During that day a man could write his wife a certificate of divorce. What if this happened to her 5 times, what if there was abandonment 5 times, what if there was a release 5 times, perhaps 2, 3, or 4 out of 5? Stop assuming the woman at the well was a loose woman who had 5 husbands because she chose to. You don't know why she was in the predicament she was in. If she was abandoned many times by men who would send her away or leave themselves, what could she do as a woman in that patriarchal day? Why would Jesus talk to someone with five husbands? It didn't matter how many husbands she had to Jesus, perhaps with people, but not with the one that mattered. Jesus mentions here in John 4:23 to a broken thirsty repeatedly divorced woman that the time is coming and it's here now when true worshipers will worship the Father in spirit and in truth! That included her! Yes she may have been married and divorced several times but she would be included in the true worshippers. She may not get married again on earth, but that was irrelevant, she had been chosen regardless and in spite of her history to be one of the first passionate evangelists of Jesus! John 4:30 says so the people came streaming from the village to see him. So they came because of the news the Samaritan woman spread. I encourage you if you are the woman at the well to finish your life as did this woman!

What about Abigail she too had a husband before destiny showed up. And when Nabal was struck dead instead of abiding by what people expected her to do, mourn and grieve for months over her dead husband, instead of doing this she packed her bags, mounted David's horse and, rode off having made the decision of lifetime to be his wife and one of the queens of Jerusalem. You may ask, how she could just go with David like that, I am sure David was on a journey and had a destination to be at, to think he waited around for a long time for Abigail to make a decision is silly. She made the decision quick. How could Joyce Meyer marry Dave Meyer after being divorced for only one year? If you walked in Joyce and Abigail's shoes it would be easy for you to understand what it's like to be married to a fool. Perhaps Abigail didn't choose Nabal, perhaps it was an arranged marriage. Perhaps she did choose him and he changed, we don't know, neither is it relevant for those reading her story, what's relevant is that a new marriage came into being that was used for God's glory. I am sure when she deflected David's anger against her first husband, was not where her wisdom and advice ceased. Perhaps David was going in her direction initially because God chose Abigail, yes the wife of another to be David's to give wise counsel not just to save his name and reputation that time but for future references. Point and case is that Nabal had a heart weigh in and failed. David would later sin out of his flesh and reap consequences distributing them through the next generations, but it says in Acts 13:22, but God removed Saul and replaced him with David, a man about whom God said, 'I have found David son of Jesse, a man after my own heart. He will do everything I want him to do. Both Nabal and David had sinful behavior but what made the difference between the two was the weighing of the hearts!

By the way where were these women's children before destiny showed up? God has been regulating wombs and seed from generation to generation. Is it a coincidence that Ruth didn't have any children before meeting Boaz? Why didn't she have any children by her first husband? Why didn't Bathsheba have any children by Uriah? Why didn't Rahab have children before Salmon? After all she was a prostitute? Why didn't Abigail have any children to take with her when she rode off with David? Why didn't Sarah have a child before it was time? Why were all the wombs of Egypt closed when Sarah's position was altered by her own husband's contributive lies, why didn't Rachel conceive until a certain time, why did Tamar not get pregnant by her husband? Why did it take years for her to receive her blessings: Because not only is God a weigher of the heart but he is also a regulator of the womb and seed.

As many children Peninnah gave Elkanah, he still preferred and favored Hannah. 1 Samuel 2:5 is where Hannah praises God as he reveals himself to her through her experience and her previous taunts by Peninnah. She proclaims that the childless woman now has seven children, and the woman with many children wastes away. The Lord gives both death and life; he brings some down to the grave but raises others up. There is a pattern in the word of God regarding women who were barren eventually giving birth to mighty men of God in the bible who have been used for vastly important assignments of the Lord. If you are a modern day Hannah, fret not and let your heart not be troubled, you could just be ordained for a special child. You can learn a lot from Hannah who vowed to God in her distress and God answered her plea!

The Bible demonstrates more toward women who have had issues with husbands, or who are widows, or who have been married much more than it does regarding men who are widows. In order to be a part of the Sanhedrin council that Saul was a part of you had to be married? Where was Saul's wife? Could the man that churches almost give more honor to at times than Christ sometimes be divorced? Where ever his wife was it was irrelevant for this assignment. When God has an assignment on your life such as Paul's it doesn't not matter what was conceived prior. It's coming to pass.

God is the only one who can forgive sins as he is the one who gives a release. When god forgives you and or releases you no man or woman can "UN-forgive" you or put you back behind a door God closed himself. He will open doors no man can open and close doors that no man can close. When you know God has closed or opened a door in your life don't be surprised if church people try to undo what God did because they want to see you where they believe you should be, due to their opinion. Many times people may just be trying to encourage the person to hang in there and put up more fight, however God may have closed that door in a person's life. In our rationality we tend to think it either has to be A or B, not realizing that God's thoughts are higher than our thoughts and his ways are higher than our ways. For example: either you remain married to someone with the heart and spirit as pharaoh or you will never be accepted in our churches as a minster even if you have a call on your life...those are our rules! Follow them or become victim to our A and B option.... not realizing that there is not just an A or B plan God has for your life...there is one plan, plan A... allowing everything to work out for those who love the Lord and who are the called according to his purpose. The truth of the matter is if there is a real call on the person's life the same people that will condemn and shun you will be the same people who will later respect and honor you after they see what God's purpose is for you.

There is a mindset, a stronghold/principality over the expectation of marriage regarding how it should play out according to its design before the fall of man. Nothing is wrong at all with the way God originated marriage, the issue is what occurred after the fall that can impact a covenant in a fallen world. When this area is not something you are able to relate to, it is immensely easy to misunderstand others it has.

A mindset is the set way in which one thinks. We can compare it to civil rights. Yes, minorities have been given rights within the workplace. Yes women have been given rights to work in the workplace, however they are still discriminated against, and situations are manipulated to demonstrate the true essence of racism and discrimination. Yes the laws are in force and there is a company policy stating they don't tolerate these practices but in reality they are being practice by the same companies that claim they don't tolerate them. Even though it is written in policy and understood that it is illegal for discrimination to take place, it still does because of the mindset that will not change regarding women and minorities being accepted as equals in the workplace. The same is with divorcees, yes you will be acknowledged publically on Sunday morning as equals in the body of Christ and people will appear to treat you no differently however the mindset that there is only so much a divorcee can do within the church, and that someone else will be used greater still exists. I have seen how some divorced people are treated as if they have a disease within the church. I hate to break it to you, but God will use a divorcee for his work: look at Joyce Meyer, she was married for five years to someone else other than her present day husband Dave Meyer of now over 30 years of marriage, Nelson Mandela, the same man who sat in a jail cell for years taking a stand for South Africa was divorced, Myles Monroe a great renowned author and entrepreneur is divorced. The call cannot be stopped by divorce; it can certainly be delayed and impacted but not stopped. You may say, this is an obvious and you don't have to reiterate the obvious, however this is being written so that years from now regardless of the state of the church a child of God may experience a divorce believing all the lies that the devil would have them to believe and much of it may come from church people. This is who this book is written for particularly future leaders of the church who have been taught to operate out of rigidity and being saved by works, it is also written for the one who experiences a heart breaking divorce, but there is still a serious call on your life, don't let people tell you or speak through their silence that you have been disqualified from your calling. You are not alone, many have experienced the same before you, many are experiencing it now with you, and many will experience it after you.

There is a difference between laws and understandings from regulations verses being ingrained in our hearts and minds. Divorce yes we understand there are reasons you or people divorce but in reality they could be telling you in another voice stay away from our church, our ministry, our clique and etc.

God loves all of his children, even though his love for us will never change or be altered, the fellowship we have with God can be altered depending on our hearts and actions.

God is a weigher of the hearts. Proverbs 15:11 says that death and destruction lie before the Lord, how much more than human hearts!

Hosea 4:16: my people are destroyed because of lack of knowledge: we need to ensure our brothers and sisters in the body are well aware of certain infiltrating spirits, especially in generations to come. If our children are being taught that same sex marriage is right and they won't even be able to identify naturally what marriage is supposed to look like, do you think they will be able to recognize demonic spirits like Jezebel, Pharaoh, Hamans, and Herods? Perhaps not at the beginning of their conversion, as none of us have, but somewhere moving into maturity when they get off of milk onto solid food, how do we expect to prevail against the dark forces of this world when we are not educated on them? First of all what are they? What do they sound like in the spirit? What do they look like in the natural and in the spirit? Yes the Holy Spirit will reveal it to us with discernment and through prayer, but what about practical education on these spirits, by the time someone educates one on these in the natural combined with the Spirit of God's discernment much more time can be saved without having one go through unnecessary things to finally be aware of certain spirits.

Let's look at a young lady named Tameka who struggled growing up.

Tameka was born in a broken single parent home, her family never went to church or followed the Lord's ways, they instead did whatever they wanted and lived lawless. Tameka began having sex at an early age, drinking and smoking, and getting into trouble with the wrong people. Why? Do you think she deliberately did these things because she knew it was wrong? I'd be surprised if she did what was right according to God's word coming from the brokenness in which she did. Of course we have a God given conscience but just as Eve was deceived in the garden of Eden, Tameka's mindset was not rooted and established on whether it was wrong or not, but the ideal of "it's not that bad, or it's okay".

If our God given conscious was enough after the fall then there would have been no reason for Christ to come and die for his people. Apparently that was not enough. Tameka engaging in premarital sex was normal in her mind where dysfunction became normal. Nobody had ever stopped to correct her, everyone around her was doing this, she didn't have education on living right, eventually she became saved and the Holy Spirit began to teach her of the impact that sin has upon one's life. She was reaping the consequences of sin she had sown in ignorance. There was a blindness beyond her conscience that Christ was fully aware of would be there before she was ever born. One of the best strategies of the enemy is knowing that what you sow is what you reap, if he can have people sow in ignorance he knows yes they may wake up and smell the coffee but by the time that happens they will already be reaping their harvest of sin which will delay their destiny and perhaps interfere with the power of the Holy Spirit within them developing against his kingdom. We as churches have the inclination to make people like Tameka feel condemned not realizing that what she sowed was in ignorance and it's our job as the church to help her tap into the power of God within her and get herself together. Instead there is an attitude that Tameka can only do this in the church or go thus far, realizing that attitude is an aide to the enemy that would want to keep her paralyzed in not exercising her gifting. God said no there is not one that is righteous no not one in Romans 3:1. Yet when you encounter mature saints in the body of Christ that used to be Tameka ten or twenty years ago, not being able to empathize with her or take the time to lead, teach and direct (Titus 2:4) sadly they have become so high and mighty they feel, believe, and act as if they are so much better than Tameka. Nothing is sadder than someone not reaching down and back to grab another who is encountering the same struggles they had to face. The hand you are reaching back to is literally your own, and we owe it to God to do unto others as we would have them do unto us (Luke 6:31, Matthew 7:12, Golden rule).

Satan was insane in thinking that he could do and be what he wanted and still be in heaven with God. So it is today, people are insane just like Satan in the fact they believe they will cheat on their spouses and not get caught and if they do get caught they expect grace and mercy to be given and still receive the same benefits and fellowship as before. If our fellowship with God is predicated on our actions why in the world do people think they can repeatedly step out on their spouse or continue to abuse emotionally, physically and psychologically and still experience the same fellowship? Partly because they are getting away with it and the spouse is not drawing any boundaries because of the need to be attached to someone. People will get away with what you let them: God understood this. Israel was getting away with too much as she continued in her adulterous state. God had to show yes even I being full of love, mercy, grace, and forgiveness have boundaries and limits too! Just as there are consequences to sin and wrong living, there are consequences for oppressing or manipulating God's children, and bringing offense to a covenant that was made to another and or with God. Therefore he turned Israel over to their depraved minds for them to reap the consequences so that they would understand what they were doing, in order that they may be saved. God continued to eventually reconcile to Israel but he did have to take action. God will never reconcile with Satan, that is what that is. What if Satan stopped all the evil he is doing right now and repented before God? Some people will tell you to keep praying for Satan, for there is a possibility you may win him over with prayer, and that is a truth. Another truth is that God knows Satan will never repent or align himself up rightly, therefore he was dealt with the way he was dealt with. This is exactly what is happening when we tell people to go home and pray for your spouse…if that spouse is a child of the devil it does not matter how hard you pray, they don't belong to God. It may seem like they get away with much, but there is a day coming where God will handle that person. God is a God that gives much warning and chances before bringing judgment, therefore if judgment is brought that person had a number of chances to turn it around, however being stiff-necked, stubborn, rebellious, and hard hearted will bring upon the judgment of God.

Satan of course does not want you saved but if you are saved, the concern is not so much you being saved and forgiven as much as it is you having power. He wants to bring havoc everywhere before going to his eternal dwelling place.

Love Weighs Out Over All!

When Jesus came to the earth and died for us because God so loved the world, he proved that love outweighs all his other attributes. Did his holiness stand in the way of God giving his only begotten son? No it didn't. The finished work of the cross tore the veil in the temple in two giving all access to whosoever will, to come boldly before the throne of what? Of no mistakes? The throne of good deeds? The throne of being perfect? The throne of keeping God's commands? No….It's called the Throne of Grace. Jesus didn't mention a lot about grace when he was on earth, yet he was grace incarnate. The fact that he met Saul who later became Paul on the Damascus road and gave the kingdom assignment to him to spread the news of Christ and the grace was made available for those walking in Christ. Not grace to be taken advantage of, but to stand before and be right with God while following him forward. God didn't take his grace lightly when he allowed whosoever will to approach his throne of grace boldly, so why man believes that he can take it lightly is beyond me. I am not referring to believers who take advantage of God's grace, that in itself is a mess and it's not God's desire. I am referring to "man" or people who think that Grace is sort of kind of enough, making it as if the grace and the blood of Jesus was not enough. How dare you devalue the finished work of God? His grace is amazing because it was a gift undeserved. Did God come and do this just so that his plan could work, as some militant duty to redeem you? His response to the cross was militant, but the motivator behind that was love. It's one thing to be militant just to be militant, it's another thing when you are operating in a militant manner because you are passionate about love, loving others, and seeing them saved and changed for the glory of God. There is certainly a difference in the two when it relates to obtaining the right spirit. I believe Jesus did what he did for us to redeem us, justify us, advocate for us, and so much more, but **I believe above all he did it according to 1 John 3: 16. He so loved the world that he gave his only begotten son that whosoever will believe in him shall not perish but have eternal life!** If you believe that coming to the mature place in Christ means the less loving you are to people then you are immature yourself. Yes! There is much processing in becoming mature in Christ especially in the area of discipline and managing your emotions and feelings, but that never means shutting down love and compassion. Yes at times we are to disregard our feelings in order to obey Christ if it is something we may not want to do etc. But this never should be communicated to a believer to throw your feelings in the trash. There are times when we need our feelings to take a backseat if our feelings interfere with an instruction from God, yet this does not mean that God does not care about our feelings, there are several scriptures that clearly indicate that he does. Emotions are not a result of the fall, feelings are given to humans by God. Know that God cares about you and he cares about your feelings. A lot of this is situational as well. For example, if you have feelings for someone else's wife or husband, then guess what you can do with those feelings? Throw them in the garbage! No you cannot act on that! Hagar was sent back to submit to the authority of Sarah in Genesis. Regardless of her feelings she did what the lord told her. I'd like to look at this a little more in depth because it wasn't just the fact that she was told to go back, there are many things to look at here. Please note that Hagar didn't just run off and away because she did something wrong and had issues with submitting to authority, what we fail to realize is that Hagar was being put in a predicament created by her authority that was not godly nor his will, nor did she have any control over what happen. I am not saying she had to make Sarah upset when she became pregnant, perhaps she had a lot of built of tension over the years from the way she was being treated by her authority, we don't know, but what we know is that the issue stemmed and originated from her authority when Sarah had Abraham sleep with Hagar to bring Ishmael who Hagar never asked for. But God! He saw her and she knew he saw her and what she was going through. There are several scriptural references that confirm that God cares about us and everything pertaining to our lives including our feelings. How many times in the New Testament do we see Jesus having compassion or being moved with compassion? Compassion derives from a person's bowels. When you go to the restroom to relieve yourself it is because something is moving in your bowels. Compassion and love can be felt in your bowels and it will move you just like it moved Christ and gave him passion rooted in love for us. The tax collector in Luke 18 beat his chest because he felt his situation, he was moved, he felt and the result was that God heard his prayer over a religious Pharisee and the tax collector, a sinner, who made contact with God, was justified before God more over the Pharisee who compared himself with a law that could not save him. The Holy Spirit is a helper and comforter who brings conviction as a result something felt by the sinner or believer to move or direct in the appropriate way. The Holy Spirit, God himself feels. Ephesians 4:30 says do not grieve the Holy Spirit. We don't even see God as a person. No he is not a human being like you and I, but he is a person and he can be grieved. God gets angry, he grieves, this is one of the reasons he hates divorce, because he can witness firsthand on how divorce makes someone feel, God was separated from his bride Israel due to continuous chances offered by God that were rejected. God is full of compassion, he is moved. He made all things for his pleasure according to Revelations 4:11 and Colossians 1:16. How many of you know pleasure can be felt. Qoheleth, writer of Ecclesiastes says there is nothing better under the sun than to eat, drink, and be merry, how many of you know the result of those things includes feeling. God cares about your feelings, even if man doesn't. Why would God give a woman a clitoris? (This is not a children's book). It has been medically proven, that there is no medical reason a clitoris should exist in the woman. In fact some countries practice circumcising women so they won't feel the pleasure that God put in her naturally when engaging with her husband. How can God give a woman a clitoris to enjoy the gift of sex (Clifford and Joyce Penner, authors of the gift of sex), and man turn around and cut it out because he doesn't want her to feel something God designed her with. This is a clear indication God cared about the woman's fulfillment. There are several aspects to intercourse, reproduction, spiritual elements of it, and so forth, I am referencing the result of sexual stimulation, and that results in one feeling something. God gave sex to humanity not only to be fruitful and multiply but so that we could enjoy pleasure just as he made all things for his pleasure. For the adults who are not married and sexually free, let us reference 2 Corinthians 1 starting at verse 2, May God our Father and the Lord Jesus Christ give you grace and peace. All praise to God, the father of our lord Jesus Christ. God is our merciful father and the SOURCE of all comfort. He comforts us in all our troubles so that we can comfort others. When they are troubled, we will be able to give them the same comfort God has given us. For the more we suffer for Christ, the more God will shower us with his comfort through Christ. Even when we are weighed down with troubles, it is for your comfort and salvation. How many of you know that in order to be comforted or receive comfort the prerequisite to this is to be uncomforted. One who needs comfort feels a particular way. I don't believe that way is feeling good, for if you feel good, there is no need to be comforted. God is showing us that he cares about us, what we go through, and he is with us, and that he is the source of all comfort. Isaiah 61 depicts several examples of those who mourn and how the story won't end there for those in Christ. You see the turnaround from mourning to dancing. To make one want to dance you have got to feel something. Ask David, he danced out of his robe before the city! Ask real praisers, it bubbles up, you can feel it, Jeremiah said it's like fire, shut up in my bones, you can feel the Holy Spirit. One of the reactions and results of Holy Spirit is typically a burst of enthusiasm that is felt. No wonder why in Jeremiah 9:17 Thus sayeth the Lord! Call for the wailing, the mourning women that may come! We have already confirmed that some feelings do get us in trouble! I speak for myself! But on the other hand, there are some feelings that usher into wailing and mourning that enter into the presence of almighty God! Notice he didn't call for the wailing men. Not that men don't wail or mourn, but the woman is built in a different kind of fashion to enter into God's presence and get in touch with God quicker and more passionately than some males who don't feel as much. They call women emotional. This is how God made women. I believe this was initially in Adam but when God took Eve out of him, I believe some of the characteristics taken out of Adam are manifested in this area of feeling, note that is my opinion from my relationship with God, my experiences, and revelation God has given to me. Yes, I know this doesn't speak for all men and women as you may have some men who wail and some women who don't feel a thing, but I'd argue the majority is as such. It is true that some religious people enter into a misery so thick that they begin believing that because they are miserable they must be pleasing God if they ignore feelings that won't change their circumstances, and as a result they teach this to others whether that be consciously or unconsciously, and it damages what God has placed in a person as God never called us to be numb people walking on earth. Yes obedience is key, and in order to be obedient we must disregard certain feelings at times, but that doesn't mean God could care less about how we feel, and it doesn't mean there won't be another time in life to fully embrace what you feel.

Notice it says that God so loved the world, not God so loved the church. God loves the church as we are his bride, however he is compassionate and loving and these characteristics are responsible for the amazing grace and mercy that some believers take lightly, and also some leaders don't elaborate on in fear that it will give people a license to sin. What do I mean by this? It is true, we live in a day and age where grace is being preached erroneously, and people believe they can live any kind of life they want because of grace. This is being taught incorrectly according to how Paul desired for us to receive the message of grace. I believe that if a person is truly saved then at some point even if they were taught an erroneous lesson about grace, after studying the word of God for themselves, undergoing real sanctification, and being filled with the Holy Spirit, then they will understand and know what this really means and line their lives up accordingly. Anyone who has been taught the message of grace and learns God's word to see what the message really meant and still carries on living any kind of way is responsible for themselves. The point here is people are going to do what they want to do regardless if the right or wrong message is taught. Just because someone is taught the right message does not mean that they are going to adhere to the instructions that were taught rightly according to what grace really is. It does not matter how many times you drill something into someone that person still has the power of choice and free will, and they are going to do what they want to do anyway. If they go on believing, "Well, grace is there if I need it". It no longer becomes an issue of what someone taught them, the issue now is that they believe after having studied the word of God for themselves that they can just live however, and let their blood be on their own heads. Pray for them; however it may not be the fact that they are just lost and confused. It could be that they just don't have any desire in living right. A lot of people who adopt this type of lifestyle (I can live however and still be saved), really don't want to live a Christian life, and this is so hard for some believers to get through their mind. Everybody does not want to be saved, face it. There are a number of souls that has chosen to reject Christ, some are rejecting him now, and some will reject him later. We are to be light and salt in the world and point to Jesus as he is lifted up, he will draw all men unto himself (John 12:32).

It amazes me that you can even put the word "but" after acknowledging the grace of God in my perspective. There is no if, and, or but about it. It sounds as if the idea of God's amazing grace is being taken lightly and that it's sort of important, BUT that we must work overtime to keep it when that is far from the truth. There is no "but" when it comes to God's grace. We are all here not experiencing the wrath of God because of God's grace, and we are saved through faith in God and by his amazing grace that saved us (Romans 3:10). You absolutely have to do your part in appreciating God's grace and not taking advantage of it, however keep in mind you didn't have a single thing to do with receiving the gift of God. It was a gift that Jesus paid for. The acronym for grace we often say is God's Riches at Christ Expense! This is absolute! I don't ever want to take advantage of God's grace and I never want to act lightly toward the fact that I am saved by grace and by no work of my own (Ephesians 2:8-9). Galatians 3:23-29 is where we know we are God's children through faith, not works. Galatians 6 is where Paul gives his final advice to believers: and it reads Notice, what large letters I use as I write these closing words in my own handwriting. Those who are trying to force you to be circumcised want to look good to others. They don't want to be persecuted for teaching that the cross of Christ alone can save. And even those who advocate circumcision don't keep the whole law themselves. They only want you to be circumcised so they can boast about it and claim you as their disciples. As for me, may I never boast about anything except the cross of our Lord Jesus Christ. Because of that cross, my interest in this world has been crucified, and the world's interest in me has also died. It doesn't matter whether we have been circumcised or not (physically). What counts is whether we have been transformed into a new creation. May God's peace and mercy be upon all who live by this principle, that they are new people of God. Paul is confirming there must be a circumcision in the heart of a person. For it's not what goes into a person such as unclean foods according to Jesus in Matthew 5:11, but it is what comes out of him that defiles him, and that of what comes out of an uncircumcised impure heart will displease God.

Those who take grace seriously, that is thanking God for his grace and living a life that appreciates it without living just any kind of way, even though that person may fall short at times, because they are not perfect. These individuals have apparently had a change in heart, their heart has been circumcised, and there has been a real change to take such a stance. Perhaps those this has not happened to yet, have not undergone this particular transformation. Maybe they will at some point, perhaps they will never? We don't know. Our job is to lift up Jesus, and he is the one who saves as we point to the narrow road to him. What I am saying is, you cannot force anyone to do anything. People will do what they want to do and live how they want to live if they have ultimately decided to reject Christ and his way of life. The bible clearly tells us that God wishes that none would perish, but we know the reality is that people are perishing daily. It may not always be because the gospel wasn't shared right with them, or that they needed more time, a possibility is that they may have not acknowledged Jesus before men, and as Jesus said in Matthew 10:32 he will not acknowledge them before his father in heaven.

We know that a house divided cannot stand and two cannot walk together unless they agree. What does the enemy want the body of Christ to do? Divide in beliefs! Oppose one another in what we believe. God did not intend on division to be in his body. This is one of the main reasons this book is written because one side of the body of Christ saints are preaching live any way you want and it's okay. This is so wrong! This is leaders leading the people astray according to Isaiah 9:16. The other side is people being taught that they can live a perfect life without ever making a mistake because the Holy Spirit lives within us. The Holy Spirit does live within us and even being filled with God's spirit it is still possible to make a mistake and fall short. Not habitually, however we are never to act as if we have arrived in life. This approach repels people because it seems as if they will never measure or amount up to some standard that God dealt with when he poured out his blood as the ultimate sacrifice for us. This side usually teaches on many important things but the love of God is not as commonly elaborated on. Why are many being deceived? Why are many falling away? Many people do not feel loved by the church and they don't feel like they can even reach the bar the way the word is being thrown at them in a bad spirit and a serious lack of love. So what now? What do we do? Don't you know that Satan loves the fact that either side that is taught is going to lead the believer down a road that won't give them the full benefit of holy fellowship with God being reassured that they are loved, and saved. Jesus said I give them eternal life, and they shall never perish, no one can snatch them out of my hand. My friend if Jesus told you this, then believe him. If you choose to live your life any kind of way, let me assure you, you will have to give an account, but you have to take in to consideration 1 Corinthians 6: 9-11 which says, or do you not know that wrongdoers will not inherit the kingdom of God? Do not be deceived: Neither the sexually immoral nor idolaters nor adulterers nor men who have sex with men nor thieves nor the greedy nor drunkards nor slanderers nor swindlers will inherit the kingdom of God. **And that is what some of you were. But you were washed, you were sanctified, you were justified in the name of the Lord Jesus Christ and by the Spirit of our God.** If God has justified you, no one can condemn you; people may try with all sorts of subliminal messages yet know who you are in Christ! Notice that the scripture ends by telling the believer that they are washed, sanctified, and justified in the name of Jesus and by God's spirit. Therefore, don't forget to let the believer know verse 11. If you participated in any of the aforementioned things that will cause you not to enter the kingdom of heaven as a believer, keep in mind the scripture acknowledges that is what you WERE. Meaning if it is a part of your past then let it remain as it is, the past. Do not practice the same now that you are a believer.

There is the mindset that if I tell the people they have grace or exhort on grace and mercy, it's assumed that everyone is going to run rapid living their life just any kind of way outside of God. That is not always the case. Yes it does happen. Those individuals have to give an account, but don't hush up the grace of God because of your fears and your thoughts that people are going to do whatever. Any person whose heart is not circumcised will do whatever anyway. Grace is to be proclaimed on the mountaintops, not whispered as some secret knowledge that we have it. It was not secret when the streams of grace and mercy was being poured out of the side of Jesus as he was high and lifted up on a cross at Golgotha. That is exactly what the enemy wants you to do. He wants you to paint the picture that grace is something that isn't enough, that salvation as not given only by grace through faith in God. He also wants believers to think they can live however they'd like because it's there. **BOTH**

are wrong! I understand both perspectives, but both are not demonstrating what God wants the believer to know. He wants the believer to be free in him, by adhering to the boundaries that are set up so that we may maintain holy fellowship with God, because holiness is beautiful. God also wants us to know how much he loves us and forgets our sins. There are several scriptures that talk about how God remembers our sin no more, he stomps on them, he casts them into the sea remembering them again no more, he puts them in the small of his back. There must be a balance. Please forgive me I will never take God's grace lightly by acting as if it wasn't enough. Neither will I live my life just any kind of way.

Just as those who name the name of Christ can at times take advantage of God's grace, there are some believers that have you thinking you can live Godly in and of yourself without the Holy Spirit which is just as incorrect. We don't always know if someone is filled with the Spirit of God. If they are not, why are you surprised that they are living how they are living? It always amazes me when someone who was brought up not seeing the good example of a Godly marriage, dates when it's their time, and marries the wrong spouse, to go to church, for ministers to declare "You picked wrong". My question is, did you expect that person to pick right? With how they were raised, the situations they may have faced, and don't forget the enemy who's the master of deceit. I'd be surprised if they picked right! That just sounds like something to tell someone who has a self-inflicted situation as such, oh well, we don't care, you're on your own, but then go on about how we are supposed to help one another, not leaving anyone behind struggling, and make a difference by loving.

Yes it is true that a person with the heart and spirit of Pharaoh is indeed sick and they too do not know what they are doing to an extent, however when given the opportunity many times they refuse to accept God and honor and walk in what is righteous. Someone who has been provided the necessary guidance and principles over long periods of times that still chooses to reject Christ and his ways is not of God, in this case they are not keeping God's commandments because they really don't love God and even though they may not be aware of the full impact of their actions they don't even have a desire to get it right, this is what makes the difference.

We understand that people get strung out on drugs, and alcohol, and get addicted to pornography but when it comes to being unevenly yoked there is no excuse for that. There is usually some type of rehab or Alcohol anonymous or 12 step program but for marrying the wrong person, there is not as much help for those who have chosen to marry the wrong spouse. It may appear that some churches care as they redirect you to counseling, etc. however others just say you're on your own, you should have known better, you picked wrong, and your choice is a reflection of yourself, instead of looking at them in the eyes of Jesus which says Father forgive them for they know not what they do. It almost seems as if it's more acceptable for someone to receive help for other life threatening circumstances, but not as much for marrying wrong. I have learned that true authority comes from a pure heart. Through my experiences I have learned to view everyone in this light including my ex husband who I am not labeling as being saved or unsaved only the behavior that was demonstrated after our slate was wiped clean and after years of sitting under some the best preaching, teaching, and counseling around. Perhaps those were seeds being planted for him. I can safely say that there was not a filling of the Holy Spirit and there was much maturity to be developed but that does not mean that he has not and will not grow in those areas. Prayerfully he has and will, as I have overtime, nevertheless it should not be counted against me that I have acknowledged dangerous behaviors towards myself and potential children over time of being with him. I have done more than just acknowledge it; I have chosen to do something about it after trying to make it work on a number of occasions. I don't care how much you wait and have patience when waiting on someone to love you back that does not know love, is like waiting for a ship at the airport. Through much prayer and the leading of the Holy Spirit it would not be benefiting anyone at all in the body of Christ to see two people not being able to climb out of a hole they are drowning in. If you are trying to keep from drowning and you have someone pulling onto you trying to keep you down that's a sad situation. All people have something good about themselves, as no one is "all bad", the issue comes when the bad begins to outweigh the good significantly and nothing is being done to address it. Usually people want to get help when the house is ninety percent burned down to the ground, instead of when the flames start catching fire.

What we see is people trying to lead others to Christ with the wrong tools. The tool of do what I tell you to do, the tool of if you fall you must not be saved for real, the tool of beating you into submission and firing all kinds of hits to you from the pulpit are all the wrong tools. A hammer and a nail goes together right? Use a screwdriver to put in a nail that is 10 inches long, and see how effective you are. A screw driver is a great tool, but the tool that is best used to get that job done is a hammer. It doesn't matter how many times you beat that nail with a screw driver. It's not going far. Use the tool of love to usher people into the body of Christ and allow the Holy Spirit to convict in areas necessary. When the vision, mission, and ministry are not really going anywhere we may sometimes need to check what tool in our tool boxes have been used the most, and appropriate the tools according to what should be used. God understood how original intent could be impacted by a small little moment. Look at Adam and Eve in the Garden of Eden. All it took was one little moment for all of creation to be thrown out of sorts. All it takes is one moment for someone to go to prison for life. All it takes is one moment to ruin a great reputation it took years to build. All it takes is one moment for a covenant to be broken, which by the way can only be maintained if both parties keep their agreement. One cannot do it alone, even though this is what is taught.

Scales of the heart is for a deeper spiritual aspect of issues that are causing divorce and separation in marriage in addition to the obvious of not preparing right. The word says do not be unevenly yoked but what about after this happens now what, the church will tell you well you should not have done it not understanding why you did: yes you chose, but how did you choose, in ignorance due to home of origin, circumstances, other? Regardless people are being condemned who have made decisions in ignorance, but I have news for you if this is you, when Jesus looked down from the cross when he was dying for our sins he saw you marrying who you chose out of ignorance (if this applies to you), even though people will not be able to empathize or even care, the King of Kings and Lord of Lords saw you and prayed for you right there in that moment, he prayed for everyone who would ever make a decision in ignorance: Father forgive them for they know not what they do. This includes believers who are labeling and judging others, he prayed for you also: father forgive them for they know not who they judge or label, father forgive them for they know not who they are joining themselves to, father forgive them for they know not what diseases they are inflicting in their bodies, father forgive them for they know not the costs of rejecting me, but my life being sacrificed will serve well for those who are willing to accept me, whosoever will.

Jesus knew there would be cases where sexual immorality would be encountered and answered their question in Mark 10:9. This was asked in regards to the topic "for any reason at all". He knew they would be quoting him here on marriage for years to come, and thought it necessary to include that the results of a covenant that can be broken in a fallen world, even though there would be more issues such as abuse and abandonment along with the wheat and tares being joined together. All of this was too complex and Jesus was not going over all of that with children of darkness who didn't accept what he was saying and doing anyway. Why share your wisdom with people who don't fear God. Jesus has a way of communicating to the believer personally that if you are in him he has you covered, you have to trust him, it may not be in the outcome you expect but he has your back and is watching every abuser in your life whether that is behind closed doors at your home or on Sunday morning from a ministry you are serving in. Jesus knew that if you were in him he would take care of anything that rises up against you anyway. The spiritual law of praise is so powerful, anything on you or around you that is holding you, if you are in Christ I promise you it's just like the law of sowing and reaping, yes you may reap your consequences or you may be in a season of something that God is using to simply demonstrate his glory in the end, nevertheless you can't walk in praise and worship and remain connected to anything unlike God. You could look up and be carried away by angels, before you know it you were somewhere and God will flip the page and you will look up somewhere else safe and intact.

God will shut doors no man can shut and open doors no man can open even if they tried. There will be people who will try and tell you what you qualify for and what you don't as a divorcee and who you qualify for and who you don't but listen to God's voice and walk in peace, for you were called to it. This is not for couples who are trying to make it work in their marriage. There are many other books that will help them, this book is specifically for those who are separated and are not reconciling, divorcees, and those who will be ministering to divorced people within the church, or even church members who encounter divorcees regularly, believe it or not whether you want to or not they are in the world, and they matter, God loves them, and has assignments for their lives just as those who have not experienced divorce.

When you start picking and choosing people you want and don't want to love because of reputation, some self-examination may be necessary. Don't say, we are going to help the homosexuals, the murders, the pedophiles, the adulterers, but when it comes to those who picked the wrong spouse, we want nothing to do with you. If we are the church, we are to help everybody, not just the ones that make our ministry look perfect.

Does the blood not cleanse us from all unrighteousness? Is the blood of Jesus not enough? Does God require our works for us to be saved? No. The blood cleanses us from all unrighteousness, the blood is more than enough, and God does not require works for you to be saved. He desires for you to work for a reward in heaven that will be given to you at the Bema Judgment seat of Christ. Thank you Bishop for clearing this up! Many preachers are telling believers that they we will stand before the "great white throne judgment". I say speak for yourself! That is not a place I will never stand for judgment. That is for the world and non-believers. We will be before the Bema Judgment seat of Christ not being judged for our sins and mistakes which the blood of Jesus washes them all away according to 1 John 1:17, past, present, and future sins with respect to salvation! (Meaning that I don't intend on taking advantage of, neither do I take advantage of the blood that was shed for me and the grace, mercy, and salvation that Jesus said I'd have if I confess with my mouth and believe with my heart that God raised Jesus from the dead). The goal is to bring balance!

We will be judged at the Bema seat of Christ to receive a reward and a crown to worship Jesus with for all of eternity. I reiterate, if you are in Christ, you will not be condemned for your sins, you will have to give an account, but you will not be condemned according to Romans 8:1. What does it look like you ask? Well let's just say, some will reach for a crown on their head and it may be a weak crown, some may have a sturdy crown. The quality and value of your crown depends on your work you did for Jesus on earth. 1 Corinthians 3:13 says our works will be tried by fire. I always love when I see a church's symbol that represents gold or something solid that their works represent, verses wood or hay or something that can easily be burned up in the fire. Prayerfully their works match their emblem. I believe we will get to the New Jerusalem/Heaven and there will be people you'd never expect to be there, and won't see people there you'd expect to be there. I believe that those you'd expect to have a crown like the equivalent to a BMW may have crowns of cotton. Others you'd expect to have crowns made of paper may have a crown in the finest gold! That is why we are not to judge anyone before the last day according to 1 Corinthians 4:5. Just because you see someone who is renowned in the gospel on earth does not mean that they will have that same status in the New Jerusalem/Heaven.

It's almost taught that the spotless blameless blood of Jesus and the gifts of salvation, grace and mercy through faith in God, is not enough. Truth be told before Jesus left us with the Holy Spirit no one was capable of doing anything except having faith in God, trusting him, and receiving his grace and mercy. It is preached that no one in the Old Testament had the indwelling Holy Spirit. What I believe is 1 Samuel 16:13 as it says So David stood thee among his brothers, Samuel took the flask of olive oil he had brought and anointed David with the oil. And the Spirit of the Lord came powerfully upon David **from that day on.** I don't see where the scripture says the spirit of God came on David and left after this or that, it says from that day on. I believe that David was the only person in the Old Testament that had the Spirit of God on him or in him from the day it came on him all the way into God's glory. This is not to say he was perfect and had no issues. We all know he wasn't, yet we all know it was due to his relationship that made things right at the end of the day. Many scholars believe the Spirit of God never left him as the Spirit of God never leaves a believer who receives God's Spirit at conversion, which would have only been possible after Jesus died on the cross and sent the comforter which is the Holy Spirit. Thank God for the Holy Spirit that can now help us, and the same thanks is to God for grace and mercy which the believer is **not** called to live by from day to day, but it's there if needed for unintentional sin, and truth be told intentional sin. We are not to take advantage of God's grace. God saw fit to bless us with new mercies every morning according to Lamentations 3:22-23 which says Because of the Lord's mercy that we are not consumed, because his compassions fail not. They are new every morning. Great is thy faithfulness. They are there, however we are not to take advantage of them!

Because we have the Holy Spirit now does this mean that God decided to withhold the mercies that the word of God clearly indicates are new to us every morning? God doesn't just give us new mercies every morning for no reason at all. He saw a reason for it to be extended in addition to his compassion and love. We are not to take advantage of his mercy and grace by living day to day outside of his will and word, however God is God and he sees what we don't, therefore if it is made available by God every morning and I have done something unknowingly or unconsciously excuse me while I thank God for extending to me another mercy! Feel free to talk about me all you'd like, but God who is supreme over all has lavished his love on a thousand generations of those who love him and keep his commandments. Thank you Jesus that I have the opportunity to keep your commandments because I love you, and thank you for your mercy and grace that keeps me in position as your child if I mess up, which we all have. Some believers expect you to wallow in condemnation after the revelation of your sin, however I encourage you to embrace what God, not man saw fit for you to have when you woke up this morning. Once again, I don't encourage or believe you should be taking advantage of God's mercy, but I don't think believers should take light of God's grace, mercy, and love by acting as if it's not needed, useful, or good enough. Praise God for the gifts he has paid for and extended to us because they didn't come cheap as to why you wouldn't want to take advantage of them!

You ask, well how can it be both? Shouldn't it be one or the other? God's grace, mercy, and love is more than enough because even though Jesus said in John 14:15 that if you love me you will keep my commandments, there is no deed you can do enough that will grant you salvation, grace, and mercy. Your actions play a part in your love relationship with Christ not in what he has already done for you. God's love for us is not predicated off of our love for him. John 14:15 is an indicator of our love for Jesus. If we love God we will walk in his ways. I agree with this wholeheartedly. I also believe that without his spirit you cannot walk in his ways in and of yourself. According to Acts 17:28 in him we live, move, and have our being. John 15:5 says for a part from Jesus you can do nothing. How we keep the Lord's commands is through the power of the Holy Spirit, especially living in a temple of flesh and a world where the presence of sin is everywhere. This is often forgotten as many are walking around with high chests playing the sport of demonstrating how much they can do or not do in and of themselves. When this is done around new believers or those lost or struggling this does not please God. There is an arrogance that's disguised in "confidence" that I can do this or that and you can't.

I can appreciate the teaching of my Apostle on the patience we should have with those that are not where we are. Some areas could be in education, spiritual maturity, physical strength, mental and emotional strength and much more. I hear what you're thinking. "So if we are to be patient with those that are not where we are, how does that speak to unevenly yoked marriages?" I'm glad you asked. It can be just as frustrating for your spouse if they are less mature than you are spiritually, compared to your maturity in Christ, especially if they are attempting to do better and grow themselves. The other side of this is that they could be frustrated because they don't desire to live a Godly life at all, and they are frustrated because your life style convicts them with where they are, and it could be a reminder of what they will never walk in by choice, and that is a life that pleases God. That will be discussed at later section of Scales of the Heart. One thing is for sure, God is the most patient being ever to exist, however even though he is beyond patient, he has limits and boundaries. We all know what happened to Satan regarding the Lord's patience. There was none for him; he was kicked out of heaven, with no reconciliation plan in place. Depending on the type of situation at hand this will determine the case by case circumstance that will in turn produce necessary results according to God's will. We are never to put people down about where they are regardless of where we may have matured to. Love clearly understands this principle. There are more people talking about love, but not demonstrating love. How can this be? I believe many believers have no idea what love is. I'm talking about the kind of love that Christ had for us when he died on the cross for us over two thousand years ago. He didn't die on a cross just to complete some deed, action or achieve some goal, but he LOVED us, just as the Father loved us just as much as he loves his son according to John 17:25-26 and 1 John 3:1.

Therefore when Jesus said if you love me, you will keep my commandments, he understood the show didn't stop there. If that was the case there would have been no need for Jesus to even come to the earth and redeem people. Hadn't God given the children of Israel his commandments, laws, and ways during the time of Moses? If those that loved him during that time and after would have just kept his commandments then all would have been well right? Wrong! That's just it! They were not able to keep his commandments even if they did love him because they didn't have the indwelling power of the Holy Spirit to help them. Those who lived before Jesus came had no idea of the impact and the sin levels that were present among them and that which was being increased over time. Yes, the more time that goes by, the more of a falling away there is, higher and greater levels of sin are present with in the world. Think about the old days where technology wasn't booming, there wasn't all the riff raff from day to day with hectic schedules. People valued family, life, and there was meaning to doing the right thing. They worked off of little but were happier, and had more peace. Today we have so much technology, forever busy with the world's demands on our lives and yet have less peace than those before us who had much less stuff than us. What happened to just loving and living for Christ being content with what we had? Notice I didn't say complacent, this content I am referring to is found in 1 Timothy 6:6 (Godliness and contentment is great gain), where there are many merchandising ministries that will have you believe this scripture shouldn't apply today after encouraging people to run after the world and all it supplies. God set the children of Israel free from Egypt not to accumulate stuff, but to serve him. God is not setting you free for you to buy the hottest house, car, jewelry, and so forth, but it is so that we must serve him. I am not saying don't do well. Thrive and leave an inheritance but make sure your hope is built on nothing less than Jesus blood and righteousness...build your hopes on things eternal. People are putting more emphasis on the temporal when the word says the things we see are temporary and the things we don't see are eternal. This is not to say do not enjoy your life. God gave Adam his wife Eve before the fall of man and before death crept into the world. He gave the gift of relationship which he saw was good and fit before the fall to be enjoyed as well as after the fall. As we look to heaven as this isn't our home, it is okay to eat the fruit of your labor as stated in Ecclesiastes after you have tithed, and to enjoy what God blesses you with.

Both Ingredients Make the Real Difference!

How can the same God who said if you love me you will keep my commandments be the same God in Luke 23:34? While he was dying on the cross he looked down on the people and prayed Father forgive them for they know not what they do. God understood that no matter how much people tried to do the Word, none would be able to unless he died and sent the Helper which is the Holy Spirit to aide them in his instruction of keeping his commandments to show we love Jesus. You may say, well now that person is saved so that does not apply to them. It doesn't stop there! After someone has given their life to Christ and has accepted in their heart and life Jesus as Lord of their life, they have his spirit, but now they need to be filled, which is a process! In this process there is a transformation the new believer under goes being sanctified or set apart where God forges you into the refiner's furnace to burn off all the dross and mess off of your life prior to you becoming saved and or spirit filled. In addition to being filled the person needs to mature in the things of God, the word of God, and consistently going to church, learning to serve and being faithful when serving. They may have never tithed before. Just because one is converted you can't say at that initial moment they now know what they are doing. That is not true. Truth be told they could be making all kind of mistakes as they are learning, growing, and maturing in God. There does not come a point of one having fully arrived, because none of us have, however there will come a point where you will know exactly what one is doing and there won't be any question about it, because the Holy Spirit will seriously convict you as you are now maturing in Christ.

Transformation for many people takes time and does not happen instantaneously the moment after conversion. The miracle of you receiving the Spirit of God and becoming a new creature in Christ does happen immediately, however for most, there is a process of transformation that occurs in the area of sanctification and becoming mature in Christ. This occurs according to Romans 12:2, Do not be conformed to this world, but be transformed by the renewing of your mind. This is one of the largest benefits of the mind as a believer in Christ, that God uses our mind so that we may be transformed. What is being done in the Spirit is essential, yet because our spirits on earth is wrapped in flesh, we are not in heaven just yet, and as long as we live on the earth, we must choose our thoughts and be renewed by the mind. Therefore whatever God gave us; there is a reason for it. If God didn't see fit for us to have a mind, he wouldn't have given it to us, along with emotions, and free will. This is another reason Jesus met us where we were instead of trying to meet us where we should be. Always meet people where they are, the impact of this initial connection with a relationship in mind to be built is what will aide others in not staying where they are, but reaching up towards Christ. Each person is in the furnace of refinement for different amounts of time depending on their history, their heart, their learning state and progression of maturity, in addition to the assignment that God is preparing them for. The new believer is learning new ways, new thoughts, new everything! This person has been operating in the flesh all their lives, whether that is for eight years, twenty years, even fifty years, and now they have to learn a new way of life which is not easy at all. It seems as if this is supposed to happen quickly for those who are genuinely saved, however I believe you can be saved and not Spirit filled for years. It depends on the individual, where they are, what bondages they perhaps may be under, what their history may be, so many factors are associated with each case by case situation that really only God sees and judges as he tells us not to judge, because He sees the big picture. Real Salvation at certain point will have the proof in the pudding sooner or later where fruit will manifest. There has got to be a change! For me to tell someone they are not saved is not my business, however if your actions are continuously indicating you're not, and you claim that you are, if those actions will affect my life directly in any way shape or form, I need to consider where I am with you, my future, and so forth. You being saved is not the issue of addressing things where action is needed to create boundaries and limitations for health and safety.

The issue that cannot be ignored or pushed under a rug is if the actions are not being corrected overtime, especially with corrective action measures such as always in God's Word, going to church consistently, serving in ministry, and tithing, taking life enhancing classes to grow and mature. If one is doing all of these things and there is still no change, run for your life! The issue is a matter of the heart, and one's soul cannot be saved according to God's word unless a heart circumcision is done and that is available by choice. There is a rejection of this opportunity in their private life and the evidence of that is for all to examine. Note, I said examine, not judge. They have done a great job at masking who they really are in refusing to apply all that they have been given the opportunity to benefit from spiritually. This also explains that salvation is not in any of the before mentioned things. None of those save you. God chooses whom he reveals himself to according Romans 9:18. Why would God harden the hearts of some? Because they never belonged to him, even before the foundation of the world. God saw that they would never be included in the "whosoever will", because he saw their heart that reflected the "whosoeverwon't". It can be confusing to see someone doing all these things but there is no growth over years. You have to pray, fast, and seek the Lord and spiritual guidance on a situation like this impacting your relationships. You have to continue to forgive that person to no end, yet know that doesn't always mean you have to place them back in the same position once occupied. This is the thin line of judgment that many misunderstand. The sad reality is that it is a possibility that the person's heart is just not one that God predestined before the foundation of the world as having said yes to Him. In John 17:9 Jesus clearly says that I pray for them, I don't pray for the world (even though he so loved the world), but for those whom you have given to me (referring to the Father), for they are yours. It is clear here to see that there are people who do not belong to the Father or to Christ. These are people that God knew before the foundation of the world who would not accept his son as Lord and savior of their lives. Looking to verse 12 in the same chapter you will see Jesus say, while I was with them, I protected them and kept them safe by that name you gave me. None has been lost **except the one doomed to destruction** so that Scripture would be fulfilled. It is clear to see even in this passage that there are those who have been doomed to destruction in the beginning, before the foundation of the world. I don't want to discourage your faith, I want to be real with you. There are people that have been married over thirty and forty years to discover that the person is never changing. The person may attend church regularly and know the word of God; however it is still a possibility that they don't know the God behind the word. I hate to have to point this out because we are people of faith, and the only thing you may hear is one perspective, not realizing there is another biblical truth. God said he is not pleased when we come to Him without faith. The same God kicked Satan out of heaven, not because God had lack of faith that he couldn't get it together within time, faith was not the issue, but because

Satan was dangerous to have around the angels after rebelling against God and encouraging other angels to rebel against God too (One Third of Heaven's angels is a lot). God encourages faith, but he is also not tolerant of his boundaries being broken repeatedly. Satan rebelled on a number of levels, (particularly five) the 5 I wills of Satan are: **I will** ascend into heaven (the third heaven where God's throne is), **I will** exalt my throne above the stars of God, **I will** sit also upon the Mount of the Congregation: ruling mankind, **I will** ascend beyond the heights of the clouds, and **I will** be like the Most High God. Satan was clearly insane. Because Satan behaved and acted in ways that he should not have, caused him to be kicked out of heaven. Anything is possible with God right? Can't God forgive Satan if he chose to? Forgiveness is not a factor in the matter, the heart has weighed out significantly in regards to Satan's insane desires to be something he should have never fed into. God knows there are some thing you cannot play with, and must be addressed quickly, Luke 10:18 is where Jesus said He saw Satan who fell like lightning from heaven. So here we see the real origin of the fall. It started when Satan fell from heaven like lightening and hit the earth, then Adam and Even fell afterwards. The point is, anyone who is insane enough to think they can sit in church and bible study, serve in ministry, read God's word through their natural ability, and even be granted a title or position, have no apparent change over time, not live a righteous life according to the scriptures, not according to something they've worked out personally with God, this person is insane to think God is not going to deal with them just like he did their father: Satan! Someone like this is not a child of God, but of Satan. John 8:44 says for you are the children of your father the devil, and you love to do the evil things he does. He was a murderer from the beginning. He has always hated the truth, because there is no truth in him. When he lies, it is consistent with his character; for he is a liar and the father of lies. 1 John 3:10 says so now we can tell who are children of God and who are children of the devil. Anyone who does not **live righteously and does not love other believers** does not belong to God. If you are joined to someone like this, I have to give you some real news. That is you have to remain in that relationship if you married them, and if they desire to stay with you according to 1 Corinthians 7. If they are not a believer and want to leave then you are free to a biblical release from that covenant as the New Covenant of Christ indicates. You may be frowned upon by religious people, but it is written that per the circumstance that Jesus calls you free and to peace. If Jesus saw that an earthly circumstance can affect a powerful covenant this is important to realize, because many will tell you the circumstances don't matter, and in regards to faith, that is truth, yet in regards to marriage God himself acknowledges circumstances that can impact a covenant, man may choose not to, and tell you to disregard it due to their opinion, yet Jesus addresses this because it's real. Apparently Christ saw something beyond worst (for better or for worst). This will be discussed in another chapter. I tell you the truth, if you joined yourself to someone who won't live righteous, or won't leave, or let you go, remain there, endure the suffering, and pray to God that your spouse will be converted by living a lifestyle that witnesses the gospel and the Word of God. I guarantee you, after a while if there is no change, the scales of the heart will weigh in and if it is God's will for you to be released I promise you, nothing and no one can keep you joined with that person not even yourself. When God determines a thing, it's done. You can try to oppose it if you want, you're in for a rude awakening and additional unnecessary strife. The truth is it may not be God's will for you to be released. If not, then there is a reason that God sees for you to remain, and you have to trust him as He is with you. Yield to the suffering, yield to the process, yield to the heartbreak and live your life for God and focus on what you can do in the relationship to work on yourself and be the light in your marriage and home. Nevertheless, nothing is hidden from God and all will be vindicated whether in this life or in the next. I have to be honest; God does not release everyone in this situation. The weighing of the heart determines the deliverance. You may see the person as having a bad heart, but God may see potential, perhaps they will convert, however if it is highly likely that there will be no conversion of the spouse that does not want to live a saved life, it may be that God saw that person before the foundation of the world as not accepting or receiving Jesus in their heart, and perhaps that could be the reason why some are released. This is what I believe from my experiences and testimony that we will review in a later section. I can tell you that consistent righteous living, praise, and worship, and prayer and fasting will break off any chain in your life that is not good for you, people don't understand when that's a spouse. Yes, you may have picked him or her to be your spouse for whatever reason, but tell that to your broken chain if you are released from a relationship on the basis of abuse, adultery, and abandonment. We will discuss these in a later section of the book.

The point here is that love outweighs judgment! Romans 3:25 states that Jesus whom God set forth as a propitiation by his blood through faith, to demonstrate his righteousness, because in his forbearance God had passed over the sins that were previously committed what does this mean? That the wrath and judgment of God was appeased by the blood of Jesus Christ. Romans 8:1 says there is therefore now no condemnation to those who are in Christ Jesus, who do not walk according to the flesh, but according to the Spirit (The spirit of God is love, joy, peace, patience, kindness, goodness, faithfulness, gentleness, and self-control) what does this mean? That if you are in Christ Jesus according to 2 Corinthians 5:10 that means you must give an account as we appear before the judgment seat of Christ, that each one may receive the things done in the body, according to what he has done, whether good or bad. The "Judgment Seat of Christ" is not the "Great White Throne Judgment". The "Judgment Seat of Christ is the "Bema Judgment Seat of Christ" where you will give an account if you are in Christ and are rewarded for your works which will be tried by fire. The word clearly indicates the Judgment Seat of Christ is not a place of God's wrath towards the believer in Christ, because Jesus was the atonement and the ransom paid for those who are In Christ Jesus. The Great White throne judgment is a place for the "world", the unbelievers, and those that repeatedly reject Jesus Christ. Revelation 20:11-15 depicts this judgment which is NOT for the believer, those who are not in the book of life at this judgment will have a different eternal fate than the believer who is In and Covered by the powerful blood of Jesus. 2 Timothy 2:15 says to study thyself approved so that you will rightly divide the word of TRUTH. We can never point the finger to others who teach erroneously if we do the same. Teaching the good word of God with a bad spirit is a misrepresentation of what God desired for the body to be encouraged and edified. God's grace, mercy, and love, is a gift that we had absolutely no part in earning or receiving, that's what GIFTS are. Yes you have a part to play in not taking advantage of these gifts, but you and I never had one part to play in how they were poured out by a loving God. When the veil was torn in two at the Crucifixion of Jesus Christ it gave access to those who are in Christ to BOLDLY come to the throne of (judgment?) No! To the throne of Grace is where we are able to come, where the Love of God outweighed immeasurably his wrath and judgment. God still weighs the hearts of men continuously. That has not changed, you will reap what you sow, and your fellowship with God is predicated on your actions, behaviors, and heart. In John 10:28, Jesus said, I give them eternal life, and they shall never perish. No one can snatch them out of my hand! If that is you, give God a shout of praise that you will never perish because you can do all things through Christ who strengthens you including overcoming. John 15:5 says apart from me you can do nothing! Including overcoming. So when you do overcome it is only by the power of the Holy Spirit and not in and of yourself. It is by the Lord that you even overcome. People will judge what overcoming looks like in your life if they don't understand where you've been, where you are, and where you are going. Especially if you overcoming doesn't precisely reflect how they overcame. Rest assure that because your testimony doesn't mirror their personal testimony, that does not mean you are not an over comer. Differentiation without separation testifies that we all have trials and tribulations but those trials and tribulations are idiosyncrasies and should never separate the body of Christ. There is a diverse Kingdom work, meaning if we all had the same personal testimony, with the exact same ministry then what kind of world would that be? My testimony may not be yours and yours may not be mine, but I am never to criticize where you are as if I know what you've been through, or what God is doing in your life, because truthfully I don't. Judge no man until the last day according to 1 Corinthians 4:5. God is love. Love outweighs all, including judgment for those in Christ.

Restoring Love

Compassion is the ingredient that is often left out today in the body of Christ. Jesus didn't die on the cross as some sole act of duty and look down on the people and say father forgive them because they don't know what they are doing, completing the assignment just because it was the thing to do. His attitude was not militant like that. I believe that God carried out his assignment like a faithful soldier, as we are to as well, but I believe he had compassion on us and loved us as to why he did what he did primarily. It was Christ's passion to reconcile man back to God that led him to and through the cross. If Christ had passion, why are we told not to have passion? This is not the passion that rots the bones. This is the passion of the call, the passion to love, the passion to live in Christ, the passion for the abundant life. Usually it is because one cannot differentiate between one and the other, so it's just tossed in a box or out the window. God was passionate not only in the New Testament but in the Old Testament as well with regard to His bride Israel. Jesus prayed father forgive them for they know not what they do because he felt the ignorance and lack of knowledge that was operating which was keeping them from a loving compassionate relationship with Him. Looking back to Matthew 9:36 and Mark 6:34 it says that when Jesus saw the people that he had compassion on them! Compassion is something one feels. Real compassion that is. It comes from the bowels, from our belly. This is why when we bring forth springs of living water it has to come from a stirred up heart felt place. When we worship in spirit and in truth it is not out of derived law, but it is with the entire being of a person who is worshipping in spirit and in truth. When a healthy saved married couple engages in intercourse other than the act of reproduction occurring, there are feelings and drives built into us by God that are a result of the intercourse that God intended to be experienced. If God built that inside of us, and if one knows what it's like to experience the feelings of sex that was given to married people, as a gift of pleasure in addition to reproducing, then why do we believe God doesn't feel? His thoughts are higher than our thoughts and his ways are higher than our ways. We believe that because when it comes to "business" and to carry out particular instructions that because some feelings may not matter, that God does not care about our feelings and that He does not feel (which he does, and there is scripture to support this statement). Throughout the entire Word it is evident that God cares about his children. He understands them, and can relate, after all he made all things for his pleasure Colossians 1:16. This is not to be confused with us being obedient to God and his instructions in our lives. Yes our feelings can get in the way with what God told us and it is better to obey God and disregard our feelings than to operate out of feelings alone, as this can be dangerous because one shouldn't be driven by their feelings, yet God does care about us. God is love, and love is missing from some people who name the name of Jesus today. People can be more interested in their allegiance to a reputation or a man or woman in the Gospel who models the way of life in a particular mannerism, instead of that to God and the essence and fruit of the Holy Spirit. How can you say you are a believer yet you don't have or know love? When you see the people coming what do you see? Does the first ten minutes of your interaction pinpoint on all their deficiencies and shortcomings first? Have they engaged someone who spends the first hour of ministry on everything they are doing wrong in life? Are you quick to point out the negative? Are you anxious to yell at them for things you swear they were aware of doing in their "god given conscious"? Are you degrading people and labeling them having known absolutely nothing or not enough to make your accusations? Or are you excited, motivated, and thrilled to pieces to get ready to love God's sheep without measure? It's sad when love is the last thing on the list when it comes to dealing with God's people. Often times this revelation is missing. It's just like someone who doesn't have the revelation of children trying to tell you how you should be raising your own. This doesn't mean someone who doesn't have children can't help or aide in some areas. It's just like someone not having the revelation of going to a secular job all day that sucks and drains the energy out of you, which will affect other areas of life, but doesn't understand why you just can't make it happen with other areas they may excel in. It could be perhaps they have much more time and flexibility than those who have more restricted employment. This is not referencing the man or woman of God whose full-time profession is to cultivate the Word of God in the lives of God's sheep, or those who have been called to a full-time ministry position by God. It is like the revelation of proclaiming one thing, yet having your children live something totally different. A woman raised her son in the fear of the Lord teaching him all the Lord's ways, and surrounded him in the right environments. One day when that child became an adult, the child chose another path in life. The woman now has the **revelation** that no matter what you do or don't do, you cannot control another free moral agent. Prior to this revelation it was easy to talk about how children of God should behave, until she was able to personally bear witness of her own child's life that didn't mirror the Word of God that was extended to her son. The point is, it's easy to tell others how they should be living, yet when the opposite results hit your home, and affect your life, it's different. It's often assumed if you love them then they will take advantage of grace as stated before, which I understand does happen. For instance, for the married people reading the book, I'm sure you can recall a time when you made love to your spouse even though issues were not resolved. There could have been something major that happened that impacted you and hasn't been discussed or address, however because you love your spouse, you make love to them anyway regardless of what the issue is. I am not saying this is always easy, but I have been there, and so has God, and so should ministers of God's words. Don't let people's actions stop you from loving them. You may have to love them from afar depending on the situation and according to the New Testament scriptures on Church Discipline, but when people come to your ministry do they leave feeling loved in addition to being filled with God's spirit? My word of advice is after you've ministered, preached, or taught on all the dynamic powerful teachings on the holy spirit, tithing, faithfulness, don't let love just be mentioned for name sake, just as passionate as you may be about the other topics, don't quiet down or lose your vigor when you come to the topic of love. I've seen this many times where people will show you clearly what they are passionate about because they are excited about it, and they are always talking about it. Examples are money, power, deeds, being filled with God's Spirit. When it comes to love, we sometimes quiet down and lightly brush over it, only to go back to exhorting about having power or reaping a harvest of seed we have sown. No my friend, just as you were shouting about power, I'd be glad to hear you shout about LOVE. If that is not something you'd be comfortable shouting about, why are you comfortable about exhorting other areas? What you may not be comfortable with is an indication what you may not be familiar with. As stated, there is nothing wrong with exhorting many different things, it's actually encouraging to experience the impartation and motivation that's being demonstrated, however don't hush up when it comes to the LOVE of God.

Tone is so very important. When we are witnessing to non-believers and new believers and even mature believers. Sometimes it's not what is being said, it's how it is being said. This small barrier is not always so small when received and perceived incorrectly. How is your consistent tone? Is it love? Is it militant? Is it uncertain? Is it rash? People need to have the fear of the Lord which is the beginning of wisdom, but not by you instilling fear in them by screaming at them every time you're ministering. It does not promote a welcoming environment for people to want to come back or even interact with someone they are now afraid of. It was never intended for followers to be afraid of a leader. Reverence, honor, and respect are needed and I'm sure appreciated, but let's not mistake that for fear. No sheep of God should ever be afraid to interact with a leader or minister. Jesus was welcoming and he was gentle. He didn't even forbid the children to approach him, so this new thing today where you have to fill out paperwork and jump through hoops just to hug a leader or thank them for their encouraging message is not Christ like.

It demonstrates the world's leadership and we are advised by Christ in Luke 22:24-27 that our leadership should reflect that of a servant leader. For examples, Husbands are called to lead. It's heartbreaking when you find a man that leads in everything except serving and submission, especially in the home. Submission is beautiful when done right, however to be the head, leader, and the first, means that you're the first to submit and serve. (Men, don't throw my book in the trash just yet.) If God made you to be the example for your family, are you exemplifying serving and submitting? Or just giving orders and instructions with the impression that serving and submitting is for women only? Do you have to be the mastermind behind everything? Or do you consider your family. Gentleness, compassion, and love, are some of our Lord and savior's most essential traits and they are missing today from the lives of many who name the name of Jesus Christ. If this does not pertain to you, your church, ministry, family, praise God, pray for those it does apply to.

A friend of mine shared her experience coming to Christ. She said that in the morning she'd be getting ready for her day at work, and she would have the television turned on but the volume was turned off. During the same hour every morning she'd see the same preacher on television but she couldn't hear what he was saying as she just turned it on for a little light in her room. The volume was turned off. She couldn't help but notice the minister's body language during his sermons. Every morning she looked at this man and thought; it looks like he is ready to fight someone. He seems very abrupt and threatening. I'd never want to meet someone who is portraying their nonverbals in this manner, let alone even hear what they have to say. One day she turned the volume up to hear what he was saying and it sounded excellent. She couldn't believe the same man who was pointing his finger and jumping at the crowed every ten seconds was the same man that delivered a loving word. Needless to say my friend began turning her volume up in the mornings to hear a great preached word to help her begin her day, and that eventually led to her going to church, becoming saved, and being an active member leading a ministry. My point is of course we don't judge a book by its cover, however be mindful of what you're projecting. For we represent Christ in what we do and say, but keep the little things in mind. Are you representing him in your tone, your body language, non-verbal communication, facial expressions, etc? I know this may sound ridiculous, but keep in mind that could be the very thing that will reproach someone from even wanting to receive the great package you may have for them. Thank God she turned her volume up so she could hear, but what about those who don't turn the volume up? What are they to be impressed by? It is more than what is being said, it's the entire package. Yes be angry with the devil, but ensure others understand the anger is not towards them, it's toward the enemy.

Today many will have you so figured out without knowing anything about you, yet telling you all about yourself. It is usually assumed that if you are a new member or trying to find the right church then you are not good at submitting to authority and you are not in alignment spiritually. This is a truth. A person's church membership does not equate to their relationship with Christ, it does not show that they could or could not be rooted and grounded in Christ not Church. Church is definitely appropriate for the mature believer and as they would be expected to serve in ministry and give back, however life is not always a linear equation that allows for that. One that is brought up in church order all of their lives, may not get this, as "life" does happen. The wandering church member you are labeling could be a young man or woman, a middle aged person or someone that is elderly. It is not your job to label and judge or act as if you've known them for years even though you know very little based upon what you see and discern, your job is to demonstrate the love of God and any advice, instruction, or guidance should be done in love. How many wanderers did Jesus run into during his years of ministry on earth? When did he label them or judge them. Yes, there very well could be a percentage of people who don't do well with authority and who have removed themselves, however we are not to place all people you encounter new to your congregation or those who may be transitioning in their live in that percentage. Never judge one's life based on the chapter of life you walked in on. For that is stereotyping. Some have left because of hurtful experiences within a church, whether that was years of abuse and negative encounters or only a few months, everyone is not to be put in the same category or box. Some have left because perhaps God only intended for that person to be there for a particular season, maybe for them to grow and mature and to contribute where necessary in serving, but maybe God has ordained them to finish somewhere else. We don't always know what God is doing. It is true, many people put the "God said" or "God told me to do this or that" on a decision. I have news for you, sometimes it's accurate. I know you may choose to believe it's just the person talking from self will, and that is a possibility, another possibility is that God did indeed instruct that person. It's not edifying to judge people's arrivals or departures as if you know what God should be doing with them, you may not, and it's not your job to tell someone where you think they should be, you don't know where God may be calling them to. People often try to open closed doors and close open doors that God has supernaturally closed or opened for His children. Where God has put a period it is not your job to put a comma. We are to love, not just soften our voices for five minutes in a two hour sermon sounding like you know love, but to actually be careful how we deal with God's sheep. As a leader I'm sure you know you will be accountable for God's sheep. He will ask you, how did you handle my sheep? How did you love my sheep? Are you handling God's sheep gently as he did and does, gentleness is sometimes the fruit of the spirit that is missing and mistaken for sensitivity, however there is a difference. This isn't to say that when one is called to ministry that their skin shouldn't be tough, as there will be many attacks, blows, and hits, sternness doesn't have to take residence in overall interaction when it comes to balancing sensitivity. You don't have to gravitate to one or another only. Why not implement both simultaneously? This is something I just don't get, I would think the more mature a saint is, no matter the position, status etc, the more gentle and sensitive they are to others, not necessarily putting forth kindness as weakness, but being strong as a lion and as soft as a dove knowing when and how to execute both. You may say, you can't take advice or biblical feedback from someone who has made a mistake contradictory to God's Word. Usually this comes from one who is very naïve, inexperienced, or very religious. Religious enough to adhere to a murderer's writings (Paul) yet disregard and even put down one who has never shed blood of another, let alone droves.

Growing in God

When I was about six years old I discovered a treasure in my grandmother's room. My grandmother had this movie in her collection called the Ten Commandments. I watched the movie at her house for the first time and fell in love with God all over again every time I watched it. Every time we went to my grandmother's house, while everybody would be in the living room, I would sneak upstairs and go in my grandma's room and lock the door and put the three hour movie in. I wouldn't come out until it was good and over! I mean until all the credits ran through at the end. Overtime my family caught on and would say things like, here she goes again, right upstairs to watch the Ten Commandments! I quickly became identified with The Ten Commandments in my family. Years later throughout life, I was known as the church girl, and after going through a serious sanctification process at the age of twenty they named me "The Extremist" for the gospel. I was not offended by this by any means in fact I embraced it because as you grow in Christ there should be evident changes that others can clearly see. You may be viewed as being a Mr. or Mrs. Goody two shoes, or perfect patty, or stuck up but count it all joy and press on toward the high calling of Christ Jesus because it is evident that you have chosen to follow Jesus. During that time in my grandmother's room is where I really began to know God for myself outside of church. Yes, I had been to bible study, vacation bible school, I sang with the other children in the gospel choir, I had a children's bible and I read it, but nothing clicked for me like watching the Ten Commandments.

I would memorize the lines in the movie and later on when I heard the scriptures in church I knew them like the back of my hand not from memorizing them from reading my children's bible, but from watching the movie! I'd love to be able to say that I learned all my scripture as a child from writing them repeatedly, or from reading my children's bible every night. That sounds good and perhaps more appropriate, but I thank God she had that movie upstairs in her bedroom! I later asked my parents if I could be baptized when I was eight years old at the Baptist Church my family attended. I remember putting my white robe on with the other children who were also being baptized and we went into the basement of the church where the baptism pool was. All these people were standing around and I was afraid to get into the water with the Pastor. My biological father passed away a few months prior to this event; however, the man who raised me, my dad, grabbed my hand and went into the water with me so I could be baptized.

From that point on I recall being flooded with dreams often where I would see all type of spiritual activity. I didn't know what I was dreaming about at that time, but over the years I have held on to a few dreams that won't erase my memory and I can clearly see that God was speaking to me in my sleep even as a child. I could also see things in the spirit during real time that I later realized was not the norm to see outside of dreams.

Years later, as I allowed sin in my life, my spiritual gifts began to dull and they were barely effective after so long. I know it can be hard to hear me say that I have the gift of discerning spirits yet I failed to accurately discern choosing the correct spouse. Yes ha ha absolutely true, but you have to look at the indications of why the gifts are not operating as they were intended and where someone was at in their life when they were making certain decisions. The prophetic joke of someone's gift not operating when you think it should have is indeed humorous. I encourage you not to forget that the man or woman with the gift is but dust without being filled with the spirit of God. Some people will be able to receive this message in the book because it's not coming from someone who has it all together or deem them self as never missing the mark.

For example, The Apostle Paul that we often lift up more than Christ at times had a season where he was executing Christians by the droves. He was declaring in many ways that following Christ was not the way! This is the same man who came back to the people he was killing trying to convince them that he got the correct revelation after a Damascus road experience. The same man who was killing Christians, was now going out preaching and declaring the same gospel he was condemning others for. This is the exact thing the enemy wants to do with your life and tried to do with mine. He wants to find your strengths and have you ignorantly sow into the things contrary to the will of God for your life, so that by the time your Damascus road experience comes, you're already disqualified. Sound like a smart plan doesn't it? As my spiritual father would often say as he lowered his voice in a Barry White Tone: "The devil can't stop nothing!" The good news is that nothing can thwart the plan of God on your life if God has called you. The call can be delayed and derailed, but the enemy knows that it's coming to pass. It's just a matter of time. He doesn't want you to know or believe that, but you ought to call the devil what he is and that is a liar. Regardless of your history, if you are in Christ his story is written in our history! Do not dwell on the past, and when other people keep bringing it up to you as you embark pressing on towards the future, stand firm in your mind by renewing it and be transformed with your identity in Christ and not in your past.

Save yourself from proving to people what you know God has revealed to you regardless of your past that may be contradictory to what God is calling you to do that's revealed to you by his spirit. Get used to looking crazy and being uncomfortable. Get completely out of yourself and obey God regardless of the past or what you may have done. Yes, you will be talked about, lied on, despised, rejected, and labeled, however God has a way of silencing all the judgments coming your way.

People may look at you and say, why should we listen to you of all people, you did x, w, and z. They don't know that people had a choice to either listen to Paul or not. They could refuse to listen to him because his past seemed to make him non-credible, or they could have said I know he has had a contradicting past, but the man is right and my life can benefit from the truth he is giving. The same is with your story. People can choose to be impacted for the better from what you are imparting, or it can just be their loss. It is an encouragement to me in knowing that the disciples that Jesus handpicked were people who had serious issues. Did he have to do a credit check on them? What about check the last ten years of their lives? No, he knew what they were capable of doing even though they were hard to teach at times, Jesus saw their end from their beginning.

So we have come to the conclusion and reality that there are children who are raised by parents who may have not taken them to church, and or implemented Godly principles and living anywhere in their lives. Just as we mentioned earlier how a man of God can have a child who is rebellious and chooses to go in the opposite direction he raised him in, there are children who didn't grow up learning or knowing anything about God yet they are the faithful members of the church. These children mature to be ministers within the gospel teaching and executing God's word through the power of the Holy Spirit. Point and case, be careful who you put your mouth on because you don't know what God will do with them. Just because you may see them in a club or on the street at one season of their life, don't hold them to that moment because God has a way of using the least likely candidates for grand kingdom assignments. The major thing that qualifies you with God is a right heart! The enemy desires for you to be remembered at your times of broken fellowship, or before salvation, or at anytime where you were not living according to God's word, however if God forgets your sin, then so should you. More so be sure that you have done a true repentance. That is confessing your deeds and wrongs before God out of your mouth, not silently, doing an about face and turning from that thing and moving toward God without going back to it!

Many people grace pulpits across the world today, not on the basis of where they came from, but on the basis of their direction called by God. People will look at someone and of course want to know immediately where do you come from? What does your past look like? This can certainly be of importance because recognizing a family's honored reputation or a ministry's honored reputation can explain why there is moral character, godly values, and perhaps mantle or anointing present. By no means is this how God calls and chooses those he desires for his purposes. God does not go down the checklist that man does. He does not need to know what family you were born into, or what ministry you are from, if any. God does not need to check your references, or have verification from any entity to bring you before great men for his glory. This is something that believers today still don't get, and that is **GOD DOES NOT NEED TO GET YOUR PERMISSION TO BLESS WHOM HE CHOOSES, TO APPOINT WHOM HE CHOOSES, OR TO USE WHOM HE CHOOSES.**

It amazes me when people walk around like God has to come to them to get their permission to arrange things how God wants to do it. For example, a pastor has a daughter who is a solid believer, well taught in the word of God, and lives her life accordingly, perfect? No! But she is someone that God will use mightily for his purposes. Now there will of course be some screening, observances, questioning, and caution when it is time for her to get married. The candidates will as expected have to deal with what comes with the approach of the young lady, her family, and her call. She certainly has free will and can choose whom she wants, but God does not need to get her parents' permission to join her to someone he believes will be great for their assignment together, and has ordained before the foundation of the world for her, all for his glory.

Now it will be nice to have her father's blessing, and it creates a positive accepting environment if the family and friends accepts him, but it's not a need as much as it is a desire. Speaking of the topic, I believe that God gives us all free choice when it comes to a spouse; however I also believe that if you have an assignment on your life where there is a call to lead God's flock, or a very high calling, then nothing will be able to stop that, including marrying the wrong person.

The call may be delayed or derailed, but the course isn't changing. This may sound ludicrous, but it will be discussed later when we look at certain people in the bible with the heart of God and the agenda of God and how situations were manipulated specifically by God for their ordained courses to be fulfilled.

Again, the big picture is that everyone is not raised in homes where godly principles are the core of the home, these people sow and reap in ignorance then go to the church to be edified and encouraged, but are torn down again and again, particularly by someone who has no idea what it's like to be born in a home like theirs. This is not to say that their home of origin didn't have any issues, but it's not always likely that the issues that occurred in the minister's home are the same and as detrimental as those who may be in the congregation and not in the pulpit.

On the contrary this is not true for all leaders, some have been through very little, and others have been through ten times as much, and would never qualify to be what God has ordained for them to be. The case here is that it is easy to sound like you understand, however you can never understand what you haven't lived through from an experiential stand point. Yes, from an intellectual perspective, absolutely, but not from an experiential perspective. I am not saying that it's best to experience things in order to learn them as in my introduction I stated that there are various ways of learning lessons in life and that Christ is the best teacher as he decides what is allowed in your life due to free will, or what will be best for you at that moment.

For example, if you are always talking about how you and your husband, or your wife are always happy and living the abundant life because you chose the right spouse please note, you will never ever be able to fully identify, understand and empathize with someone who chose the wrong spouse in life. Therefore, it is easy for you to judge and condemn someone else who chose the wrong spouse, because you are not able to identify with the consequences or feelings of choosing wrong. Yes! Be glad that's something you can't empathize with as you wouldn't want or need to if that doesn't apply to you, but don't pretend you understand what it's like to choose the wrong spouse when you're "telling off" those who did.

If I have never done drugs in my life, I would find it very easy to reprimand someone who is strung out on drugs because I cannot relate to what they have done, yet I know it's wrong. Take someone who was delivered from drugs and give them the same assignment, they may have a totally different approach to helping the person strung out on drugs because they have been there themselves. They know what it feels like to do wrong and choose wrong, and there is no way in the world that they would make someone else feel even worst then what they are probably feeling and experiencing because of their decisions.

The good thing is that God will cause all things to work together for the good of those who love the Lord and who are the called according to his purpose according to Romans 8:28. This too is being taken lightly in addition to God's grace. This means that all things work together for your good if you belong to Christ. The good, the bad, and the ugly. I pray that you will believe that no matter who tells you otherwise.

Looking back when I was nine years old my mom and dad were facing some serious issues in their marriage and it ended in divorce. My twin brother and sister where leaving home as they were eight years older than me. My brother off moved to Pennsylvania to college and my sister moved to Indianapolis with her boyfriend and their son. That left just me and mom. We were leaving our beautiful six bedroom house and nice neighborhood to start a journey I'd become familiar with later in my life. We settled in an apartment and started a new chapter in life. She and I began visiting a non denominational church and joined soon upon visiting. The family that I knew was torn apart and there were only a handful of relatives that lived where we were located, as the majority of our family remained in the south. I was not that close to my biological father's side of the family although I knew who they were.

That same year we began visiting a new church and we eventually joined. I wanted to go to a youth retreat the church was having at an out of town campsite. My mother was told that I was not of age and I would not be able to go. This is the very first time that I prayed to God. This situation moved me so tough that it led me right to my knees to actually talk with God for hours at a time. I would wake up in the middle of the night just to remind God of my prayer as I heard in church that you can't stop praying! Here is where my prayer life began. I prayed and prayed and I believed with all my heart that God heard me. I was even looking for results when we would go to church. I thought someone would just walk up to us at church after I prayed and tell us I could go. No one walked up to us at church, but a few weeks later my mother just so happened to get a call from someone at the church who said that I would be able to go to the retreat as long as I was closely supervised by the chaperones.

This is my life story! I have always been and still to this day am usually the youngest person in practically every group I am associated with in life. Being around people older than me has always been my reality, in school, in clubs, in my social life, in ministry, unless I was teaching the youth. Even though I was learning a great deal from being positioned this way I was still making decisions that reflected my age at certain points in my life. It has taught me not to hold a child to something an adult should be held to even though they may be just as intellectual and understand much knowledge, they are still a child and will make decisions out of a youthful immature unprocessed mindset. We often see this when appointing young ministers. The young minister may have the knowledge of God down. However they have not been processed in life's situations. This is not to say that their situations have to mirror someone else's, but it will be evident just like you tasting a delicious looking pound cake to discover that the baker forgot to put in the vanilla.

Nevertheless, I thought it was awesome that this great big God answered a ten year old girl's prayer. It's a good thing I went to the retreat because one night my pastor preached to the youth and I had an experience that no words could describe. I had never encountered God in this way before. I passed out after praising God so hard in worship. I remember the tears kept coming and I had my first face to face encounter with God. I went home from the retreat and I prayed to God telling him, that no matter what I am going back to at home, at school, and in life, to please do not let me wander too far away from you.

Talk about God being faithful to that prayer. Even to this day, I look back over my fairly young life and I see his hand all over it keeping me from things and people and manipulating situations so I will remain close to him. This is not to say that I was covered from every trap of the enemy that was set for me, or wandered from the steps that God ordered for me, but I know it's a contribution to me being delivered from every trouble that rose up in my life afterwards. Sad to say, but I did break my fellowship with God during my teen years. It was just me and mom, and mom had to work a lot. The main structure I had in my life was school and church. This is why I loved to go to church. I was hungry and thirsty for structure and boundaries and I could find this at church. I liked the rules and I was determined to follow them to a T. Of course I fell and didn't realize at the time that I couldn't do that in and of myself, but I desired to get it right.

After my mother had been through enough of her own struggles and heartbreak, having raised twins alone, and another bad marriage and still me to be responsible for mom had to work and pay the bills. You are not able to understand this unless you have been where she was. Having experienced divorced for myself there is a reality of how people do not understand why most divorced women work a lot. As a divorced woman I know what it's like to ensure all the bills are met and have little next to no energy at all by the end of the day in addition, to protecting myself, and I don't have children, so I can't imagined how she pulled it off. Hats off to you mom! I can compare the time in my life when I was married now that I am divorced. When I was married I had a full plate, but being divorced that plate is three times as much. I know what it's like to work all day long and support myself without children, so for her to do this with me at the time I know it was not easy. I found myself hanging with the wrong people as a teenager because of the love and acceptance I thought I obtained. I was saved and in Christ, but I wanted friendship and to be accepted and just like many others I found love in all the wrong places.

During elementary and middle school girls would pick on me throughout school because I was "cute" so to speak. I learned that my physical appearance communicated to them that because I was light skinned with pretty green eyes that they could say anything and do anything to me as if I was too girly to fight back. Boy, were they in for a surprise. After defending myself in school I along with the other students learned quickly that I had the ability to fight. A reputation was being built for me that I didn't want anything to do with. I was the pretty girl who could fight. I didn't even like fighting. I tried to avoid it at all costs. I remember fighting girls not in anger but in peace. I saw the beasty character come out of the girls that hated me and while I was fighting them back, I couldn't help but love them at the same time. Yeah right you say! I remember having a major peace with every fight that I physically fought to defend myself. I was never angry or beasty like, I just defended myself, looked up in amazement that I won and went on about my business. When I fought back it wasn't to hurt or harm them more so it was to stop them from their hate. There were times where I had to fight just to get home from school on many occasions. This is also an area of my life where I experienced God showing up for me. I learned to identify him in my life by him rescuing me. I had come to know him as rescuer as a small child and later as a teen and young adult. No I didn't come to God only to be rescued. I walked and talked with God even in my mess. Eventually I turned full circle when it came time for me to rededicate my entire life to him at the age of twenty. In my time of distress with childhood enemies, he always showed up for me. I didn't grow up in a home where people physically fought and I don't know where I had learned to fight, but one thing was for sure, I knew how when the time came. My first fight was when I was I in the fourth grade. I was walking home from school and a girl that was harassing me for weeks wanted to fight me after school that day. Her name was Destiny. It was the first time I had ever fought anyone and I'll never forget that experience. Our classmates deemed our fight as a tie. She was strong and I had no idea that I had an ability to fight her off. She was displeased that she didn't get a first place ribbon by the crowd by our fight, so the next week she followed me home again with the same crowd as before. This time, I fought Destiny and there was no tie, I won slightly at the end as she ended up falling on the ground, I drug her down the street to the stop sign on the corner of my block. That wasn't the end of it. The next week, she came back, with the same crowd. That was the last time I fought Destiny. The last time I fought Destiny, it was made very clear that she should never follow me home from school again. I tell this testimony of mine, because that was a physical fight, but I have been fighting destiny, my destiny for years, and it mirrors the exact stages of my physical fight with that young girl. My soul often waited for the final round in certain trials and tribulations where at the beginning there was a strain and struggle, but by the end, momentum has picked up and it becomes automatic to triumphantly be victorious overcoming all opposition to my destiny in God.

One day when I was on the bus headed home from junior high school there was a large crowd at the bus stop waiting for me to get off to fight someone I never met a day in my life. Apparently students at different schools were putting together boxing matches for me that I knew nothing about with other girls who were challenging a reputation I could care less about. I had never seen this girl one waking moment of my life before I got off the bus. She was standing there waiting for me to get off the bus with a big lock in her hand that she had wrapped up in a sock. The reason I knew what was in the sock, was because by the time our fight was over I had taken what she planned to beat me with, and I beat her with it to later open it up and find a lock on the inside of a sock. This was my entire elementary and junior high school experience. My mother had to put me into a different school because it was getting out of hand. That wasn't the best solution we discovered because the new school I went to was not teaching me anything I hadn't learned at my previous school. So what do you think happened? Correct, I had to go back to the same school where all the conflicts were occurring. I'm glad to say that in high school this pattern ceased and I actually enjoyed normal school years without having to watch my back every day after school. I understand how people come out of experiences where the enemy will try and take what you did to defend yourself with the intent of imposing a nature on you that will be unhealthy for your life. I am glad that it didn't prosper and grateful that stage of my life ceased. How could fighting be something that God used for my good?

I didn't realize it at the time but I felt that God was with me with every fighting encounter I had as a youth. God used what I had been through to teach me and prepare me for some of the strongest fights coming in my life that were not at all physical. When it came time for me to fight in the spirit in my life to break away from things that should have killed me, my spirit learned a new warfare, however the feelings of pulling through brought me back to when I had to fight as a youth, and that was don't give up until it's over. This also had a negative impact later in life, when I was fighting for things that I should have let go a lot earlier. To have fight in you is great! Especially for this kingdom walk, however there are times when we don't discern well the things we are fighting for. Many people hold on to things that God is trying to kill because we don't want to give up the fight. For example: David fought in prayer over a child that God was going to kill due to the circumstances associated with him committing adultery with Bathsheba and killing her husband Uriah in 2 Samuel 11. No matter how persistent David was in prayer and apologetic, the very thing he was trying to hold onto was the very thing God was killing no matter how long David stayed on his face. This is imperative for those in abusive relationships. You can pray all you want and fight all you want and perhaps there will be some positive results according to 1 Corinthians 7:16. The other possibility and reality that many church people won't tell you because it is viewed as being pessimistic is that you won't win them over. It may take you 20 or 30 years to finally figure out that you are still fighting hard and strong yet it's not for the right fight. The spirit of God will lead and guide you in making the necessary decisions along with much fasting, prayer, and reconciliation. However if a man has been beating his wife for years and they are in their sixties and seventies and he is still beating her, chances are, he is not going to stop, even though there is a chance he may. If this is you I encourage you to seek God for what he will have you to do. I have learned when to hold it and when to fold it.

My grandmother told me about a woman who was beaten black and blue and ran to the church for help for the church to ask her when she got there, "What did you do to him to make him beat you like this". Automatically without hearing what happened it was her fault that her husband took his fists to pound on her, as if he had no responsibility or accountability in his actions. It always makes a ministry look good when couples that face abuse, adultery, or abandonment reconcile. If you reconcile, you're applauded and even handed a ministry of your own. If you decide to leave, you're constantly reminded how you're wrong not to go back to the situation because after all didn't God forgive you for all you've done wrong? If God has forgiven you, then why won't you forgive? It is often assumed that because one forgives, they have to put that person back in the same position they once held, and that is not true. I can forgive from a distance with boundaries. As beautiful as reconciliation is, it does not always happen. There are many people in the bible that God didn't reconcile to. It had nothing to do with an unforgiving nature, more so than it had to do with the nature of the one that was out of fellowship with God.

This is to be likened to success. Just because you are successful does not mean you are successful in the eyes of God. There is nothing worse than being successful in the wrong assignment. Yes you accomplished all you desired to do above and beyond, but what does God has to say about your success? Are you successful in his assignment for your life? When your assignment lines up with his assignment true success is guaranteed! Success is also not success unless you earned it fair and square! Many have reached their definition of success while believing it was done honestly. That's not always the case. In today's Christian culture there is popular beliefs that you have to do things a certain way and look a certain way and make this amount of money or have this much education because that's real Christian success. That is far from the truth. It is important to have your home life, your emotions, your finances, your education, and spirit life right, don't get me wrong. However your hope should not be built upon those things. As it's preached, my hope is built on nothing less than Jesus blood and righteousness, I dare not trust the sweetest frame, but wholly lean on Jesus name, Christ the solid rock I stand ALL other ground is sinking sand!! We are in the world but not of the world. Why invest all of your time and energy into a world you don't plan on being in forever. Yes we have to be here temporarily, but the enemy will have you focused more on your temporary place than where you are going and that's eternity. So why invest all of your strength, time, and money into the world's system which is coming to an end according to Matthew 24:14?

Keep in mind I was going to church faithfully as a youth while all of this was going on. There were many days my mother had no idea of the fights I had got into, neither did I tell her. It was a part of my norm and I was used to carrying things alone by that time with no one to talk to at home. I prayed to God often, and I became quite learned in doctrine and scripture from church; however I was missing the boat in other major areas. The sin in my life wouldn't make room for the Holy Spirit to fill me so that I could get all of what God wanted for me.

My family is originally from the south. I have heard stories about my great grandfather and his father before him were preachers that assisted Doctor Martin Luther King Jr. and the Civil rights movement in the south. There are also a few licensed ministers in my family in Birmingham, Alabama, however this is all that I am aware of.

My mother's parents were born and raised in the south. I was not born in wedlock, and I didn't have a relationship with my biological father at all. I remember after receiving results from a paternity test when I was eight years old that the man I had seen from time to time was in fact my dad, and that it was being arranged for us to begin spending time together. Soon afterward I got all dressed up to spend time with this man who I only had a few memories of to discover later that evening that he passed away the same day I was to spend time with him and meet an older sister I never knew I had. I later was able to meet my half-sister and two half-brothers at his funeral a few weeks later. I didn't have a relationship with him, but I always had a hole in my heart from not being able to know or even talk to the man that helped to conceive me.

Between the time I was born and the time I was three years old my mother married the man who raised me, the man I still consider and acknowledge to be my father today.

The house hold that I was grew up in was my mother and father, my brother and sister and me. We went to church on Sundays and I can remember a few times where we prayed together as a family occasionally. There was not too much discussion about Jesus and God at home, but we learned when we went to church on Sundays. I saw my parents bend over backwards to make sure we had food on the table, clothes on our back, and the bills to be paid. They were facing many struggles of their own lives. We had bibles in the house, but I don't remember us ever coming together to read them. I don't mention this to beat up my parents in any way or reprimand them in a manner that they didn't raise me good enough. I have watched my parents grow leaps and bounds over the years in the area of their walk with Christ and I am glad to know that He is continually doing a work in them. What I share is not where they are today as it is capturing a season in time when I was a child. I am mentioning this because everyone who attends church regularly is not necessarily raised in a home where biblical principles are being lived out and encouraged consistently. This is not always due to parents not wanting to implement this type of living. I am forever grateful to my mother who taught me how to create a beautiful atmosphere and to wear your smile for the glory of God regardless of what the past looks like. My dad, who taught me to be strong and was financially supportive to me in ways many fathers are not to their biological children. Thank you. My life wouldn't have been the same without you! I love you! I have watched my parents grow beautifully in the Lord as they have also watched me over time.

Sometimes depending on what kind of spiritual chain/bondage one is living under, release and change is not happening until the bondages are broken, and order is set. There are many parents today who are doing the best they can, going through many personal issues that their children do not see or would understand and it's reflected in their homes. This is why we all need Jesus, because he helps where parents can only go so far (Psalm 27:10). I understand how you can go to church for years and have issues in your personal life and at home that do not mirror or line up the Word of God. Again, this is not due to just simply choosing to live this way, **there is a battle going on** and if there are areas in one's life that are not free from sin and bondage then prayerfully Jesus will work out the rest. I am a living witness that God will show up for you when no one knows what you are going through.

I remember going to church as a child but I didn't really understand everything the preacher was talking about when we were attending the Baptist Church we were members of. For a very long time I thought that our way of life at home was normal regarding being believers and being saved. Many children believe that their home of origin is the norm, and many times it's not. Most people come from dysfunction. Over the years after maturing in my own spiritual walk and lining my life up with the Word of God, which by the way didn't occur over a linear three step process. I was later able to recognize that my parents did the best they could at the time with where they were. They both came from broken homes and had their own home of origin issues. A person can only deposit what has been deposited into them, therefore if you discover later that you didn't receive things while being raised in your home that you wish you had, this can assist your perspective to understand that important elements may have been absent due to them not receiving them as well.

There are many positive contributions that my parents have made in my life, and I can honestly say that I wanted for nothing tangible. Like a lot of other homes in the church, godly principles are not necessarily embedded and practiced within the home consistently. It is important to note that just because you were not raised a certain way does not limit you to raising your own family in the manner you deem essential. I look forward to teaching my children the things of God and backing it up with a lifestyle that mirrors the same. This is not to say a perfect, flawless lifestyle, because no one is perfect, but I will certainly strive to instill Godly living in my home when God blesses me with the family that he is choosing for me.

The past is the past and no one can go back and change what occurred or what didn't occur. I have come to grips with this through Christian counseling and grief recovery classes that have helped me dramatically to overcome my childhood and my past. I have overcome situations that were passed down to me due to generational bondages and home of origin issues, that didn't start with my parents, but long before they were born where they were also affected by the same. There are also situations that were self-inflicted on my part. I mention this because Scales of the Heart will attest that people do make decisions that are self-inflicting knowingly as well as in ignorance. It is said more today that people are creating their own Ishmael's which I agree with, however I believe that some are originated in knowledge and others are birthed in ignorance. Many will often tell you that you are where you are because you chose that route or course, which I also agree with, but the reasons as to why a person may have chosen or did what they did is not always examined or understood, neither does it seem as if there is any care or concern for the decisions that were made. I believe Christ looks at why decisions and actions are being made and he weighs the heart of a person (Luke 23:34).

How can the same God who said if you love me you will keep my commandments be the same God who prayed for the very people who was not keeping his commandments? He prayed to his father: Father, forgive them for they know not what they do. Was this for sinners only? I believe it was certainly for sinners. What about for believers? I also believe it was for believers to a point, because at conversion a new believer does not know a number of things relating to living a Christian lifestyle until they have gone through a transformation process. Is this not contradictory? I believe it is in a rational sense, but spiritually we cannot contain God and all that he is. Can God hold you accountable for your actions and at the same time be praying for you, while loving you enough to give his life for you? I believe this to be so. This does not merge well with rational thinking that says it has to be one or the other, because it does not make sense to us that God can be both of something. There are some absolutes with God which we can clearly see in the word of God. Does God want you to be hot or cold? Yes! He will vomit you out of his mouth if you are lukewarm. Is God holy or isn't he? Absolutely he is holy! Does God care about lukewarm people? Yes he does! Does God want to save those who are not holy so that they can become holy? Yes he does! See, as ministers within the body, we often project one side and not the other. God's greatest attribute is love! This can be contradictory to him carrying out certain pronouncements to those who **CONSISTENTLY AND ONGOINGINLY** are breaking his commands and don't have a desire to line their lives up with the word, especially after having been extended the opportunity and the grace over time. So how can a loving God who is love, destroy a people or even divorce a person, place or thing (Satan, Israel, Adam and Eve). Because even though God is love full of mercy and grace, he has limits and boundaries. If those boundaries are repeatedly broken just as a covenant is broken repeatedly God may add a different road to the course he intended from the beginning. You may say, God never changes his course! I agree. I believe the destination is just that the destination, but we see clearly in Exodus 13:17 that God led the Israelites along the long way for a purpose. Then it came to pass, when Pharaoh had let the people go, that God did not lead them *by* way of the land of the Philistines, although that *was* near; for God said, Lest perhaps the people change their minds when they see war, and return to Egypt. He led them the long way so they wouldn't be afraid of the fight that was ahead. Be encouraged my friend! If God has led you along the long way, it can be due to your decisions, to test your heart, or so that you will be processed for the fight head! At the same time it could be for other reasons you may not know or be aware of that only God can see and understand.

We can often follow Christ's example in many things, except the very compassion he had for people who were sinning in ignorance. I have learned that this too is a form of sickness. Scriptures are being thrown at people left and right without compassion, love, and understanding. There is a need to preach the holy unadulterated word of God so that people can understand they can't live for God any kind of way after they become saved, but it's not always coming from a place of compassion and care. At times it is apparent by the manner and tone that it is coming from a condemning place. No one is going to admit that they are condemning you or even believe they are, as we all know that it is wrong for us to judge and condemn but that is exactly what is happening. Condemning and judging someone is easy and sloppy, to show someone their error in love takes more strength and energy because the Spirit of God will give you the ability to articulate your correction for the individual in a way where they still know that God loves them and that he understands. Delivery is so impactful. This is not to be in the same category of rebuking the enemy, or casting out spirits, or exhorting boldly the gospel of Jesus Christ, this is regarding showing someone their errors.

Man looks at self-inflicted situations and says well, you made a mess, too bad so sad, you should have known better, but the King of Kings and Lord of Lords who is Supreme over all, creator of all things looks at the same self-inflicted situations you created in ignorance and prays for you. When Jesus was being crucified on the cross, and they nailed his hands and feet to the cross, he didn't look at mankind and say you are doing this from your God given conscience that you were born with, and you should know better not to do this. He didn't say you know exactly what you are doing, and the mess you are creating. No, he prayed and said father forgive them for they know not what they do (Luke 23:24). This has been taken so lightly. Other scriptures are held in high esteem over the very thing and reason Jesus came to the earth.

You might say in ignorance? Yeah right! Those people know exactly what they were doing when they were killing Jesus. I beg to differ, just like Christ did on the Cross. This is the very reason he came, which was for the sick. Not just the sick people on street corners and in the world, but sick religious people who are operating in everything except truth and love. Ignorance is a sickness and you must be delivered from it. The only way to be delivered from this sickness is not just by being saved, but by being filled with the spirit of God. It may appear that when someone gets saved that they are immediately filled with his spirit of God. Sorry to tell you the truth, but that is not so, you receive God's spirit immediately when you get saved, this we call conversion, however it takes time for your life your line up with God's word, then become sanctified and set apart from the world, and then you have to continually ask God to fill you with his spirit daily.

It was not just a prayer for those people that day that were crucifying Christ. That prayer reached back in time to the Garden of Eden. He prayed for Adam and Eve and mankind, father forgive them, even though they sinned in the garden, they had no idea what they were doing. Why didn't God stop it, because God is so loving that he chooses to limit his sovereignty to extend to you free will and choice? In the garden he placed two trees. One was the garden of the knowledge of good and evil, and the other was the tree of life. Right there before the fall of man, choice was given by a God that we understand to be in ultimate control. Is God in control of everything you may ask? Ultimate control that is, however due to free will there is some type of control people have over situations and circumstances that are not necessarily caused by God more so than he allows them.

Be encouraged my friend, if God allowed something in your life even though he didn't cause it, the difference of the outcome is if you belong to him or not. If you belong to God know that he will work it out for your good according to Romans 8:28. This does not mean go and do whatever you desire because knowing you belong to God is a free ride to lose life! There is a balance and a responsibility you have in lining your life up with his word if you belong to him. If you choose to live your life with the attitude "that gives me a license to sin" then, by all means, no one can take your free will from you, but be prepared for the consequences and the setback that's coming to you. I'd ask the question, if you lived that kind of way and declared such a thing, I'd wonder if you were saved at all. Not that I would judge your salvation as I am instructed not to judge any many before the end time according to (1 Corinthians 4:5). The fruit of your life may identify you with the goats/ tares of the world that Jesus said he will separate from his sheep and wheat, but only he knows. I agree with my spiritual father when it comes to pantheology. What in the world is pantheology you ask? This is referring to the end times or eschatology. It's the fact that no man knows the day or the hour according to Matthew 24:36. There are many prophetic timelines in the bible, and you must as a believer discern the times you are in because that is very important as a believer and for the church, but when it comes to Christ's return, it will all pan out in the end. That will save you from trying to figure it all out in your own strength. Know that He is coming again, and he is coming quickly, live your life everyday as if He is coming back that day, being ready! Trust and follow God, and obey him. I wouldn't be right if I told you to obey him in your strength like many are taught. You cannot obey God unless you are doing it through his spirit. This is why the filling of the Holy Spirit is important. You may be aware of times in your life where you were saved but not filled with his spirit and that is okay for you to acknowledge that because it brings you out of denial and positions you to receive truth which Jesus would want. He would also want you to take a new position of being filled with God's spirit every day. How do you do this? Cut out all sin in your life. A believer is not sinless but the closer you grow to God the less you sin. If a pastor tells you they don't have any sin in their life at all, and they will never sin again in this earth, begin to pray that God will lead you somewhere that will hold you accountable and understand that you without His spirit, you are but dust.

It may be perceived that I just told you to go find some place you can get away with everything, that is not what I am stating. I am saying that a place that will preach to you nothing but grace having you believe you have no part on your own is misleading you down the wide gate to destruction. It is true you didn't have a part to play in the gift of grace being available and extended to you initially, because Christ paid for it, but you do have a part in honoring it and God by remaining in good fellowship with God as you carry his name. We see in the Old Testament how God lavished mercy and grace many times on people, yet there is a turning point in the New Testament when Christ died on the cross and sent the Holy Spirit as a helper to believers. It was not until Christ died on the cross that the veil was torn in two and there was access to come boldly before the throne of grace. This major work is a part of the finished work of grace in this aspect. Paul received the message to take the good news to all non Jews (Gentiles) which came directly from God almighty, therefore grace is not to be taken lightly that Jesus didn't support grace as much. Just because he may not have spoken much on it during his time on earth does not necessarily mean that it wasn't important to him. It was important enough where access was given to those who didn't have it prior to boldly come before his throne of Grace. If you are somewhere and you are burdened with trying to uphold an unrealistic standard to be a child of God in good fellowship with God, I am praying for you, because that kind of environment and teaching will do nothing but make you feel like you just don't measure up resulting in a bondage robbing you of true freedom in Christ that is aligned by boundaries. This is true in a sense that none of us measured up according to Romans 3:10. It is true that people within the church can walk around bragging about how they are better than you because they have the power to abstain from certain things and practices compared to you, without ever realizing there could be a difference in maturity and where you are spiritually. There is also a side where someone is just flat out sinning wanting others to feel sorry for them; this is what the Lord does not approve of. So is it wrong to go about bragging about how strong you are in your own power compared to those who are newer in Christ? Yes! You're doing it not in your power but in God's power so stop bragging. Is it wrong to live your life with a license to sin? Yes!

Trade that license in for the abundant life in Christ where there will be trials and sufferings, yet you will count it all joy as you watch God deliver you from all your troubles according to Psalm 24:19, keep in mind that is for those who belong to God, and if you say you belong to God you will keep his commandments, it doesn't mean you are going to be perfect or fall sometimes, but the fall should be a struggle forward that was unintentional or unknowingly verses something you ran full fledge to do. God's blood covers you. Thank God with all your might that you are covered by the blood of Jesus that makes you white as snow! While doing that don't forget to honor this with right living instead of taking advantage of it.

There is a renewed filling that needs to take place for you to walk in victory and overcome the enemy daily by God's spirit. We overcome not by power and not by might but by the Lord's spirit. This is a process. It can be a short time to get here for some, and others it takes longer. You can be filled with God's spirit today and not tomorrow. The goal is to live consistently filled with the spirit of God and you must seek him and ask him to fill you and line your life up with the word of God and get rid of all sin that you know of and pray that God will keep you from unconscious sin. Confessing our sin is also essential to being filled with God's spirit when necessary, yet God doesn't want us sin conscious, more so that we are blood bought and saved by grace through faith in God and not works.

My Road to My Transformation

In high school my cousin would often play the role as my big brother in school. When I came in as a freshman he was a junior. He and his friends always made me feel safe and special because they played the role of being my big brothers at school. They looked out for me, respected me, and had my back over the years through school. It wasn't until near the end of my senior year in high school when I had run into one of my big brothers at the mall who graduated with my cousin Lance. We had lost touch over the years as they had moved on to college after high school, while I was finishing up. We exchanged phone numbers and agreed to stay in touch and went on our way. He and I talked a few times on the phone catching up and reminiscing about High School and made arrangements to have lunch. The only relationship we had in high school was just that of "big brother and big sister" and that never changed at anytime down the line. He kept telling me about how he joined a fraternity in college and how excited he was to be a part of this new venture in his life. I had no clue about anything fraternity or sorority related and I thought that it sounded great from listening to his experiences.

Before we left he said that there was a guy on his frat line he wanted to introduce me to. A few weeks later I agreed to meet his new frat brother and I could see perhaps why he thought we would be interested in one another. On the outward appearance we looked like we could have been twins physically. He was the exact same skin color, had the exact same hair type and color as me, and he too had the same green eyes as me. Overtime we began a relationship as I graduated high school and went into my freshman year of college. This was the period of my life where I fell away from my walk with God the most. I went to clubs and hung out all night with friends. My home church wasn't in the same city I was attending college that year. The funny thing is when I showed up to the parties people would be talking to me about God when I was trying to party. I felt the Lord's presence on me heavily during this year of my life when I backslid. You may not understand if you haven't experienced this, but if you have, you know exactly what it's like to be in the club partying and praying for people at the same time. Hence, that is not the place or the right approach to prayer, more so conviction of the Holy Spirit.

It is often assumed that when young believers graduate from high school and leave their parent's home they intend on intentionally living for the devil. That thought or intent never crossed my mind when I left home. As you move and live away from your normal surroundings as a young adult, you develop a new network and influence grabs tightly to you, more so for those who were not raised in homes where their parents were ministers or who stayed connected to the churches of their hometowns. The forces of this world will grab and suck you in to the college lifestyle and then it becomes a fight the farther you drift away. If a door is open to sin, the enemy hones in during this time, like no other. He knows that a youth does not have to have the mindset that they are coming to live for him (the devil). Eventually, if the surroundings around them are just right, it won't be long before a gradual tight snatch is occurring. This is exactly how you can witness even children of ministers go off to college or leave home and live a totally different life. It's not that the Word of God is not in them, it is a real battle. This isn't to say that some do have the mindset that they are just going to do whatever they want because they are "grown" now. Don't place all youths in that box, because many who don't have continuous guidance end up only doing what they were taught or what no one corrected. It is just like being in an unevenly yoked relationship. There is a literal BATTLE going on. If you don't know what that is like you cannot empathize with some of the struggles and forces that some have had broken off of their lives. Usually when they come to the church either for the first time, or to reposition themselves in God's house, they are not always welcomed well. Sometimes you may have no idea what someone has had to fight off of their lives to get to the house of God. The father of the Prodigal son we read about in Luke 15 rejoiced when his son came home, just like heaven who rejoices over one sinner who comes to repentance than ninety nine who need no repentance (Luke 15:7, 10). The brother of the prodigal son was faithful and lived his life right, which was great for his life, but he couldn't even see the need to celebrate his brother coming home from going astray, instead all he could see was the wrong choices that was made. Truth be told, the percentage of those youths who fall away from the faith severely outweigh those who remain connected after graduating high school. Everyone who falls away does not do so with the intent of living for the devil.

Meanwhile, back at the ranch, what I soon discovered was that it wasn't as clear to hear the voice of God during this time in my life when I fell away. I stayed on campus during my freshman year of college and didn't come home until it was time for the Holidays. My mother moved to Iowa and I was in college with my boyfriend who had become like family at that time as his family was also in another city. Our parents were both in different cities and we had only each other. I was his family, and he was mine. He supported me, and I supported him. I wasn't that close to my siblings and my mother was gone. I stayed in touch with my dad after the divorce and he was always there if I needed him. My boyfriend was one of the most respected young men around on the college campus that is. It seemed like he had a type of authority when he walked in a room that demanded respect and I was drawn to that. He made me feel safe, and people respected me just because I was his girlfriend. Overtime people just associated my identity with him. They didn't even call me by my name; I was called his lady everywhere I went. It felt like a privilege to be his "woman". Everywhere we went together we received star treatment. He was popular, good looking, he had resources, and it seemed like he really loved me. After the school year ended I received notification that my financial aid would not be enough to cover my dorm for the next year of college coming up.

I couldn't afford to stay on campus after my renewed financial aid was submitted for the next year. My mother was in Iowa, and my boyfriend at the time kept saying that I could move in with him. That's what I did. I moved in with him. As terrible as this was I didn't understand the impact of doing what I was doing. I knew that you should be married to have sex and that shacking up was not good, but I didn't really understand why until I began to line my life up with God's word. You might ask, didn't you grow up in the church? How could you not know something so simple? I knew about theology, doctrine, and a lot of other things that are essential for one's walk with God, but I didn't have knowledge or examples in major areas such as witnessing a godly marriage and kingdom principles implemented fully within my close settings. The disconnect was obvious, but I thank God that he didn't give up on me, and because of my sufferings I was able to learn and line my life up right. Psalm 119: 71 says it was good for me to be afflicted so that I might learn his decrees. I share this to be transparent with my life so that if there is someone else out there that was raised in church or is being raised in church that is struggling in areas due to unwise choices or serious lack of knowledge or examples, know you're not alone. People may cross you off their approval list, but know that God isn't through with you yet! Struggle forward and back it with actions by doing God's word even if you feel like you're going to die. You will die, to your flesh, but God will raise you up again to a new life in Him. I promise you! It's worth every bit of sacrifice. Knowing the word and lining your life up with it is two different things. The bad news is that I shacked up. The good news is that I started going back to church consistently when I moved back to my home city, and it didn't take long for me to make a stand as a result.

I went every Sunday and didn't miss when I moved back to my home town. I even started going to bible study on Wednesdays. Every time the church doors were opened I was there. I joined counter culture club, and started fellowshipping with people that were going where I too wanted to go. I would come home and tell my boyfriend that I am getting my life in order and I wanted him to also. So he started coming to church with me. No one knew we were living together, but we were. When the first semester of my sophomore year was over, I told him that I would be finding an apartment of my own and I have decided to live right in every area of my life, and follow Christ. I finally understood the impact of living outside of God's will and I was absolutely convicted! I had to get it right! It seemed like at the time I moved in with him, all the light bulbs came on, and I finally started seeing sprouts from all the seeds that had been planted prior in my life. The word of God had been richly poured into my life by those that taught me his word. During my sophomore year of college was when I moved back home and I transferred to the college of my hometown. I finally received the revelation of God and his ways, and how impactful it is to live right, and how impactful some of my choices had been. It was like I was waking up for the first time in my life. The good thing was I knew the word of God which was a great help during this time of my life.

I had narrowed it down to two apartments to choose from and had my boxes ready to start this purifying journey with Jesus. That's exactly when my boyfriend proposed to me. I said yes and was excited to follow Christ with my soon to be husband. We lived together before marriage for almost one year and upon grasping the order of God we abstained from shacking and waited until we got married for any intimacy. This is of course out of order but it was major mile compared to where we were. We did all the necessary premarital counseling at his home church. We didn't attend that church but it's where he wanted to get married. We attended my church regularly, but we got married in his hometown because his family and friends severely outnumbered mine and the wedding and reception would be there.

I remember waking up on my wedding day without a voice. It was the strangest thing I had experienced in my life. I was fine just days before and I was not sick. That night at my rehearsal I noticed my voice fading away. I tried drinking tea and eating cough drops throughout the day when I woke up in the morning in the hopes that I would have a voice for the ceremony. I greeted over 200 guests at my big done up wedding and reception without a voice to speak up. I was beautiful and everything was in its place, all except my voice. I remember sitting at the head table at our reception with all of our guests trying to talk to my new husband who could not hear me over the all the fun him and his frat brothers were having. My reception didn't seem like a reception at all, but more so a big fraternity and sorority event. There were all types of people he invited that I didn't know from college and from the "Greek world". Some I knew, others I didn't. I just didn't feel like it was about us, and after pulling him to the side and straining my voice to communicate this to him, I'll never forget the embarrassment I received at my reception of my husband yelling at me in public, walking away rudely to get back to his "peeps". My eyes were being opened and it was too little too late.

Throughout our marriage my recollection of going through my entire wedding day without a voice constantly played in my spirit. It was God's way of clearly telling me that he could not hear me. I always reflected on this in times where it didn't seem like anything was getting through to him. Had God heard my vows? I know the people didn't so I was told after the ceremony and at the reception. Did I just go through the motions of a wedding? I pondered this in my heart throughout our union, especially the first time divorce was threatened by my husband that first year.

That was the beginning of our union. It was over before it ever began. You might say, Lady Joy was you not having a voice a clear indication not to marry him that day? Perhaps, but I also believed that I needed to be placed in a boundary so that I could get what I needed for my spirit and development with Christ. Yes I could have learned the same on a better course, however with my home of origin, the decisions I was making, I could have been led down a much worst course than the one I was taking, and I believe that God saw what I needed. He didn't cause it or plan for me to marry him, but he allowed it and used it to bring me to a place of maturity. God knows exactly how to put boundaries on his children so that they are not destroyed and where I was at that time, I needed to be in a boundary. It was time to grow up, and I reaped the consequences sown in rebellion and ignorance, like many people do. Just to note there is a difference between being blind and being ignorant. I believe people have a combination of both and Christ clearly understood the difference as he prayed on the cross for those who were blind to the fact that they were killing the Messiah.

We spent so much time together being around other people, when it was just him and I, he never really had anything to say. It was like pulling teeth to get him to communicate with me. He said it was his pain and his "stuff" that he didn't want to talk about, and I wanted to respect that at the same time wanting to know what he was referring to. You might be thinking how sad. Couldn't you have avoided all of this from the beginning? Yes I could have, however life is not linear. It's not like you just go from point A to point B and life is over. There are so many ups and downs, failures and victories in life and church people act as if your life is not linear with no hang-ups then you're really not saved. The vicissitudes of life are real. Job 14:1 says that the days of man are short and full of trouble, this is a true statement. In Christ we are blessed with every spiritual blessing and we have what we need to make it through this life in victory to overcome, yet that does not mean problems and trouble are going away. You just learn to live above them, however it doesn't' denote that they are there, and some of them you have to address, and this is not to say you are allowing them to rule over you. I know I was saved, but I needed help. Thank God that he helped me and saw the best in me, even when others didn't. There are so many testimonies like this within the church, but sometimes it's covered up so well that you'd never know the couple that seems to have it all together went through similar challenges as those who may have exposed their struggles more openly, even if it meant helping someone else. The risk of exposing the issues and ruining reputation is greater than others being helped. This is the exact occurrence in today's settings. The reputation is so much greater than any one person or few persons being truly ministered to or cared for. Sometimes we operate and teach as if there are guarantees in life. It is always critical to note the importance of the original intent. For example, the woman was originally created with the intent to give birth to children before the fall of man, yet due to the fall it is a fact that some women leave this earth never giving birth to children. This could be due to a reproductive issue on behalf of herself or her spouse (important to note here that some men also were created with seed that was intended to reproduce after its kind, and yet men too leave this earth never reproducing offspring as it was originally intended for them to do). This could be due to someone making a decision that they just don't want to have children, this could be due to the Lord determining someone should not have a child for whatever reason that may be, and as we know the fruit of the womb is a blessing from the Lord. God could also desire and will for people who have faced this to raise other children who perhaps may be fatherless or motherless. Perhaps it's just not God's time to bring forth a child **yet**. I am not saying that someone who has been given a negative report from the doctor cannot conceive and bring forth life, for we know with God all things are possible, my point is that there were many things intended originally from the beginning, yet due to how the fall has impacted this earth not everything will turn out the way it was originally intended for. Just like we were intended to live forever before the fall, yet we will be in the flesh which was not always bad before the fall, yet we are in it until we are called home. Yes we have the Holy Spirit given to us that will help lead, guide, direct, and place us back into a place of dominion and power which we received once Christ made this available to his believers as we are sons and daughters of God, yet many facets of life are being affected by the fall until we leave this earth. Even though there were original intents from the beginning of time we see in Genesis we cannot ignore the fact that people are victims of rape and molestation, murder, adultery, abduction by thieves and so forth. These things were never intended from the beginning yet they are happening every day, even though we have the power to overcome them all. The wheat and the tares are growing together and will be separated when Christ does this work. Believers certainly have the ability to overcome for their lives and will be delivered from all of their troubles according to the word of God. Another example is that there are evil people who prosper and good people who suffer on the earth. There are people who never smoke and get cancer anyway, and then there are people who smoke like a chimney and never get cancer. Just because one goes to college does not guarantee them a job immediately after graduation in that field. I am not saying that person will never work in that field however I am saying that just because one gets a degree it does not guarantee them a secure job in that field. Just ask over fifty percent of college graduates who can't even find a job in other fields let alone the field of study that was pursued in their studies.

There are people who do exceptionally well in life, and stay out of bad places, get an education, walk with God and even minister to God's body who have been murdered like a villain. There have been real testimonies of people being gunned downed on their way to bible study. In Ecclesiastes 8:10-13 it explains that wicked people are buried with honor and treated as if they are good in this world, and good people are treated as if they are wicked. The point is there are no guarantees in life, even if you take all the "correct" steps to a goal. I recall getting ready to graduate college and right before I was about to walk the stage about a month or so prior I received a notice in the mail of a young lady who was trying to sue me. The young lady filed a lawsuit against another company and made an accusation against me because her business was failing. She was trying to sue several people who she wanted to blame for her company diving and I was one of them. She was very close to my age and decided to start her own home health company. I was hired as an administrative assistant for her new home health company and she had just rented office space. It appeared that her business had just taken off during the time she hired me and she took upon herself to take extravagant vacations and trips away from the office to celebrate. I'd get calls and emails from her instructing me to tell her staff when they came for their paychecks that she couldn't pay them on several instances. I was accused of soliciting her employees to work for another home health company that her very own human resource manager began who worked for her long before I started working for her in administration. This was one of the worst things I ever went through in my life. As I have grown and matured, I learned that this was nothing to really fret about, however when this was occurring I almost lost my mind. Having to be brought before a court and judge for something that I never did was heartbreaking. I had never experienced any issues with the law before in my life and I was horrified to have read her accusations against me. I had gotten straight A's in school, tried my best with every club and organization I belonged to. I hadn't made all the right choices but I decided to rededicate my life back to Christ and all you know what was breaking loose. I heard God say in my spirit that there is nothing you need to worry about because the truth shall set you free. One day during the lawsuit I received a call from my lawyer who advised that the young lady wanted to make me an offer. The offer was if I was to go before the court and say that the other company came to me soliciting me to leave her company and work for theirs. She wanted me to lie about something that never took place, and if I agreed to it, she was going to cancel her case against me. I knew in my spirit what I heard from the Lord, and that was to tell the truth. I turned down her proposal and said I cannot lie and bear false witness and that I guess, I'll see her in court. I told her she doesn't have to cancel her accusations against me, and that God would see about me. I know it must have been silly to her at the time for me to decline her offer; however when all was said and done, exactly what I advised came to pass. This was also a great witnessing opportunity for my lawyer who called me after I declined to share that he knew in his heart that I was a true believer for handling the situation as such. She had big time lawyers that I could never afford and they were all over six feet tall. I had no money for a big time lawyer and didn't know who to reach out to until the Lord ordered my steps to a short statured Caucasian witty lawyer who happened to be a believer, one I couldn't afford but he just so happened to represent me anyway (I don't know what it is about short men who are full of power who have been ordained to help me in life, but I thank God for them. I thank God for my Bishop and my angel TL). Month after month went by and week after week and time was getting closer to the trial date. I knew I had heard God but I was prepared to go before the court with God's word he spoke to me when exactly a few days before the trial. I received a notification that the judge, not the plaintiff dismissed me from the lawsuit after thoroughly reviewing the case determining that I had nothing to do with some of her employees leaving to go work for the other company. Not only was I released from the lawsuit, my lawyer gave me a generous settlement that I know only God could have been responsible for. I went in fire and came out cold. I came to know Luke 12:11 by experience. The Lord says when you are brought before the synagogues, rulers, and authorities; do not worry about how you will defend yourselves or what you will say. For the Holy Spirit will tell you what you should say. Jesus says in Matthew 10:18 that it is on His account that you will stand before governors and kings, you will be brought before trials and that these are opportunities to witness about Jesus. This is one thing to read about it in God's word; however it's another story to live this out by experience. Mark 13:9 also describes the same. That experience taught me a lot. Grateful that I have a clean background and have never committed any kind of misdemeanor or felony, I certainly have a new respect for those who have had to face similar situations or who have been falsely accused. It is not easy to go before a court being accused of anything terrible when that doesn't reflect your character at all. My faith was stretched and I saw God fight for me, and guess what we won. If God be for you, who can be against you? Being persecuted for Christ's sake can be viewed as a paradox according to Psalm 128:1-2 which describes the prosperity and blessings of the believer. It is important to note that the persecution and the blessings go hand in hand in our walks with Christ. This experience was three years before I was divorced and it prepared me to walk in settings where I would immediately be accused. I learned how to stand in assurance knowing that God is with me, for me, and watched him fight for me. I know that anything that will rise up against you if God sent you and is for you will ultimately not prosper and every mouth raised against you will be silent. It's actually become interesting to me at this point in my life. It's as if I look to see what God will do next to silence the one who is accusing me now. It never fails, but He always confirms I belong to Him.

All the while in my marriage over time the revelation became clearer in the direction we were headed. We went to a marriage class for three years faithfully, we went to church on Sundays and Wednesdays, even Saturdays. We got into ministry, we went to counter culture club, we were being mentored by successful couples and I set a home environment of praise and worship within our home. I was now a wife, working a job, in school full time, and serving in ministry. It was here that I realized you can have people in ministry serving Sunday in and Wednesday out but they are facing intense trials. I am not just referring to my situation, there were others in my ministry who too had a full plate and was facing all types of disheartening situations. The point is if you think that perfect people are the only people who are to be in ministry, my prayer is that you will graduate to reality. Yes there are times when we need to sit down, get counseling, or exercise church discipline for those who need it, but if we all were sat down due to not lining up with God's word perfectly, there would be no one left standing, because we all would be sitting down.

I came out of the world completely. I had battled something major in my spirit and that was pledging for his sister sorority. He had loved his fraternity so much and it seemed like the thing that brought him joy more than anything and I wanted to make my husband happy. I was pulled in another direction, and that was the Lord's way. I wanted to be completely souled out for Christ. God kept putting in my spirit that it didn't matter how successful I would be with that process or any process. There is nothing worse than being successful in the wrong assignment. I prayed and prayed and the Lord said to me loud and clear, you either choose me or choose this. I chose the Lord and never regretted it. Even though this was a test I believe I had passed from God, I was still in a marriage with someone that didn't want to be as extreme as I was. We would cross over into the New Year at church to rush out so that he could stop at the club and wish his peeps a happy new year. I remember sitting in the car alone, having just left the church at that New Years hour, after refusing to enter into the club with my Ex. I prayed, I worshipped, and Jesus met me there in the car by myself. I couldn't understand why we had to ride by the club to tell everyone happy new years, when they were not riding by the church to make sure we were celebrating new years as well.

Do you know what it's like to damage your life and have to take every bit of the consequences that come with that? If you don't, please don't act as if you can empathize, because you can't. If you married Mr. or Mrs. Right, you will never be able to seriously empathize with someone that married Mr. or Mrs. Wrong. Please don't try and beat anyone up over the head that has chosen Mr. or Mrs. Wrong because you have no idea what they are going through. Perhaps you wouldn't have made it half way through their testimony, it so easy to judge, instead think of ways you can demonstrate how you care for them in spite their wrong choices. Perhaps you didn't choose to marry the wrong person, but do not act as if you have never made a wrong major choice in your life. If you feel as if you haven't I pray that you will be delivered from a form of sickness. I know that my experiences have made me ever so sensitive to other people and their lives.

There began my wilderness experience after all this time of just going to church. It wasn't until I actually moved back to my home town after my first year of college and positioned myself in a marriage that was not healthy that I could finally hear God's voice loud and clear in my life. This was the most broken time of my life, but I was so close to the Lord and I could feel he was close to me. I grew in the Lord like a wildflower during this time. Everything that was deposited in me earlier seemed to have taken root and sprung up during these years of my life. I thank God for my wilderness experience, and wished my marriage would have lasted a lifetime as marriage is designed to last, however I am all the more certain as God has confirmed overtime that I am to move forward forgetting those things that are behind, pressing forward toward the mark of the high calling of Christ Jesus. After studying the blood friendship covenant my entire being was shaken to its core when I got the revelation of what God had done specifically for me. I may be deemed nuts for sharing it, however He told me that He set me apart from the foundation of the world and he would not allow me to spiritually ratify a covenant with one I was not ordained to be one flesh with. The revelation was that my voice carries my blood, which carries my spirit. On the very day that I was to pronounce and ratify a marriage covenant with someone my voice was GONE. I believe with all of my heart that God knew what would happen and the result of that marriage. To people it looked like a covenant took place, and there was certainly a contract involved, however God revealed to me that he kept me in a way that only he could do in withholding my voice at that very moment. I don't believe that God was caught by surprise by my divorce, even though I was. I know that God is in the details, and I know that he loved me enough to do for me what is not always normally done. I am sure you have your own testimonies of how God came through for you personally in a custom fit way. Rationally it may not make sense to others, yet, God revealed this to me.

Anytime it was just him and I alone he quickly gathered his things and said the famous words of "I'll meet up with you later". I found myself alone all the time. It was where I grew up for real. I never went back to another club or bar, I threw away all music except gospel, and I cut away all unhealthy friendships and relationships. I was always at church, sometimes I went to services alone, but that was okay. I prayed to God about being filled with his Spirit and began speaking in tongues for the first time in my life, it was like a metamorphosis was going on when I was at home alone during that wilderness of my life, I would look in the mirror to meet someone my soul longed to be introduced to. I saw myself maturing and growing immensely. The warfare was serious.

I would often watch TBN. He would come home and complain that I was watching too much of that God show, yes the same man that was going to church, in ministry, at every service right alongside of me. I'd go into the basement to watch it there so I wouldn't disturb his preference; he'd follow me and pull the TV cord right out of the wall. I was becoming self-righteous so I was told.

My husband was never home with me, but always off with his frat brothers or in his home town where his family was. As sad as I was about this, I was excited about Jesus and enrolled into every class I could at church. I came to serve whenever I was needed. I went on retreats and revivals and was fine being married to who I was married to. It was what it was. I had Jesus and he was enough! I got used to our life, I prayed for things to get better. I never stopped praying for him, and would often tell him about things the men were doing at the church that he could partake in if he'd like. He eventually did for a little while, but after a point didn't find interest in being consistent. I didn't always feel safe. There were many times where I'd wake up at two or three AM in the morning and something would say go downstairs. I'd go downstairs to find my front door unlocked or barely closed.

There was one day in particular I thought would have been the game changer in our marriage. One day I told him not to go to his home town that particular day and he grabbed his keys off the counter got in his car, blasted his music and hit the highway. A few hours later he had an experience I thought would have changed him for the better. He was coming out of the barbershop and a pedestrian was walking and he hit the guy. He got out of the car and as he was headed toward the guy, the man pulled out a gun and started shooting at him. He shot up his car and wouldn't stop shooting. He came home that day with five bullet holes in his car, the same car that I had often laid hands on, on my way in the house from work. All bullets passed him even though he rode back on Route eight with a completely cracked windshield. I knew that was the thing that would wake him up to the behavior that wouldn't cease. Sadly I was wrong.

Looking back, I understand what happened between us. I was growing rapidly and he was not. I was okay with that and just wanted us to work, even if that meant later down the line. I thought perhaps we will have children and I can focus on raising children and praying for my husband's light bulb to come on, as I was growing and maturing myself. We had both been under the same teaching and preaching and were reading the same books etc. for years, but there was no evident of change with him. I didn't understand how anybody could sit under the awesome teaching we were under and still remain the same for years. During our marriage classes, we both were able to recognize that we came from broken homes and that we could create something different for our family, if we chose to do so. We both agreed to start fresh with how we wanted our lives to look like regardless of our background. Although we agreed to this together, I later discovered it wasn't we who were following through with this or truly wanted this, it was me.

In life as ideal as it may be to prepare adequately for marriage there are many things that occur along the way from birth to the altar where one says I do that has a tremendous impact upon the rest of their lives. Those who have been taught appropriately and prepared substantially have a higher probability of a successful marriage, yet the majority learns after the ceremony and wedding has taken place as a result of the fatherless generation. There tends to be growth and maturing along the way and for some it's too late when the point of maturity blossoms. I can witness this first hand and so can many others. Yet I find it interesting that many are not transparent in the role of leading others. Instead what replaces transparency is denial and numbness to the painful realities that many live in. I'll never forget the prayer my ex spouse prayed the very last time I left our home. Although the enemy meant the destruction of our relationship for evil, far in advance before we ever got to the altar, I believe that God will and has used what the enemy meant for evil, for good so that his purpose will manifest in our lives and in the earth. As much as I desired with all my heart for our marriage to work, the reality of who we both are is grounded, and as much as we don't like to admit this, with the intent of being hopeful and walking in faith, and that is some people don't and won't ever change. Perhaps things about the person may, but the essence and the core of a person typically remains the same. This is something God understands as to why as much as he wishes for none to perish, many perish. As much as he desired to give Lucifer the authority and beauty in the beginning he had, he realized that the situation was something that would never change. Therefore adjustments must be made depending on how threatening situations may be, and as tough as it may be, it must be done. I know how this will be viewed especially by people who believe they can control other people, which by the way is witchcraft. God gave us dominion over everything in the earth in the beginning but the one thing he told us not to control is another person. How many people do exactly that? It is masked and hidden behind all types of explanations, yet at the end of the day the truth of the matter is the only person you are suited to control is yourself and even you must be submitted to the Holy Spirit who helps where the members of your body and earthly being is in desperate need of the help and comfort of Holy Spirit. I know that God used my ex and myself to help one another grow and mature in ways unimaginable, and I am forever grateful for his willingness to take me as his wife at such a young age, even though neither of us knew how to model a successful Christian marriage, there was something birthed in both of us that will result in ministering to many with similar struggles and testimonies. I pray that God be with you and the Lord will watch between me and thee, and that I see you in glory.

I understood that he went to church growing up, which was the church we were married in, but in his home too, there was no Godly principles instilled or practiced. I didn't learn until after our second year of marriage when he told me that he was not saved at all when we met or when we got married. He finally admitted for the first time that he went to church growing up time to time, but he wasn't saved and didn't know anything about living a saved life until we got married. He wanted to marry me and he didn't want me to be upset with him for knowing the truth of him not being saved. I thought we were on the same level of being saved, which was being out of fellowship with God with the intent of rededicating our lives back to Christ. I was wrong. Had I taken the adequate time and did a thorough inspection I would have clearly realized that this is not someone I should be building a lifetime relationship with, but many pieces were missing with me as well. There were so many red flags and warnings during our relationship but I couldn't clearly see them because I was too sowing to the flesh at that time and not to the spirit.

I do have one vivid memory of riding on the highway with him and I felt in my spirit that I was the only live person in the car. Of course we were both alive physically and he was driving, but the in the atmosphere of the car I felt in my core that I was riding with someone who was not conscious or alive. I mention this so that others, who may be not be where I was will not turn a deaf ear to the signs. I didn't know how to read them then as I could clearly read something like this now. Wait before saying I do! Even if you have been together for years, and have an established relationship, trust me when I say you wouldn't want to stomach half the pain that comes with marrying the wrong person. If you have already made this decision, I strongly encourage you to put all of your faith and trust in the Lord by submitting to your choice and be patient for it all to work out for your good if you are a child of God. God will either transform your spouse by your dedicated life to Christ or he will deliver you if it be his will, nevertheless God knows how much we can handle.

I appreciated him being honest with me about his salvation that night he told me the truth. At that moment I led him to the Lord. At that moment there was the loudest bang on our front door, and we opened the door to find no one there. I knew what the bang was, but didn't say anything. After this we still struggled and I expected it as we were unevenly yoked in many areas. I yielded to the consequences of reaping that in which I sowed. I didn't do the work necessary to determine if the man I was agreeing to marry was ready to be what I was expecting him to be, neither did I know how or what things to incorporate in this process. I tied myself to someone that originated in sin and ended in death. It was painful but I was hopeful. I didn't desire to be with anyone else except him. I knew things were not perfect but I wanted help for us. For the first time after 3 years I went to a couple we had come to know within our church to help us. In class they often talked about seeking help when you need it and holding one another accountable. So I went over their home in the hopes to get help. My husband was furious when he found out I was going to get help and tried to stop me from going over there. He kept yelling we don't need people we have God who can help us. He knew that things would be exposed and accountability was about to set in. I thought that getting help was the best thing to do, but he refused to come get help with me. So I went by myself several times until he later joined.

Things didn't change. For the sake of privacy every testimony of the things I had to overcome in my marriage are not recorded. I kept telling myself, things are going to get better. I'll just focus on

Jesus, church, ministry, and hopefully children, and pray for us. I knew in my heart that I had decided to marry this man and I was going to be with him for the rest of my life. No matter how many times he would come home after midnight, how he would always be with his frat brothers or in his home town with his side of the family. There was nothing I could do or say, because I chose to marry him. I remained in guilt throughout the marriage and after separating a few times, this was the main reason I went back. There was a way of escape provided and I had shut God's door every time, because I believed this is what I should endure and that I didn't deserve to be out of the marriage I chose.

As time passed, he still wanted to go places that I disagreed with going to and refrained from attending. I wanted to go to church; he wanted to go do his thing. I was no longer the eighteen year old girl he met that just graduated high school, and I was transforming into someone he was repelled by and afraid of.

The third year of our marriage I had a breaking point when things were not getting better after meeting with our mentors. I noticed a pattern was being set where birthdays and holidays would roll around and I'd be spending them alone. I couldn't find him and he would often meet up with me on Sunday morning in the church parking lot for service as if we'd been together the entire week. I recall a birthday party he had in his home town that I was not aware of or invited to, he was kind enough to bring home the balloons, a plate of food and some left over cake from his birthday celebration that was supposedly for just a few family and friends, and come to find out from pictures it was a grand event. It seemed like the more I prayed the worst it got. Infidelity was eventually admitted. I sensed it and knew it but there was just never any proof that I had, neither did I care. I didn't want to lose him or what we were trying to build; I guess I should say what I was trying to build. We went back and forth about the situation of him cheating and were finally invited to meet with my pastor about our marriage. My pastor took note of my faithfulness and offered to help me as he stated he saw a unique call of God.

It was not a pretty thing to lay all your dirty laundry out on your pastor's kitchen table. Many details were discussed openly in regards to reoccurring offenses, nevertheless my pastor was a great mediator and he didn't pick sides even though I had been raised under him since a youth. He was fair. He knew I had chosen to marry him and he knew of the issues that were occurring. He asked me one question after hearing about what was going on and he said what do you want to do? Do you want to stay or leave due to what had happened in your marriage? I answered: I am going to stay. Regardless if there was a legitimate reason to divorce I wanted my marriage to work, my husband was practically the only family I really had in that season. My dad was always there if I needed him, my mom was in between states and was only a call away if I needed her. We had something together and whatever that was, it was enough for me to hold on to at that time. I knew my pastor very well and had learned enough about him from him raising me in the Lord and being around him a lot. I could tell that he was disturbed to hear about what was taking place in my household.

He seemed very unmoved when we left but I could tell that Sunday in the pulpit after talking about adultery and infidelity that he understood where I was. It wasn't that he was okay with what he heard. All I can say is there was a prophetic word released in the house the following Sunday as eye contact was made with my husband: word for word: if you don't shape up God will take your wife and give her to someone else who's worthy. It can be said that he was "just preaching", but I came to learn him a lot better than what he lets on just by following him week in and week out. Like most pastors handle themselves to take on the disturbing news of people, it's usually addressed in the pulpit with an accurate measure of what was really felt. I learned him not from a leadership stand point, but from a sheep and shepherd standpoint. I knew my shepherd's irritations, likes, comforts, and challenges, like a lot of other faithful members.

My husband and I had another action plan this time set in place by our pastor. It was new and the material was great. There was just one issue, we both had to put our foot forwards if change was going to manifest. He had provided us with some new things to review, some really good books that helped and he prayed for us and with us and checked on us. All went well for a few months. After we crossed into another new year things went right back to how they were. There was that pattern I noticed again. He was coming to church and showing up to assigned ministry meetings but he would leave to go do his thing right after. He had learned how to put the church uniform on and be accountable to a certain point without having to change his lifestyle. It is one thing to know that people do this, but to have someone over you that is doing this in a marriage where you're directly affected it's a different ball game. At this point I began growing distant from my husband and I was angry. My anger came out sideways at times as I would totally shut down to him or blow up after trying to suppress it as if I wasn't being affected when in reality, I was. He knew that church people were watching us and would hold him accountable for the things that were disclosed, but he still found ways to work around it. He would leave with friends smelling like drugs and alcohol in the night hours, I would ask him where you are going, just to be told that I didn't have any business knowing what he does or where he goes. I didn't understand why he would portray one thing at church and exuberantly live something else outside of church. I advised him, if this is what he was going to do then to just make it plain that he doesn't want to live a saved life instead of saying he did, yet the actions demonstrated something different. I didn't know where he was at in the Spirit in regards to his maturity in the Lord, but it didn't seem too far, which I could understand from growing up as a child in church but things didn't click for me as well. This was man who was older than me naturally but not spiritually. I knew how patient God was with me as a child, I guess it was my turn. I was looking at myself in him in some ways in relation to my teen years, and wanted nothing more than for him to receive the same revelation I did.

I was not allowed to touch his phone or his laptop. By the third year he pulled all his money from our joint account and opened another. I later discovered private bank accounts and secret credit cards. He would often pull out large sums of our obligated finances when we fought. He would threaten not to pay the mortgage or bills, or buy food when we were fighting, if he didn't get what he wanted. He did just that. I lived month to month in a beautiful home we just purchased not knowing how or when things would be paid because he was not reliable or consistent. It was never the fact that the money was not there, it was predicated on how he felt. If he felt satisfied that month, things got paid, if he didn't the bills were late. He didn't like the design of a husband providing for his wife. I was told, the wife gets a free ride in the deal. So I contributed where necessary. In my marriage I had the perspective that only those who are either not born again or not far in their walks view their wives and families as a burden instead of blessing. That was until I took divorce recovery with other people who had experience divorced to discover that men who are mature believers also can view their wives and families as a burden. We are living in the days where the mentality of "every man for themselves", and "woman" for that matter. Young ladies are not left with many options. Either she can settle for less and experience a man who doesn't want to take care of her, or she can wait for a god fearing mature man of God to later discover he too doesn't want to take care of her either. This is not to say that all people fit into these boxes, but it was alarming to me to discover the latter. What makes it worse is that the "good guy" tends to put the "bad guy" or the new believing guy down as if he is better to have the same heart in the area of not wanting to provide for his family. 1 Timothy 5:8 is more relevant in our generation than ever before.

December of 2010 I was walking across the stage to earn my Bachelor's Degree. On my graduation day I couldn't think of anything other than the night before. This was the first time I was told that he wished I would kill myself and die. The warfare was certainly not against one another in the flesh, the spiritual wickedness in high places was evident in our relationship and it became more difficult to handle. It was clear that he liked his freedom and he just was not ready to live by the rules of marriage. I had become a supervisor with a great organization and I was facing some serious situations on my job where the man I was working under was doing some very inappropriate things that began to scare me and make me very uncomfortable. Arrangements for me to be out of town on weekends with him were arranged, and it didn't seem like I had a choice as they were "business related" if I wanted to keep my job. In my spirit I knew what it was. I didn't feel safe and I told my husband often that I don't feel safe being with the man I had to report to at work. The comments and actions began to confirm what was obvious to me but hidden from others. We would take road trips together for business, and it was just he and I. I made a report with human resources after many offenses occurred and after they decided not do anything about it as he brought in a large portion of their income, I respectfully resigned with my two weeks' notice. When I would tell my husband what was going on at work, he could care less.

When I told my spouse that I was leaving the job he was furious. He said he didn't care what I was facing at work; neither did he care what the man was doing to me, as long as I brought home that paycheck. I was deeply grieved to know that my husband could care less of what I was going through at work as someone who was to be my protector, but yet he was my choice in my blindness, in my ignorance, and I submitted to my choice. I worked around nothing but men as I was supervising men old enough to be my father who were all very respectful to me, having major responsibilities most young black women don't have. Why did I take the job you ask? Believe it or not, but there, is where the Lord taught me about authority. Here is where the Lord trained me in areas I'd never imagined. I was learning from the sermon series at church about servant leadership at the time I was supervising and dispatching. I learned the administrative, the operational side of kingdom principles, and even the spiritual side of leadership and authority, not by reading on it, but by leading in the position I had, through experiencing it. I was there long enough to get what God wanted me to get. It's funny how God does things. You should have seen those faces when I showed up to semi-tractor trailer garages to do business and to shadow my drivers. They couldn't believe I was the fleet manager. Yet God had a plan that no one understood, not even myself until I recognized later that the very things I learned on that job would help me later in assignments God would give to me.

I am not sharing my testimony to paint a picture of how "bad" he my ex was. In reality he had great characteristics. He was great with his hands. He could fix anything. He was a great dresser and had a lot of charisma. Young men often would be drawn to him as they wanted to hang around him all the time. I tell you these things so that you will see what I have overcome and for you to know if you have made a choice similar to mine, that there is hope for you too. I am not able to give anyone any advice if I have not overcame the same thing I am advising you to overcome. Yes we had some physical abuses within the marriage in addition to emotional and infidelity. For example, if someone's husband is physically abusing them, there is no way I can give you a word of encouragement if I am allowing my husband to physically abuse me. This happens often. Encouragement and advice is given to someone where it's not being practiced in the advisor's life. This makes it difficult to trust someone that is trying to "help" when they cannot even help themselves.

There were few who knew what was really going on behind closed doors. I had filed for a divorce and ended up cancelling it all after being encouraged to stay by church people. I saved up enough to file for a divorce, and it was not until I put divorce papers in front of him that he showed an attempt to change for real. So what did I do? Of course, I reached out to my lawyer and cancelled the divorce and lost all of what I saved to file and move on. I was excited that my husband wanted to change and make it work.

As usual for a few months all went well then our norm began of dysfunction. I went to visit him at work one day in the afternoon and he was not there. It was well past his lunch hour and the Holy Spirit told me exactly where he was. I went right to where I knew he was, and I was right, the frat house. I pulled up to find his groupies walking out to their car as I was pulling up to walk in. I walked inside and sat on the couch wondering where he was as his car was sitting outside, and that is when his friend continued to call him frantically to come downstairs because I was downstairs for him. After waiting another fifteen minutes or so he finally came down with the flushed I'm busted face. He was clearly embarrassed as his friends where in the living room with us and he began yelling at me about coming inside to find him. I thought we had dealt with the secrecy, lying, and infidelity, however I was mistaken.

This was the time of our four year anniversary. I packed my bags on our anniversary and I moved out of the home we just purchased. It was a repeat of the same anniversary a year prior. A year prior was the first time we separated on our third year anniversary, that following spring we separated when I filed for the divorce to later cancel it, and that fall I was leaving again on our anniversary, AGAIN. Each time we separated my mother was living in another state at the time and had an apartment in our town that was vacant where I stayed. It just so happened that every time we separated she was headed back out, and her apartment was available for me to come and get peace of mind again. I was able to remove myself from our atmosphere to hear God and fast and pray. I would often get strengthened and refreshed. I'd plan on moving on with my life while there, just to go right back home when my mother was headed back in town. The last time I even got my own apartment. I didn't plan on filing for a divorce this time as it's not what I really wanted, only to be away and separated was enough for me. I didn't want to divorce, I wanted to give him a chance to get himself together and be strengthened myself and work on being patient with my husband so I could go back and we could try it again. I wanted something different for my life other than what I experienced growing up. I wanted to break the generational curse of divorce. I wanted us to work, even if I carried us the entire time. This was something I really believed I had the capacity to do, how much I have grown in wisdom and understanding since then.

The reality was that I was so convicted for marrying someone I should not have. I remember when we lived together before marriage I would get down on the side of my bed and pray to God to let us get married if this is what is best. How naïve I was, there was so much more to it than just that prayer so I learned. With where I was I believed I did the best I could have regarding certain areas of blindness. It wasn't suitable to just pray, Lord let's make it right and get married, there were so many variables I hadn't ever discovered regarding what a successful marriage looks like and before that was revealed damage was already done and life had taken its course. Because of my testimony I have much more sensitivity towards those who have experienced the same. I understand what it's like to sow in ignorance and blindness and to reap in revelation and greater understanding. I know there are people who act as if they have never been blind or ignorant before in their lives, and I applaud that one percent, however for the rest of us know that God cares about you and your situation. I believe that I have a grace on my life for "crisis" ministry. The key to overcoming in all troubles, trials, and tribulations is to always walk with God. I was walking with God before I met my spouse, I was walking with God during our broken marriage, and after the divorce. Walking and serving the Lord was not something I did because all of a sudden something jumped off in my life. That was a part of who I was since I was a child even though I hadn't developed in maturity in certain areas. I did have a backslidden period of time in my life during college, but I thank God it didn't last long and he was faithful to pulling me back in. I have come to recognize the faithfulness of saints with the purpose of either pleasing man or pleasing God. I can say that I am not faithful to God and the church nor the things of God to receive recognition from people, but I am faithful to God and the things of God for my intimacy with the Lord. Bible study is good, prayer, fasting, casting out devils, and so forth are all important as we must understand particular laws and how things work, yet at the end of the day prayerfully the goal of all of this is to enhance one's relationship with God, as we who belong to Him will spend eternity with Him. I think it's great we are going to rule and reign in heaven; however I will be glad just to be with Jesus for eternity. We as believers often worship the word of God and not the person behind the word. How often have you heard The Word! The Word! The Word!? Yet Moses, Abraham, Isaac, and Jacob had no bible, but they all had a relationship with God. What was Enoch reading as he walked in close fellowship with God? He walked with God and he was naught. I love this scripture. Enoch was not reading scriptures, he was walking with the God behind the written Word of God. Even when Seth was born to Adam and Eve, it is written that this is the time when people began to call the Lord by name, yet they knew the Lord and walked with Him before the word was written. What was written was once primarily spoken orally from generation to generation. Yes, eventually writings and manuscripts were recorded yet all of it was with the intent for the soon to come new birth of the believer of the Spirit of God, to know God personally as He now lives inside of the believer. The Bible was written to demonstrate God's redemptive work to reconcile man back to God through Jesus Christ. When one becomes saved the introduction to the Kingdom is to come and know Jesus Christ the son of the living God, and when we stand before him and enter into his joy and eternal glory it is predicated on knowing him. This is not to say we don't need to know the Word of God, and it's not to say that it is not extremely vital to the believer, because it is Spirit and life (John 6:63), and makes all the difference in growing and maturing and overcoming in this life. Walking with the Lord in sincerity of heart will open and close so many doors you are not even aware that need to be opened or closed. Being content with where you are will help as well. I did not desire to be married to someone else, but only that my marriage would somehow work in the end, yet I believe being content with where I was in my heart opened the door spiritually for God to work through my experience so that I would have an expected end in that area. God can see farther down the line than what we could ever see, think, or imagine, and it's in trusting Him, that we proper. What typically would have occurred, or should have occurred to destroy or kill you will not be able to prosper in any way shape or form when you belong to God. My Ex was not God's choice for me, he was my choice. I was trying to do everything that I knew to do right when I got the revelation but it was just too late at that time. I had come from a home of origin where divorce was everywhere. My grandmother divorced a man after a few years of marriage. She married my granddad a few years later and they were married over fifty years until he passed away at the age of eighty. My other grandmother was married to my granddad that was physically abusive for 23 years of marriage. She even lost a child from the physical abuse she endured. She divorced him after 23 years of marriage. After one year of divorce she remarried him, to later separate due to the same behaviors. My mother was raised seeing this and decided she would never let a man treat her that way. She experienced divorce herself. There I was holding onto a marriage because I was trying to break this generational curse of divorce. I had a perfect life looking from the outside in. Wasn't that good enough? Over time we would get the inside right, right? We made a beautiful couple, we were educated, had great paying jobs, a beautiful house we had just bought, we went to one of the greatest churches in the city, we were popular, we were in ministry, we were so broken, so very very broken! If it hadn't been for God and those helping us within our church, I know I would have certainly lost my mind and I am sure things would have been even worse than what they were. There were so many positive things that our church did in regards to pouring into us. So why didn't it work you ask? Because no matter how much one goes to church, or how good the teaching is, it is has nothing to do with an individual making choices and having a will that overrides God's by way of free will.

That is another primary reason I decided to go back to the marriage. I was supposed to be the one who refused to divorce no matter what in my family. I learned that the very thing that I was avoiding because I wanted to be the saint in my family who represented Christ, was the very thing I'd become familiar with myself. The last ministry that I wanted was a ministry having anything to do with divorce. Overtime I have come to realize that this is a ministry that God hand selected me for. As I reflect on my family and life, the revelation God has given me is that even though I come from brokenness, I also have a heart to please God, live by his ways, and live a life dedicated to the work of the Kingdom of God. The major revelation is that I am not the only one, and there are so many where I am as well, who have become dormant to their call because of how they are put down within religious settings. Before I divorced I experienced a feeling that many married people feel but won't admit. And that feeling is, if I divorce, then that means I am not saved. This is how many people look at others or label with our rationality. Regardless of the issues that are known to occur in marriages, there is something more heroic and godly that is more so accepted in the society of church about remaining in a marriage no matter what is beyond worst. Even if it is life threatening and one's safety is in danger. Jesus Christ clearly spoke on a biblical release in the area of adultery in Matthew 19:9, however it's not uncommon for the church to communicate the message of "We don't care what Jesus said, we don't agree with biblical release of any kind". This may not be said verbally; however it can communicate in other ways. This message given is not biblical, and it brushes over what God himself indicated in regards to being released. You often hear the scripture of Jesus addressing the Pharisee's question by referring back to the original intent of marriage in the beginning, yet rarely is the later passage referenced as much as the first. I learned overtime that divorce is not something that can separate me from the love of Christ (Romans 8:31-39), and it doesn't dictate my salvation, even though it felt like it did in my mind as I was going through it. Oh how I have won that mental battle by now.

I know what it's like to be married and encounter someone who is divorced. You don't want to treat them wrong, but I'd admit I felt awkward even talking to them at church as we all know God hates divorce. I was young and didn't fully understand all the implications of that threshing. I never thought that I'd be the person later in life, that I didn't want to talk to. I say that because people act as if they understand. They will deal with you in public just for face value, but know they don't want to associate with you because you'll interrupt their image, particularly more so young adults who have never been married, newlyweds, or those very young in ministry who have no idea what challenges are faced in a good marriage, let alone a bad one. Of course they will deal with you on the basis of ministering to you, but it is like divorcees are treated as second class Christians. Yes that's right, we lift up a murder named Paul, but someone that is divorced, even for a legitimate biblical reason, we tend to place severe surpassing judgment on them, which does not reflect God's heart or Word. Not everyone is this way, however there are many who are.

I am a witness that God will bless your Ishmael and your mess. Not that they should be created, yet God reigns on the just and the unjust, even if we pretend he only blesses those who belong to him. Many people who don't belong to God are blessed in several areas because every human being was created in the image of God, even though all may not be born again of the Spirit of God. Just as all gifts come from God. You often see psychics, and astrologers and people who do have a gift, however the gift has been distorted and contaminated by the enemy, yet the gift originated from God. Nevertheless, He did bless our marriage in several ways after we entered our covenant; however there was no lasting peace when the blessings came. The blessing of the Lord makes rich and he adds no sorrow to it (Proverbs 10:22). I did experience the sorrow of being blessed in a way that wasn't originally designed by God, but He did pour out many blessings on us in spite of it all. I believe that God was giving us multiple chances to get it right, all the while opening the door for me to leave legitimately after our covenant had been broken several times. I just couldn't let it go. I couldn't let my marriage go. I was supposed to be happy with him. What gave me the strength to stay when I did, was grasping the mindset of being able to stay with him, even if it was for others, and not myself, as it's not about me. The example I was demonstrating to others was that it's okay to be treated any way by someone without any boundaries. We were supposed to have this testimony of overcoming and beating the odds. Yes, we could have stayed together and on the outside appeared to have this testimony, however I know in my knower that would have been far from the truth. I knew in my spirit that no matter how many times I went back or if we would reach that twenty, that thirty or, forty year mark, that I needed to let it go because the set ways that had been hardwired within. As a youth, there is more of an impacting chance for one to be transformed and do an about face toward God's ways, more so it is the older one gets. All things are possible with God, however the older one gets, the more difficult it can become for that individual to adjust to changes within themselves that are embedded in their core. It is one thing to know that prayer can change the most difficult of circumstances and people, at the same time realizing that the people you are praying for have to play their part as well. The bible says there will always be the poor and the rich among us, there will always be good and evil present as long as we are on this earth, and there will always be people who claim to know God, and yet do not, due to lack of evidence in their walks with Christ. You may say, you had no faith, you didn't pray hard enough. Some things you know in your knower and there are no words to explain them. This I knew in my knower and after miracles signs and wonders that became manifested in the last part of our relationship, I knew it was confirmed that I'd have to do the undesirable and allow God to restore what he saw necessary. Some books that helped me during this time were Boundaries and Necessary Endings by Dr. Henry Cloud. I understand this may be off the wall and very difficult for traditional believers who are totally boxed into life working out in one set way and that's all. Please understand it is not my goal to move away from the "things of God" which you may perceive, in fact if you studied a little deeper, you may actually see how biblical it is instead of taking one or two scriptures in the entire Word of God to disregard the many others that imply additional truths we tend to discredit. I quote Kathryn Kuhlman who said the only thing outside of the word of God that I can give to you, is my own personal experience, that is the only thing someone can give to another, is their own personal experience, always remember that! You may know the scripture to support something, yet if you have never experienced such you have no idea of the impacts and it's easier for you to criticize those who have had negative experiences. This isn't to say that experience is not a great teacher as we discussed in the introduction, but it is to say experience leaves a more memorable mark on one. For example, there may be someone who graduated with a degree in management, and there may be another who does not have the degree but who has been promoted to management by way of learning the system. The person who was promoted may get the job over the one with the degree because of the experience that person has to get the job done. If you are going to a heart surgeon, do you want the one who has learned only by way of other's experiences and from being fresh out of medical school? Or would you prefer the one who has thirty years of experience on heart surgery? All circumstances vary which require different preferences.

There were couples who were trying to help us who would often say the same thing to me. I cannot tell you what decision to make; only you can decide what you must do. My pastor finally asked a question in a class I was in of his, why are you willing to remain married to someone who is hurting you in this same way? In the church we often preach keep hope alive, when in reality hope for certain situations needs to die because if not you will be destroyed. For example if your wife continues to put her hands on you for several years, you may want to get hopeless about her ceasing at some point, come out of denial, and face reality. I know you may never hear a perspective like this in a church setting, but God got hopeless about Satan repenting and coming to reconciliation with him, in fact, God never granted Satan an opportunity because there was no hope for that situation. All things work together for the good of the Lord and the called according to His purpose because there is too much potential in the seed of God for Him to allow it to be destroyed or not bear fruit, because in being connected to Him spiritually, one must bear fruit.

Nevertheless after moving out into my own apartment what do you think I did? Correct! I moved right back into our home to try it again. This time it was the worst time. It seemed to get worse and worse after I would go back, but the last time was my "that's all folks" for me time. After I moved back things went right back to the way they were. You may ask well, where were the babies during this marriage. Disclosing what happened without sharing too many details to reserve the privacy of my ex-spouse, I'll just say we were told by the doctor that we are both fertile as ever, however fertility could have been increased by certain measures. Truth of the matter regardless of what the doctor advised, I know that God was covering me during that seven year relationship, even when I wanted to have his child.

Certain medical measures were never ever taken that the doctor advised would be needed if we wanted to conceive. When we crossed over into the New Year I started praying and fasting about what God would have me do. I told him that if he wanted me to leave this marriage that he never intended for me to be in, then He'd have to show me by signs, miracles, and wonders. I told God in my prayer that if things will remain the same this time then I will move on with my life. I very much wanted to have a child in the misery of my marriage in the hopes that I could find some peace by raising a son or daughter in the broken marriage I was in. I prayed to God, Lord bless us with a child, that's what we need, that will bring us closer together. I kept praying to God to please confirm that I am to remain in my marriage by allowing us to have a child. I fasted and prayed, and prayed and fasted and when I had settled in my heart and mind to finally leave, that's when it happened. Needless to say the very last time I was intimate with my husband out of seven year relationship was the very first time I ever got pregnant by him. The night before I found out I was expecting was a night I'll never forget as long as I live. I thought surely it must be God's will for us to remain together because God specifically answered my prayer to what I was presently fasting and praying about. We were doing absolutely horrible when I found out I was pregnant. I couldn't believe it! God heard my prayers and he was answering. I knew this would solve all of our problems and we would be happy and once the child was born, he was going to really change for the better if not for me for our child that was on the way. That baby was supposed to fix all of our problems, so I thought. I thought perhaps this would be the thing to bring us close together with another brand new start until his reaction was manifested. I was refused help in many areas after I told him I was pregnant. I remember putting a toy truck on his dresser with our picture and some baby items, to find them removed when he'd go in the room. Each time I saw them removed my heart was pierced. One of the most disheartening encounters was when he said he hoped I lose the baby because he wasn't excited nor did he want a child with me. He'd get a new wife and home I was told. I made mistakes in our marriage. I expected him to be my God, I worshipped him to an extent and when I wasn't getting the results that only Jesus could give me, he'd know it with some harsh things I's say. One thing I never did or felt comfortable doing was cheating on my spouse. We were both hurt and broken and in need of help. Regardless of how bad things got, I never sought affection or sex from another person. Sadly I can't say the same for him. He didn't believe that adultery was "that bad" so he would say, neither did he understand the level of offense in marriage it took. During this time we would often fight as we were headed to church, fellowships, and events. I remember contemplating these things on the way walking in the door to what should have been fun nights with our church body. I had to put on the mask of I'm alright, endure the card games, the board games, and laughter and jokes everyone around me seemed to be enjoying as I watched him appear to be in love with me for a few hours, only to get back in the car on the way home being miles apart.

Here we were at the beginning of a brand new year and I was at the lowest point I had ever been in my entire life. I didn't want to live. I wanted so badly to die and escape the misery I was engulfed in. I had recently heard of a young lady I was friends with in high school by the first name of Taylor. She was shot to death, and it was said that she committed suicide. I kept thinking of our friendship in high school, and understood the pain that could drive you to this insane point of no return. This was the time I was desperately in need of a more reliable vehicle and my husband refused me to receive one. I had the income from working to get one, but he kept saying no. He preferred that I drive the unreliable vehicle instead. So we went with his decision because he was the head. He took the money we could have used for a better car and had some repairs on the unreliable car I had. A few weeks later we were driving home from his home town the day after Christmas to get into a terrible accident in the middle of the highway because the car didn't have all the repairs needed at the time.

He was the one driving that day, and from that point we headed straight to the dealership where I would be able to get a more reliable car moving forward. We were on the highway and spun around several times hitting the side rail. Thank God for divine protection, but it's not a safe situation when the leader is not concerned or serious about your safety and you have to listen to the one over you. I kept thinking about Taylor and I decide one night that I was going to do the same as she did. I loaded a gun we had in the house for protective measures and one night while he was gone I said this is it, I can't wake up tomorrow and face the same old same old. I was carrying so much as a young lady that I could not bear it anymore. I called him right before I planned to pull the trigger and told him that I am killing myself before morning. His reply was I can't stop you, do what you feel you need to do, but if you're going to do it, do it and don't play about it. Why I thought I'd get a little assurance from him, is beyond me. That was that. I hung up and said okay. Not even one minute after I hung up the phone, a young lady from my church who I had few interactions with called me right before I was about to pull the trigger. She called to tell me how much she admired my fight in the Lord and how my faithfulness was an inspiration to her. Monique was so loving and kind. That night without a doubt she was my angel. She has no idea to this day, what she interrupted and how God used her to stop my stupidity. I had never attempted suicide before; neither did I ever think I would especially as a believer who knew what it was like to experience God's peace, joy, love, and so much more. You'd be surprised what things you would experience if you've never been down that road. All I can say is right before God delivers you from any stronghold, things start getting wild and unexplainable, but hold on to God's unchanging hand and you will come out of fire cold without the smell of smoke! Your stronghold may not be a life threatening marriage, perhaps it may be another serious tribulation.

The very next day I found out I was pregnant. I had received a call from my grandmother who didn't even know I was pregnant who told me that she dreamed I lost a baby and in the dream there was a big black truck in the dream. She said that the Lord put a song in her spirit for me when she woke up from the dream. That song was in my spirit over the next few months as I faced the final breaking away of the toxic relationship I willingly planted myself in. That Sunday at church, I'll never forget that service. It was the very last service I was in at my home church. I felt the power of the Holy Spirit so thick on me as I was six weeks pregnant. The mother of my pastor kept looking at me shaking her head yes, it's like she could see everything I was carrying other than the baby. That was the last time I saw her before she died. The song that was sung by the choir that morning was the same song I would hear later on the radio about midnight as I drove myself to the Emergency Room. After service I went to my Bishop for prayer and he laid his hands on me and prayed against everything and anything that would derail, steal my destiny, or come against me to hurt me. A few days later near the end of February about midnight I started to clot, and I drove myself to the ER as my spouse was in his home town. He eventually arrived. It wasn't until that moment when I was losing our child on that hospital bed when he started arguing with me that I knew me or any children that would come along would be in great danger with this man's way of thinking and behavior. We went home that night after being told that the seed implanted an eighth of a millimeter in the wrong spot in my cervix, had it been a tad bit closer above the cervix, then it would have fertilized just right according to the doctor. I do not believe I became pregnant during the time I came pregnant for no reason at all. Of all the time I could have become pregnant, why then? I don't believe the timing of my pregnancy, nor did the miscarriage happen at the time it happened just because of biology. There could be legitimate reasons according to science, but just like the red sea parted for the children of Israel, perhaps science can show a pattern of winds that pulled the water up on both sides, but I'd ask, why did it have to part at the very moment the children of Israel needed to walk through it? Why not the day before, or the day after? I believe that God rescues his children just in the nick of time so that no one can take the credit or glory, so that there is no doubt about who the deliverer is.

That following week my supervisor extended some extra days to me due to my medical condition. God had placed me at safe place working for a woman of God at my church who was well aware of what I had been going through at home. People tend to think that when a woman miscarries it happens at the click of fingers and is over in a jiffy. It took up to three weeks for my child to fully say goodbye to me as I was back and forth to the doctor's office. It wasn't long before I found a lawyer who would meet with me and filed my divorce. On the day I was headed to my appointment with my lawyer was the first time I had realized on the back of my new car were clear see through sticker letters that read T-A-Y-L-O-R. I immediately saw my old friend's face and my near death experience the night before I found out that I was expecting. I tried to take the stickers off as Taylor wasn't my name, but I heard a still small voice say, leave it on and don't take it off because it's a testament to what I have delivered you from. It's a testament that I should be dead and gone as Taylor was in the earth, but God delivered me and showed up in my Taylor moment. Till this day as I enter my car I never fail to glance at those clear letters that reminds me of my grandmother's song that I have decided to follow Jesus, no turning back, no turning back! It was what the Lord used to carry me through a process of divorce over the months and years to keep me away, as it was my nature to always just go back after a certain amount of time passed. That car sticker was my cherubim that didn't allow me to go back even if I tried. God is certainly in the details!

The experience with my lawyer was not the greatest. There were always files missing, cancellations, advise that didn't make any sense. Let's just say Jesus was my lawyer, another situation where it had to have been God, no one else advocated for me in the court room. Had I listened to some of the advice I was receiving from this lawyer, it would have went a lot differently (I needed my powerful little package), but he was booked. One day I showed up to the court a bit late to turn in papers to keep a hearing and the court literally just when I stepped to the window. As I was walking out of the courthouse a young man who was working in their janitorial department called out to me as he had a key to the area I needed to turn in my papers. He led me in around the side and took my papers and laid them on the appropriate desk for the next morning. We'd run out of pages if I listed the many ways God supernaturally showed up for me during this exodus out of Egypt time in my life. The arrangements were, that I was to keep the home, and he was to leave the house by a certain date, but after he begged to keep the house we purchased I agreed to leave, and let him stay there. Ten minutes after I agreed to give him the house in court he was telling the judge he wanted me out by the end of the week. The people in the court room were surprised at the response due to my affirmation upon giving him the home he asked for, but I wasn't. I know he was taking in a lot as well. When your heart is broken, it's true, your head doesn't work right. Even after all of this my emotions were grasping me and later that day I drove to the house with the hopes that we could give it one last shot, and as I pulled up to the house I saw his new big black truck sitting in the driveway, that I didn't know he just got. The only thing that flashed through my mind was my grandmother's dream. That was the strength that put my car back in drive to move on forever.

Divorce is terrible! The emotions, the pain, the heartbreak causes one to not think right. He didn't understand why I would was no longer keeping the cycle of leaving and coming back. That was the end of it. The last time I saw him was the day we signed the divorce papers. He was on the phone talking to his frat brothers about the exciting cruise they were planning for his celebration. There were a few occasions we had phone interaction due to the property, but he was short and sweet with his what up statements. I knew he moved on and he knew I did as well. He never reached out to me or demonstrated a desire to try it again. Good thing he didn't, because I probably would have gone back, even after all of that. One thing I learned about myself is that I would be a great asset in marriage. You may say, how can you say that if you are divorced. I can say that because it's easy to remain with someone who does not abuse you, cheat on you, or abandon you, but for you to continue returning to someone who does these things to you over and over again, I know it would be easy to remain with someone who doesn't. If you can be married to Nabal, you can be married to anyone. I learned that I would remain in the same place and put in the necessary work regardless of what would happen and the only way I'd move is if God himself moved me. The Lord will make things very clear which path we are to take in life. As I have learned we can either disregard what is being advised or hearken to the voice of the Lord, which will in return be the best choice. I took it upon myself to get professional counseling by a Christian counselor for three months which was one of the greatest times of my life. I soon enrolled into a twelve week grief recovery course. I signed up for divorce recovery sessions. I was shattered, that all of what I was fighting for came to ruin. After being told by my peers at church to save all that shouting for the sanctuary in one of our leadership meetings, I knew in my spirit that I was just cut from a different cloth, and more than my marital status needed to change at this point. I had a few dreams to go to a local body that was associated with my church and was properly released by my pastor.

That was the hardest thing I ever faced in my life, being pulled away from him. My home church, my pastor and the congregation I had known most of my life was familiar to me. I couldn't go off into the world alone. What would happen? What's out there? I didn't know, but I know an angel came and carried me out mightily. I literally felt like an angel came and grabbed me and carried me away, before I knew it I was someplace else looking at people I barely knew. My Bishop had been the neon sign that introduced me really to Christ, who taught me, who shepherd me, who helped me, who loved me. How could I ever leave his church? The burden in my spirit was greater and I believe with all my heart that it was God's will for me to walk out in a land that he'd show me. I found a place to heal and to worship. I completed my necessary requirements as a divorced woman and even got into ministry and helped in areas of leadership. God is so funny. While you're being healed he will use you. Eventually at the right time, I hearkened to the instruction of the Lord to join another local body God led me to after much fasting and praying when that season ended. My peace has never been restored in a dynamic way. I truly learned to follow the cloud of the Lord during that time in my life, something I had never done to that extent before. Following the voice of God was something that I had to learn, and I'm still learning today. I didn't always walk in this wisdom as a youth, but overtime I became familiar with his voice and obeying the Lord's instructions completely without missing a beat. Following the Lord's voice is a life-long process and no one ever arrives. Have trials and tribulations ceased from my life? Absolutely not, but I can say that I have been called to peace and no devil in hell will ever get this peace and joy that doesn't come from the world but from the Lord. Without a shadow of a doubt, I have been called to peace. For some that calling doesn't come in the form of a divorce, for some it may. God is able to deliver you right in your marriage as you remain there. You will receive a different mindset and accept things you never thought you would if you just die to the notion of leaving if this applies to you. For some, they will be delivered physically from the marriage. This example is not to be similar to someone just leaving a marriage for any reason at all. There is a difference between quitting and throwing in the towel verses God supernaturally delivering you out of a stronghold. If your marriage is a stronghold and you are a child of God who is living your life to the standard of Christ after a while any stronghold in your life will break off and away as you become filled with the Lord's spirit, and sadly that stronghold could be a marriage. This is certainly a contradiction to some scriptures as God tells us his desire is for husband and wife to remain together, yet he will break off and away anything from His children that results in oppression and destruction, including a life threatening marriage.

Once again, there is nothing wrong with the way that God intended marriage to be. The impact comes after the fall. We know the intent of marriage from the beginning according to Christ was for husband and wife to last a lifetime here on earth. Due to the fall we cannot ignore the impacts of what has occurred in the earth due to sin. Yes we can rise above circumstances through the power of the

Holy Spirit, yet just as there are consequences to breaking God's law, Jesus saw fit for consequences for those who break marriage covenants, which can in fact be broken. Many operate as if a marriage covenant cannot be broken in this fallen world. Christ specifically releases the spouse who has been offended in this area. Paul even states that if an unbelieving spouse wants to leave after one gets saved in a marriage then you are no longer bound to that person, however what's been religiously taught is that you can never break a binding in marriage, when in fact it's biblically stated in several areas that one can be released, or unbound, depending on the issue at hand.

Marriage and Divorce in the Last Days

We seem to understand when God says in his word that he wishes that no man would perish, being fully aware that people are perishing every single day. In the beginning God created men to live forever and to be with him forever and never to perish, however what God intended in the beginning is not occurring in this fallen world even after Christ has come. Because Christ has come enabling us to come boldly before the throne of grace extending redemption and salvation for men, now there is an opportunity for whosoever will believe that Jesus is the son of God, born of a virgin, who died for our sins, and lives again as our Lord and savior. When it comes to divorce some believers disregard this area as a result of not wanting to deal with it, because of the controversy it brings. It's not always easy to understand that just as God wishes and intends that no man would perish from the beginning, but the reality is that this is congruent with man and wife not divorcing or separating, the reality doesn't equate to what was originally intended or wished from the beginning. God understands this, however many people do not because they just pass down what was passed to them in terms of what is accepted and what is not by way of society. What did we just state? What God has joined together, the word of God says let no man separate. In the beginning this was the intent and God's desire for his institution to operate and remain how he intended it, yet just as God wishes for none to perish and they are perishing every day, divorce and separation is also occurring every day, even though it was not something God wished for or desired from the beginning. There are a number of results from the fall that we have looked at prior and we seem to understand them, but when it comes to divorce, many believers have no clue what to do with this area, so it's just left by the wayside. Marriage is the example of Christ's relationship with the church, and the separation of man and wife as believers are to impact for the witness of the faith to the world, which is why there is typically little tolerance for anything that does not mirror perfection in this area. Marriage is one of the most powerful forces on earth in addition to the church, and the prayer of the saints of God. Just as this is one institution that God heavily uses to advance the Kingdom of God, this is also one of the major areas the enemy attacks. Not only in the area of trying to divide husband and wife, but also in the mindset and acceptance of what is approved by and within churches when it comes to marriages, spouses, and divorce. There have been major principalities set up in the ideas of how religious people should handle divorces and divorcees. One of the most profound wisdom seeds deposited in me by my Apostle is that not only are we judged upon what we believe in regards to Christ and the things of God, but we are also judged upon the things that we support or do not support. If the enemy can get religious people who do not know the person of God to buy into never recognizing or understanding where divorce can be used as a positive in the life of a believer then a wall will be forever be set up by those individuals who the enemy uses in this area. There is nothing originally positive about divorce, yet God can use divorce in the life of a believer for reasons he sees as such. God prefers marriages that last over divorces, yet at times the best possible outcome for certain situations in the lives of God's children on earth, is for a divorce to occur. This could be a divorce that results in reconciliation or not. Sadly this perspective is not valued because it is assumed that if divorced is not mentioned, even for a biblical release, then magically a couple will remain together no matter what occurs, when this is not everyone's reality. It can be compared to the discussion of sex within the church. The idea of, if we don't talk about sex, hopefully none of the youth or singles will engage in it, when in reality they are getting more sex than some married couples. Just because an outcome is not discussed does not negate the fact or decrease it from occurring. When in fact, the divorce rate is increasing within the body of Christ no matter how little we talk about the many contributions of it, other than lack of preparation. Lack of preparation has occurred, is occurring, and will occur if individuals are not educated in time. Prayerfully teachings and testimonies will be embraced to counteract this from happening, yet there will always be marriages that occur in the body of Christ where lack of preparation has occurred. In the last days, they will marry and will be given in marriage. What do we do with the marriages where this occurs? Encourage them to fend for themselves? Or do we yoke together for the Kingdom to discover the heart of the matters? God weighs hearts heavily in the area of marriage. When the scales of justice are pronounced, it may be difficult for men to understand those results, yet he whom the son sets free is free indeed. I have often heard couples praised for standing in their marriages over forty and fifty years with comments as such. "Thank you for living the word out". I believe comments as such are true in one regard, however just because someone has remained married for a lifetime doesn't mean that the word is being lived out in all areas of their life, including the hidden areas of their marriage that are not available for surface observation. Because one has been married for a lifetime doesn't mean that they live the word out when it comes to loving others, or forgiving, or lying, or stealing, or coveting. Just because someone is divorced doesn't mean that they are not living the word out, particularly if God delivered them from someone as he saw fit. I can attest that there are several divorced people I know that are living the word out more than some married people I know, however comments are thrown out there like this and not that it's meant to be confusing or to not true, however I believe in balance. Many people who are freed from life threatening circumstances by God are mistaken as not being sorry for going through separation or divorce when this could be far from the truth. One could be crushed, disheartened, very remorseful and full of regret. The enemy wants you to continually walk and wallow in guilt, condemnation, and grief not ever being able to move on from such a circumstance. When you don't model this attitude, it will be ascribed to not seeing your faults or truly sorry for any mistakes. I believe in taking responsibility for wrong choices and consequences reaped, as I know that I have made impeccable mistakes and have felt the repercussions of them. At the same time, I know beyond a shadow of a doubt that God parted the red sea in my life, and as I watched how He delivered me and carried me, there is no person in the world that could tell me the opposite of what God has or belittle what He did for me. I don't think one should apologize for freedom, because in the end it wasn't free at all. Don't ever let someone keep you stuck in a place that God has released you in. A lot of times people are angry with you because you have the audacity to not carry yourself the way they desire for you to, because they either just don't like you, or don't want to see you free, or they are in a prison of their own. I believe this is the only way that the Apostle Paul could have been so bold. He had the revelation of grace and knowing that the one who gave Him the assignment he was on was none other than God Almighty. Knowing this, whatever comes your way, you know on the inside how God is for you, with you, and will silence every judgment coming your way. Paul was delivered from people who attacked him before he ever got their by God. Honestly, it has been a few years since my divorce and at first it was not easy! However today, I forget that I am divorced, until someone usually comes up to remind me. It's usually someone who doesn't desire to see God's gifts and calling made manifest in my life.

Let's look at a parable of Jesus in regards to separating the wheat from the tares in Matthew 13:24-30.

Here is another story Jesus told: "The Kingdom of Heaven is like a farmer who planted good seed in his field. But that night as the workers slept, his enemy came and planted weeds among the wheat, then slipped away. When the crop began to grow and produce grain, the weeds also grew.

"The farmer's workers went to him and said, 'Sir, the field where you planted that good seed is full of weeds! Where did they come from?'

"'An enemy has done this!' the farmer exclaimed.

"'Should we pull out the weeds?' they asked.

"'No,' he replied, 'you'll uproot the wheat if you do. Let both grow together until the harvest. Then I will tell the harvesters to sort out the weeds, tie them into bundles, and burn them, and to put the wheat in the barn.'"

Statistics continue to reveal the increasing divorce rate within the world, and the body of Christ. Sadly to say, the divorce rate within the body of Christ is parallel to that which is in the world. It tends to come to many as a surprise as to why the divorce rate is increasing within the church. Yes there are factors such as marrying too soon, not having the appropriate guidance and examples in the culture we live in today, choosing the wrong spouse due to self-inflicted circumstances, pressure, lack of resources, and lack of preparation however divorce in the life of a believer is rarely put in the perspective as something that God allowed for a particular reason to bring about good in that believer's life. 2 Thessalonians 2:3 talks about how there will be a great falling away from the faith and from God in the last days on earth. This is apparent in the area of same sex marriage, taking God out of schools and public affairs, our nation depending on the government and worldly principles rather than depending on God in whom we as Americans once trusted, and to the breaking up and away of the unit of the family, whether that is single parent households, babies raising babies, foster and parentless homes, and of course divorce. What we are witnessing in these last days is attributed to the scripture that Jesus will separate the wheat and the tares after they have grown up together. I beg to argue that this is exactly what is taking place in many marriages in these last days that name the name of Christ. Jesus has been separating wheat and tares throughout the earth for generations. Marriage is designed by God that no man should put asunder and that no man should separate what God originally joined together in the beginning. Jesus came to the earth fully man yet he was also fully God. In the beginning was the Word, and the Word was with God, and the Word was God (John 1). Jesus said that he will separate the wheat from the tares, and this is exactly what has been happening, is happening, and will continue to happen spiritually in the area of marriages that involve those that belong to Christ. Divorce is nothing that is new under the sun. It has been taking place before they even began recording them, during the days of Moses, and perhaps prior to that. In certain times it was common such as in the day of Moses because of the hardening of hearts. In other areas it was not as common with society as new generations came (such as medieval times and even the GI generation in American culture, however Jesus has been delivering people in many ways shapes and forms in the area of where captives are bounded, including toxic marriages as a result of the fall (such as abuse, abandonment, and adultery). Currently as it is being done in a generation of believers in today's generation that have very little understanding on divorce other than a few scriptures that are commonly taken out of context without insight on why the scriptures are there, who it is written to, and what the message is implying behind it. In order to understand the text we must always consider the context in which it was written, and why it was written. Let's take a look at the symbol of the cross. In the days of the early church the symbol of the cross was nothing to be desired as it meant severe persecution for anyone who associated with it including death. Today in the twenty first century one may see another wearing a cross as a piece of jewelry or associate with it by representing Christianity. Yes in the days of the early church this symbol was not to be worn as such. It is important to understand where the symbol comes from, what it means, and what it meant during that era, however in today's time one should not feel bad for wearing such a symbol for in today's era it often is the symbol associated in the perspective of non-believers that points to Jesus. Therefore in today's time if one sees another wearing a cross it could very well be a witnessing instrument to communicate the message of Christ without having to worry about being put to death. There may be some opposition and persecution to a certain level, however depending on what part of the world one may live in, the consequences of associating with the cross may not lead to death, and it may actually be a way to witness.

We don't understand why the divorce rate keeps increasing or why those that remain standing in their marriages are not having an impact like before on couples that seem to divorce anyway. Divorce has been viewed and understood as defeat, not overcoming, losing, and being beat. In Malachi 2:16 the Lord says clearly that he hates divorce. This scripture is often taken out of context and has been known to be projected upon any divorced person within the church. 2 Timothy 2:15 says that we should study to show thyself approved, rightly dividing the word of truth so that we are not erroneously teaching something that we believe the bible is saying. Misappropriating God's word is something I believe also that God hates. Deuteronomy 4:2 says that God does not want us adding to or taking away from his word. Why does God hate divorce? Has anyone ever asked this? Does God hate divorce just to hate divorce? No, God hates divorce because he was a divorcee himself. He divorced Israel after throwing her into captivity after a number of attempts to try and make things right with her. Israel willingly chose to follow other gods, commit adultery, and disobey and rebel against God even when they knew what they were doing and had repeated chances to repent and turn from evil. Israel was a stick necked people and loved doing evil instead of good. What "church people" fail to realize is that divorce is not something that is new in today's generation. Divorce has been around since before the times of Moses. It started in heaven when Satan lost his mind as if he could still remain in close fellowship with God and still do his own thing too. Yes God divorced Satan from the beginning and there was, is not, and will never be a reconciliation period between the two. Does this mean that God likes divorce then? No, he hates divorce, because he hates what it symbolizes, and he hates how it made himself feel to allow something to break apart that was not originally intended to part. God does not hate the divorcee or the person who is divorced, because God loves people, and no situation, circumstance, or marital status is a pre-requisite for God's love. Yes a loving, generous God, who loves people enough to sacrifice his only begotten son, is the same God that executed judgment on Satan, Adam and Even in the Garden of Eden, and even Israel. That judgment exercised was a divorce. We don't look at this perspective because the only definition we give to divorce is that between a man and woman within an earthly marriage. My friend, when Satan fell from heaven and took one third of the created angels of God along with him to form the kingdom of darkness, there was a major breaking apart and a major divorce that occurred. We need to teach people why God hates divorce, not just that he does. He hates the fact that things did not work out the way they were supposed to and God is acquainted with grief and despair himself about why a relationship was torn asunder. What do you think happened when Moses came down from the mountain with the Ten Commandments excited to present them to the children of Israel in the book of Exodus. God was ready to destroy them. Exodus 32 reads: Then the Lord said I have seen how stubborn and rebellious these people are. Now leave me alone so my fierce anger can blaze against them and I will destroy them. Then I will make you Moses into a great nation. (Here God was intending to divorce Moses from the people), but he didn't. But Moses tried to pacify the Lord his God. O Lord he said. Why are you so angry with your own people whom you brought from the land of Egypt with such great power and such a strong hand? Why let the Egyptians say, their God rescued them with the evil intention of slaughtering them in the mountains and wiping them from the face of the earth? Turn away from your fierce anger. Change your mind about this terrible disaster you have threatened against your people! Remember your servants Abraham, Isaac, and Jacob. You bound yourself with an oath to them saying I will make your descendants as numerous as the stars of heaven. And I will give them all of this land that I have promised to your descendants, and they will possess it forever. **So the Lord changed his mind about the terrible disaster he had threatened to bring on his people** (even though he just said the opposite prior). There are several passages of scripture in the Word of God that demonstrate what God's intents were on destroying the children of Israel that soon followed with thoughts of compassion and grace. Where we see the judgment and anger of the Lord expressed, if a few chapters are flipped, it is clear to see that God is ready to restore and reconcile with his people if certain conditions are met. This is just like a parent who threatened their child a whooping for doing something wrong, but by the end of the day, does not deliver the whooping to the child because of a changed mind that derived from compassion and love. It doesn't mean that God won't eventually deliver that whooping that was promised to us, but according to Psalm 30:5, his anger is but a moment but his favor is for a lifetime. God has emotions my friend. If you think he doesn't, you will see them all throughout the book of Exodus where God repeatedly threatened Israel with disaster and divorce, but several instances of repentance or intercession brought about a change in God's intents. There were times in the bible where God clearly demonstrated that the boundaries could no longer be crossed regardless of how much he loved Israel. Sometimes we have to let go of things that are killing us, even though it's killing us to let go. This is why God hates divorce. The same God who said let man not separate what God has joined together is the same God who said in Psalm 91:14-15 I will protect him or her, for he or she acknowledges my name. He or she will call upon me, and I will answer him or her and I will be with him or her in trouble, and I will deliver him or her and honor him or her. This happens in the area of marriage often and religious people don't know what to do when this occurs if a separation or divorce is a result of this. Often the delivered child of God is labeled and shunned, however this is what they learned and as a result this mindset is continually passed down. Isaiah 30:18 says that our God is a God of justice! Knowing the God behind the word of God is so important because when there are many scriptures that oppose one another it is essential to understand the context in which it was written, who is written to, and why it was written. The context in Mark 10:9 is rarely considered when the scripture is being used. This context is discussed further in another area.

It hurt God that he had to hurt Israel. Have you ever heard a parent that is about to give their child a spanking say, now this is going to hurt me, a lot more than it's going to hurt you. The parent is saying that it's hurting me to hurt you but I have to do this or you will be harmed later. Proverbs

13:24 says he that spares the rod of discipline, hates their child. This means that if you don't discipline your child, their soul could be in danger if they don't learn that it is not okay to just do any old thing they want to do or act any old way they want to act. So it was with Satan in heaven before he fell, so it was with Adam and Eve who sinned in the Garden of Eden, so it was with Israel that God had to put in place even after much mercy, grace, and compassion, and multiple chances were extended. God had to let them know, there is a line that can be crossed, there are boundaries and yes even a loving compassionate agape loving God has limits, and limits on how you handle his children. Marriage does not stop God from acting on behalf of his child. If God's child is bound to someone that is abusing his child, there is a high possibility that God will step in and act. There are situations where divorce is the best thing that can happen so that the old thing can die and a new thing can be birthed. God cannot start a new cycle until the old one has ended. This sometimes happens in separating in marriage and then reconciliation occurs with the couple. This sometimes happens if a divorce takes place and remarriage of the same spouses that divorced. Divorce does not mean final. Sometimes it does mean final, it depends on the situation as each situation is case by case, as God is weighing hearts. Jeremiah 8:10 is a place in the bible that is not a common marriage sermon heard, neither is it the scripture that is referenced to with marriage. The same God who hates divorce says in Jeremiah 8:10 that I (The Lord) will give their wives to others and their farms to strangers. Look at Hebrews 13:4 Give honor to marriage, and remain faithful to one another in marriage. God will surely judge people who are immoral and those who commit adultery. What he is saying is put any situation of infidelity in the hands of God and watch how he handles the situation for you. What God is saying, if the heart weigh in doesn't check right in God's sight, he has the authority to take a man's wife, land, and property and give them to someone worth having them, and vice versa. We see this clearly with Nabal and Abigail. Why did Nabal have to fall dead at the exact time that David was in town? How long do you think Abigail waited to respond to David's invitation for her to become his wife? Do you think she considered the town's people who would have quickly labeled her an uncaring widow who never really loved Nabal at all? After all how could she just move on with some stranger? I think Abigail had been through quite enough at that point. I believe she grabbed her belongings, saddled David's horses and became his wife and a queen of Israel to help advise and love the one God sent to rescue her. Oh wait that is exactly what happened! People kill me with certain sayings that are passed down without realizing what is being communicated. Earlier we discussed the saying "the grass is greener on the other side. This is true; at the same time there is another side to this that is also true. People fail to realize that this is situational and shouldn't be applied to everyone's situation. The grass is not always greener on the other side. In Abigail's case as well as with Ruth's, the grass was extremely greener on the other side. This goes for men and women, if your spouse is beating you, abusing you, or repeatedly cheating on you, I'm sorry, but I may be the only one to tell you this, but there is greener grass somewhere else. This is not to tell you to divorce or separate as there are many cases of beautiful testimonies that come out of people who chose to remain in a marriage as such, however, if you don't know what I have experienced and you are looking on the outside in, you may want to save that saying for yourself, because truth be told it produces guilt for those that desire a healthier life, who are entitled to one biblically if chosen. Guilt is something that is not of god, but it is of the devil. The enemy knows if I can keep you guilty, I can keep you bound. Conviction will enable a believer to come face to face with their shortcomings and prayerfully lead to repentance and changes in behavior and thoughts. One of my favorite examples of repentance is that found in Luke 18:9-14. Nothing has changed today. Let's look at it.

Also He spoke this parable to some who trusted in themselves that they were righteous, and despised others: Two men went up to the temple to pray, one a Pharisee and the other a tax collector. The Pharisee stood and prayed thus with himself, God, I thank you that I am not like other men, extortioners, unjust, adulterers, or even as this tax collector. I fast twice a week; I give tithes of all that I possess. And the tax collector, standing afar off, would not so much as raise *his* eyes to heaven, but beat his chest, saying, God, be merciful to me a sinner! I tell you, this man went down to his house justified *rather* than the other; for everyone who exalts himself will be humbled, and he who humbles himself will be exalted." The tax collector came with a real heart of repentance. He was able to see God who heard him because of pureness of heart (Matthew 5:8), yes a despised sinful man in deeds. To know the God behind the Word means you understand that God hears you if your heart is right which will lead to good deeds as you walk in the way of the Lord; the Holy Spirit will fill you and assist you **with your participation**. When Christ died on the cross everything that has been done in offense to God before salvation and ongoing confession of sins and repentance have been placed under the blood of Jesus, cast into the sea to be remembered no more, and under the feet of God who stomps on them (Micah 7:19). This is not to say go off and do what you want, but it is to say that Jesus has already died and went all the way for our shortcomings. All of our deeds and doings are but filthy rags when it is to be compared to righteousness in and of ourselves. Sometimes the higher one goes in leadership, the less they remember this. John 3:16-21 says for God so loved the world that He gave His only begotten Son, that whoever believes in Him should not perish but have everlasting life. For God did not send His Son into the world to condemn the world, but that the world through Him might be saved.

"He who believes in Him is not condemned; but he who does not believe is condemned already, because he has not believed in the name of the only begotten Son of God. And this is the condemnation, that the light has come into the world, and men loved darkness rather than light, because their deeds were evil. For everyone practicing evil hates the light and does not come to the light, lest his deeds should be exposed. But he who does the truth comes to the light, that his deeds may be clearly seen, that they have been done in God."

Galatians 4:3, Even so we, when we were children, were in bondage under the elements of the world. But when the fullness of the time had come, God sent forth His Son, born of a woman, born under the law to redeem those who were under the law, that we might receive the adoption as sons.

And because you are sons, God has sent forth the Spirit of His Son into your hearts, crying out, "Abba, Father!" Therefore you are no longer a slave but a son, and if a son, then an heir of God through Christ.

Jesus understood something many people today do not. There is no better way to get through to someone than in the manner of being able to relate. God had to save us and in doing that he had to relate to us. There are many times where we can't always expect God to come down to our level now that Christ has died for us, and we should come up to him in and by the Spirit of God by maturing and growing up in the Lord, however when people are empathized with and one is able to really hit home and relate this is so effective it drives in the crowds. People wanted to hear Jesus because he seemed to be able to relate. He walked the streets of Samaria, Jerusalem, Nazareth and much more and he was comfortable in all sorts of atmospheres and places that some believers today wouldn't dare drive around let alone be among the center of those there. Jesus was at home with the broken and the sick. He is amazing! You often have people trying to minister from a place where they are not able to relate one bit to someone they are trying to minister to. Take me for instance. I love to help with street ministry. I love it. I have never been a prostitute, strung out on drugs, or an alcoholic, but if I can just drive the ladies to their AA meeting, or to walk the streets with Rahab women's ministries to pray for strippers and lead people to Christ it gives me a rush and sparks my passion for God. Not to say that I intend on fellowshipping as dark and light has nothing in common, however in terms of presenting Jesus and winning souls to see lives changed! My point is I may not be the one to personally mentor one who has experienced this, but I can just be of other support needed in these areas. The same thing can be applied to those who have experienced divorce. One is able to extend what they can out of their experiences, however if they have never had to face divorce and praise God if they haven't, they can only minister in this area to a certain degree.

In various areas of the bible you will read about making vows and how it is important to keep the vows that you make because your word is powerful (Ecclesiastes 5:4, Deuteronomy 23:21-23, Numbers 30:2). This is critical in God's perspective. God even deems his word very highly as it was forever settled in heaven (Psalm 119:89). God is faithful and what He says he will do, he will do. At the same time God who is the word, who inspired the written word, and who is the written word stated that no one person should do work on the Sabbath. He said that we are to keep the commandments, yet He himself healed on the Sabbath, because that earthly circumstance that God cared enough about drove him to go above His Word acting as the God behind the Word to heal on the Sabbath. Matthew 12:11 is where we see Christ asking if someone has a sheep that falls in a pit on the Sabbath, would you not rescue it? Religious people would prefer for the sheep to stay in that pit to keep a law or principle, yet God being greater surpasses what is written because He is love and the relationship and rescuing of that sheep is greater than some law being kept at that moment. That is the God we serve, yet this side of him is rarely depicted.

Your testimony may not make sense to everyone and it's not supposed to. When a man or woman does not have an ear to hear what the spirit has to say in the area of their marriage, particularly dealing with their spouse, then what God has given to you, he can take away. We read in Mark 4:25 to pay close attention to what you hear. The closer you listen, the more understanding you will be given and you will receive even more. To more understanding will be given. But for those who are not listening, even what little understanding they have will be taken away. To those who use well what they are given, even more will be given, and they will have abundance. But from those who do nothing, even what little they have will be taken away. This is what we are seeing in the last days and it makes sense. I am not surprised that the divorce rate is going up. It is a sign that Christ is closer now to coming back than ever before. Jesus said let the wheat and tares grow together until he returns then he will separate them. I believe that Jesus is already separating the wheat from the tares in many areas, not just in the area of marriage. Luke 17:26-27 says that the last days will be just like those in the days of Noah, people will be eating, drinking, marrying, and given in marriages. I believe God is setting the stage for his return and the area of marriage where God originally designed a man and woman to come together and become one flesh where no one can put asunder or separate, God is delivering his children who are wheats from tares. It's so easy to say well if you're a wheat don't join yourself to a tare. What fellowship does darkness have with light? Do not be unevenly yoked. These are all principles that are true and encouraged to follow as they will save you much time, effort, and strength. There are those who are not mature in the Lord enough to adhere to them, and they may have already gotten married to a tare. Not everyone gets saved before they get married, not everyone is filled with the spirit of God before they get married either. The word clearly tells us to be at peace with one another and remain in the marriage if it is possible to be at peace, but there are circumstances where it may not be possible. Jesus knew this from the beginning as he mentioned to the Pharisees that Moses permitted divorce because of the hardness of hearts, but from the beginning it was not so. Any wheat married to a tare understands how a hard heart can impact a marriage that may end in divorce. Moses understood it, as did Paul, as did Jesus. Jesus didn't need to elaborate on abuse or abandonment when the Pharisees asked him about marriage in Mark 10 because the question was not asked with the sincere intent to really care about marriage. The question was asked to Jesus to set up a trap for him to display intents of disobeying the law that he was to follow, especially if He was to fulfill the law as He said. Jesus knew this, and he answered in such a way to shut their scheme of trying to trap him down. The answer Jesus gave was never for us to thoroughly cover abuse, abandonment, and adultery. Jesus gave a simple answer to his enemies that were asking a question with the intent **to trap and accuse him** (this is the context, and the Pharisees is who His answer was to with the purpose of shutting their trap down). Mark 10 1-9 reads: Then Jesus left Capernaum and went down to the region of Judea and into the area east of the Jordan River. Once again crowds gathered around him, and as usual he was teaching them.

Some Pharisees came and tried to trap him with this question: "Should a man be allowed to divorce his wife?" (In Matthew 19:3: For any reason at all).

Jesus answered them with a question: "What did Moses say in the law about divorce?"

"Well, he permitted it," they replied. "He said a man can give his wife a written notice of divorce and send her away."

But Jesus responded, "He wrote this commandment only as a concession to your hard hearts. But 'God made them male and female from the beginning of creation. 'This explains why a man leaves his father and mother and is joined to his wife, and the two are united into one. Since they are no longer two but one, let no one split apart what God has joined together." This scripture has been taken out of context many times as people fail to realize that the reason Jesus answered how he did, was to take his them back to the beginning to demonstrate how things were originated, even though he was fully aware of how things were after the fall, how they were presently as he was on earth, and how they would be in the future.

It's clear to understand once a person decides to follow Christ and live for God then a change must occur internally. Just as he said in Luke 9:60, let the dead bury their own dead, the same is with the circumstances of life. Follow Christ and anything that needs to be dealt with accordingly whether that is the spirit of a harassing supervisor, an unfaithful spouse, or a wicked family member, leave that situation to itself, and in following Christ all will be dealt with.

It is clear to see by the character of Jesus that he does not play about his children or sheep being abused, abandoned, or betrayed. This is evident throughout the word of God. Let's look at the greatest commandments. Matthew 22:36-40. Teacher, which is the most important commandment in the Law of Moses?"

Jesus replied, "you must love the LORD your God with all your heart, all your soul, and all your mind.' This is the first and greatest commandment. A second is equally important: 'Love your neighbor as yourself.' the entire law and all the demands of the prophets are based on these two commandments." This is enough right here to demonstrate how Christ was not supportive of anyone treating their neighbor which is their spouse in any other way than the way they'd like to be treated. If you don't want to be abandoned, then don't abandon your spouse. If you don't want your spouse to cheat on you, don't cheat on your spouse. If you don't want your spouse to abuse you in any way, physically, emotionally, or mentally, then don't do it to your spouse, because if you do, know that God sees all, and he repays. This goes for any ill treatment. If one does, then they are breaking the greatest commandment that God gave, and don't think that his eyes are not watching the scales of the heart. It is simply clear to see that just because Jesus didn't mention abuse and abandonment in Matthew 5:23 and Matthew 19:9 does not mean that he didn't care about those areas because they were not mentioned in this part of the scripture. Abuse and abandonment are mentioned throughout the word of God as testimonies are described and instructions are precisely given on how not to harm or treat other people negatively. The scales that God uses to weigh the hearts of men have been around before the foundation of time. God predestined those he foreknew. I believe that God foreknew those that he knew would willingly choose him to be Lord of their lives and their hearts lifted the scales of judgment off of their lives as they would name the name of Christ and live by faith according to the word of God. Not necessarily having a perfect life, but a heart that weighed out. A prerequisite of salvation in addition to accepting the Lord as your personal savior, and confessing our sins out of our mouths, is believing in one's heart that Jesus is the son of God. Anytime God executed judgment in the word of God it was because of a simple factor, that factor is that everyone who received his judgment received it because they ultimately rejected God in some form, many of them repeatedly. Fire has been known to destroy those that God judged, the earth has been known to swallow up those with bad hearts because of the judgment of God, and flooding waters have been recorded to demonstrate what the judgment of God looks like to those who have hearts that God does not approve of. What is the opposing factor? It is those with a good heart that catches God's eye! You can see that one heart that God finds righteous (Noah) is enough to outweigh the thousands of hearts that flunked the scales test. When God sees a heart that reflects his own, he gets passionate, he gets overjoyed and he gets serious about salvation! All he needs is one. All he needs is a willing and loving heart that will be the remnant. Just look at Noah. Look at Gideon, yes he had some trust issues, but his heart weighed out. David messed up in some areas as we all know with Bathsheba, but the boy's heart was RIGHT. His heart broke the scale! Yes, consequences came, don't hear me incorrectly as if there are no consequences in breaking God's instructions, but know that the heart will make it right. Jesus who was the heart of the father had a heart that saved whosoever will. 1 John: 11 says Dear friend, don't let this bad example influence you. Follow only what is good. Remember that those who do good prove that they are God's children and those who do evil prove that they do not know God. If you are married to someone who is proving that they don't know good by their actions then it's clear that they are a tare no matter how faithful they are to church or ministry or leaders. Actions speak louder than the confessions made. (Matthew 15:8, Isaiah 29:13). In many cases when people apologize for the wrong they have done with their actions you will be able to see if repentance was sincere if they refrain from doing it again. Other times an apology is received however their actions speak volumes that they are not truly sorry.

Does the offender feel bad? Perhaps, but even devils fear and tremble according to James 2:19, but they do not change! So it is with people who do not have been circumcised in heart.

Exodus 21:10 says if a man who has married a slave wife takes another wife for himself he must not neglect the rights of the first wife to food, clothing, and sexual intimacy. If he fails in any of these three obligations she may leave as a free woman without making any payment. The point here is that God does not approve of a woman being neglected and abandoned.

God sees the difference in an accident occurring verses something that could have been avoided that got out of hand because of choosing not to acknowledge and respond to the situation. In Exodus

Scales of the Heart

21 starting at verse 28 it reads if an ox gores a man or woman to death the ox must be stoned and its flesh may not be eaten. In such a case however the owner will not be held liable. But suppose the ox had a reputation for gorging and the owner had been informed but failed to keep it under control. If the ox then kills someone it must be stoned and the owner must also be put to death. We of course are not in the Old Testament but it is clear to see that there is a difference from something happening by accident and something happening after an amount of time has passed that allowed a reputation to be built. This means that some continued to neglect an issue that was dangerous and harm was brought to another person's life. In relation to marriage, this is why many fail, because by the time help comes, the impact of the damage is beyond critical. There are not just a few flames in the house; the house is burned down to a crisp. When issues are ignored and people are encouraged not to deal with their circumstances because they don't matter this is where the fabric loosens and unravels, and when there is an attempt to put the garment on, it falls apart to the ground. When walking in faith we must rise above our circumstances, this is not to say we should not deal with things in reality that can affect our lives.

Another example in God's word that Jesus does not support those who oppress his children and remain in sinful lifestyles is 1 John 3:4-10.

Everyone who sins is breaking God's law, for all sin is contrary to the law of God. And you know that Jesus came to take away our sins, and there is no sin in him. Anyone who continues to live in Him will not sin. But anyone who keeps on sinning does not know Him or understand who He is.

Dear children, don't let anyone deceive you about this: When people do what is right, it shows that they are righteous, even as Christ is righteous. But when people keep on sinning, it shows that they belong to the devil, who has been sinning since the beginning. But the Son of God came to destroy the works of the devil. Those who have been born into God's family do not make a practice of sinning, because God's life is in them. So they can't keep on sinning, because they are children of God. So now we can tell who children of God are and who children of the devil are. Anyone who does not live righteously and does not love other believers does not belong to God.

It is clear to see that God is not interested in a child of Satan, even if they are joined to one of his children. It's a terrible thing to be joined to someone living in darkness, but God has made it clear that the marriage is sanctified, however that doesn't mean an unbelieving spouse is saved because the other spouse is. Salvation is something each man has to come to him or herself, and yes not even your believing spouse can grant you access to heaven and in the family of God almighty.

God can use a bad marriage to prune you. This does not mean that that is the only purpose of the marriage. God designed in the beginning many things to function in a specific way of order, yet due to the fall there are a number of results from the fall that have things in distorts, marriage is absolutely one of them. If it is God's will for you to leave a marriage that will depend on many factors. God did not intend for any person to leave a marriage from the beginning this we know from Mark 10:9, what God joins together let no man put asunder. What he is saying is that from the beginning it was never intended to be separation, however separation and divorce does happen, just as people who perish does happen. Jesus came for those sick and those affected by the results of sin, people drowning in their own consequences of sowing in ignorance and reaping in epiphanies. God bless you and keep you if this is not you, I praise God for your life, yet there are ten times as many people other than yourself that toxic marriages apply to. He came for the woman who is being beat behind closed doors, he came for the children who is being molested by a father, he came for a husband who watches his wife sneak in and out in the midnight hour to be with her lovers, he came for his children, his own that would accept him along with Gentiles alike that had a willing accepting heart. People need to realize heart weigh in day is coming and if we look at Romans 8:29, he has done this before the foundation of the world. Yes there are the Calvinistic and Armenian perspectives and scholars would have you choose one side of the spectrum. I believe we serve a God that surpasses rationality. I believe that God knew exactly who would accept him and be circumcised in heart, and he knew exactly who would not accept him and would refuse circumcision before the earth was even formed. If we look in Exodus it is clearly stated numerous times how he hardened Pharaoh's heart. Why would God harden someone's heart? Because it would make no difference hardening someone's heart that is already hard. God saw Pharaoh before the earth was made and knew he didn't belong to him, he knew that he would not accept him or walk in his ways, therefore why wouldn't he harden his heart if Pharaoh was already moving toward the destination of his eternal dwelling place (those doomed to destruction: John 17:12). God used him to show what happens to people with hard hearts that reject God and abuse God's people. Exodus 3:19: But I know that the king of Egypt will not let you go unless a mighty hand forces him, as it was with Pharaoh it is today. There are many people living with the spirit of Pharaoh dealing with God's people in the very same modernistic manners, nevertheless God will harden the hearts of those already harden just to show his glory: Exodus 7:3: But I will make Pharaoh's heart stubborn so I can multiply my miraculous signs and wonders in the land, before there is any deliverance or rescuing just note Exodus 7:4. Even then Pharaoh will refuse to listen to you, so I will bring down my fist on Egypt. Then I will rescue my forces my people the Israelites from the land of Egypt with great acts of judgment, when I raise my powerful hand and bring out the Israelites the Egyptians will know that I am the Lord. This is what is happening today in some of the marriages that are ending in divorce. No it does not contribute to all of them, some are divorcing because neither parties were or are in Christ, they are just divorcing due to the World's standard of living, some are divorcing because they are not real believers, and some are divorcing due to being unevenly yoked, some are divorcing because no matter how much they try to stay in a marriage to honor and please God, to keep their vow, to be safe in the eyes and perspectives of people God can see it is not good for them to stay in the marriage or relationship. When Moses began to get the people of Israel to cooperate with their own deliverance they rebuked him because they had to make bricks without straw. They wanted to stay in Egypt and when they were finally delivered they wanted to go back. This book is for the people who fall into the percentage of divorces that reflect God coming to pick you up and carrying you out of Egypt regardless of, if they wanted to stay there or not. God sees too much potential in you and will use you for much but he cannot if you remain in Egypt, not if you choose to remain in Egypt because if you choose to or not, it won't stop God from coming for what belongs to him: Isaiah 43:1-3 says But now O Jacob listen to the Lord who created you. O Israel the one who formed you says, do not be afraid for I have ransomed you. I have called you by name, you are mine, when you go through the deep waters, and I will be with you. When you go through the rivers of difficulty you will not drown. When you walk through the fire of oppression you will not be burned up, the flames will not consume you. For I am the Lord your God the Holy One of Israel, your savior. No matter who you marry or when you marry if you are in Christ and you are walking in his ways and lining your life up with is word and yielding to any suffering coming your way whether that is being persecuted as a believer identified with Christ, or if that is reaping a harvest of consequences sown in sin knowingly or ignorantly. After a while weigh in day is coming for both you and your spouse. God will look at the couple, and he will separate the wheat from the tares if this applies to that couple. God will often restore a couple if that is what's best for the kingdom. Other times he will separate a wheat from a tare within marriage if that is what's best for the kingdom. If one of the spouse's may be more useful outside the marriage for the Kingdom of God than in the marriage, it may not be a surprise that that spouse was delivered. This is exactly what is occurring within marriages in the church, and no one ever discusses this perspective. Our minds have become so myopic to thinking that if a divorce occurs then the couple didn't try hard enough, someone didn't pray hard enough, someone had a lack of faith, when God is a God of the present and he is constantly sweeping homes weighing hearts. God knew from the beginning whether we did or not, acknowledged it or not, that there would be some that belong to him that would join with those who are not his, and he had a plan for a way of escape from the beginning. There are some divorced people I know that are more faithful, dedicated to God, spirit filled and more loving towards God's people compared to those who have been married to the same person all their lives. When God chose to come to the earth from the beginning in the situation of Adam and Eve falling, he made up his mind he was coming for his own one way or another. You being joined to an unbeliever or someone claiming to be a believer: someone who has on the Christian uniform but their actions are coming from the devil's playbook. This is not anything the Lord has not, and cannot handle, deal with and deliver you from, if it be His will. There is a difference between giving up, throwing in the towel, and quitting verses God supernaturally closing a door in your life. When this happens in the life of the believer, many times that believer is misunderstood by Christian society as conforming to the world's system and ways, when divorce didn't start with men it started in the heavenly realms when Satan was kicked out of heaven. I believe that divorce is something that God can use for the percentage of his children tied into marriages with those who have the heart of Pharaoh. Yes you have a person with the spirit of Pharaoh married to a person with the spirit of a circumcised believer. What do we do in this situation? The ideal situation is to remain unto death and make it work: 1 Corinthians 7:16: Don't you wives realize that your husband's might be saved because of you? What we fail to emphasize in this scripture is the word might. Meaning it is probable. God is not violating the will of another person. Some churches will tell you to go pray heaven down for your spouse's salvation, not realizing that those prayers are variable based upon the will of the spouse. Many wives are told to hold on because their spouse might be saved and this is a possibility and it is great **IF** this takes place, however the other side of the spectrum is not painted as much as the first. The truth of the matter is that he may not be saved and this is sad, however it is truth. No matter how much you pray for Pharaoh to change for the better he is not, that is a sad reality that even God himself understood. We should always have faith and believe it will come to pass what we pray for, particularly regarding the promises of God made to us at the same time understand when it comes to prayer that involves other people, you and the other people must be participants inviting God into the situation in order for results to manifest.

God understood appropriating something that has gotten out of order. When Satan was kicked out of heaven, he was not placed on the outside gates of heaven, but removed totally and completely from the third heaven. There was not a separation that took place, it was a divorce. The first divorce in existence was that of God kicking Satan out of heaven, because God understood what sometimes we don't. God understood what Satan had become, and the impact he had on one third of the angels. Did God forgive Satan? We know he didn't and he won't because Satan is insane. We know Satan will never be restored to his old position of being the anointed angel of God. In fact he has a new destination for Satan according to God's word which is the lake of fire for him and his angels for all eternity. God understands that he could not let Satan back into heaven, but instead released him to the consequences of his own choices. God is love, he gave him the opportunity and position from the beginning that flowed not out of who Satan was, but out of God's characteristics and traits. Even if Satan did mess up, God was willing to risk it. Even if man and woman did mess up in the Garden of Eden, God was willing to risk it. Even if Israel did mess up, God was willing to risk it. Even if you my friend did mess up, God came to the earth and he did more than risked it. If people do not understand your testimony as a divorcee and that you could be in the percentage of rescued divorcees that God himself delivered you and brought you out, then hear me, it's okay. I thought when I was divorced that everyone must know that God delivered me because of what I believe God is calling me to. They must know right? Wrong. God will handle it all if you just trust him and place your life and reputation in his hands. After a while, once you move into what it is he delivered you to, which should be some kind of assignment for the Kingdom, those insecure feelings will disappear and you will be so ensconced into your assignments for God, you will forget all about your fears, because they will drop off of you like flies.

You alone knowing God delivered you is enough, trust me; he will restore, reestablish, confirm and strengthen you according to 1 Peter 5:10, all for you to lift him up. Just know that the only one who truly understands is the one who showed you that he understood the moment he took the nails in his hands and feet, and bled from his side, for his cry and prayer was father forgive them for they know not what they do. Some church people will always tell you, you know and knew exactly what you are doing, not ever taking the time to understand perhaps they did not. God understands when you do things in ignorance, he is praying for you, and his blood covers you, if you are waking up to the reality that the enemy has lured you into hell, along with your own choices and consequences, fret not, go to God in prayer, line your life up with him regardless of what your pharaoh may be doing, I promise, he will keep you, cover you, and if it is his will he will rescue you, you cannot make this happen yourself, you have to yield to where you are and trust God to allow his will for your life to manifest. I have to be honest in the fact that his will may include you remaining with your spouse for the rest of your life. If this is the case for you then know that his grace is sufficient and he knows and understands why that will be. I know what it's like to feel what you are feeling if you are going through a similar testimony to mine. You are not alone, and you will make it if it's God's will for you to remain or to leave. If it is God's will for you to be delivered, there will be a way of escape, perhaps many, it will be composed of many miracles and wonders that are beyond rationality if God is certainly calling you out. You will know what to do, and know that He never intended for you to marry that person in the first place. He never intended for any marriage to end in separation or divorce, yet he will use anything including death and divorce to come for who are his, and those that have proven that they have the heart of Christ. The spiritual law of praise is something to reckon with for all believers, particularly those in prisons. No matter what jail cell you are in, if you praise him long enough, hard enough, and consistently because you love him, not to get anything out of him, that could be 5 years, 10 years, 20 years, or 1 hour, I promise you that anything that is holding you in chains, has to break up off of you, especially if you have no known sin in your life, you're living in a manner that pleases God, know that the foundations will be shaken where you are. Follow the voice of the Lord as his instructions will lead you. Please do not mistake me for encouraging people to get divorced, I am not, I am pro marriage as I continued to go back to a bad one. It didn't stop God from weighting the hearts and a new course was set for my life. It was new to me when it happened, but I do believe that it was predestined before the world ever began. It is not an easy thing to tell those you come into contact with why you are there, or why you are where you are especially in new settings. Coming right out and telling them the truth, that you were praising and worshipping God like you were losing your mind day in and day out is what broke everything off your life that God never intended to be there. Nowadays that is not sufficient for people, and that's okay. It may be scary or uncomfortable for them to receive; yes I am even referring to church people who name the name of Christ and are fully aware of the gospel is for the sick being healed, blind eyes opening, the dead being raised, and captives being set free. The last thing modern church people are anymore which is sad is spiritual. Miracles do happen, and bondages are broken off of God's people in several areas including that of a marriage detrimental to God's child.

Remember, that you have nothing to prove to anyone, you may have a testimony to share but you have to walk in peace knowing that God has called you to peace. Romans 12:18 says if it is possible, as far as it depends on you, live at peace with everyone. We brush over the word possible, meaning it's possible to do this and with some people it is not possible.

If you are married to someone and they don't have a hard heart but they just messed up, why not forgive them? Why not give them another chance. Church people are quick to tell someone leaving their spouse to forgive them and go back as if in going back demonstrates the only demonstration of forgiveness. The famous line used is "after all, God forgave you for all you did", not understanding that they could be encouraged to go back to someone with a hard heart that's unwilling to change. It is difficult to understand this if someone does not know this from experience, so it becomes easy to tell someone to do this. Yes, going back should be encouraged but only to someone who is not hard hearted. A hard heart is dangerous. Forgiving someone is releasing them from the offense that they have extended to you. Forgiveness does not always mean that you reinstate someone to the same position they had before. For example, let's say you have an uncle named Ray Ray. Uncle Ray Ray comes over and steals every time he's in your house. You always forgive Uncle Ray Ray, but Uncle Ray Ray is no longer allowed in your house without supervision, if at all. Or let's say you have a business partner that undercuts you and throws you under the rug on a business deal. It's possible to forgive that person, but you may not do business with them again moving forward. The same is with marriage covenants that have been broken by the offense of adultery, abuse, and abandonment. It is possible to forgive and I encourage you to forgive. It is not always easy but it's worth it, and God requires us to forgive so that we too may be forgiven of our sins. Sometimes there is restoration into the same exact roles before the offense occurred and sometimes there is not. If someone is not restored to the same position, that is not your place to judge one as not being forgiving. The Word says do not dwell on the past, it says to press on towards those things that are ahead, it also says do not worry about tomorrow for tomorrow will take care of itself. Yes. All that is certainly true, yet that does not mean you should ignore factors that can impact your tomorrow. Because you received a bill and its due tomorrow, this does not mean ignore your bill and don't worry about tomorrow or don't pay your bill because it is due in the future.

Let's look at Mrs. Pineapple who comes to Mr. Pineapple to confess the fact that she has been unfaithful to him by having an affair with her co-worker. Right after she discloses her secret to her husband, the next thing she says is "Since it happened in the past we should do as the word says and forget it and focus on moving ahead". Keep in mind, she cheated yesterday. Now if this is the response from Mr. Pineapple then it is settled, they are moving forward. But when one is using the word to get over on another person God will weigh the hearts involved. It is not wrong of you to choose not to ignore factors that will impact your future negatively and act upon them. Yes these factors could have saved you from marrying the wrong person, but because people give up on you doesn't mean God does. God sees all and knows all, and human beings do not. God reviewed Israel's track record of disobedience when he threw her into captivity: because if it was not acknowledged or addressed and corrected the future would have been even more negatively impacted by the hearts and actions of Israel.

Sometimes, some people never take the time to unveil what they are encouraging someone to go back to, because they think they know for sure how that individual's life should look like in the end, even though they are not God. People are advised to go back to someone that will change and to embrace the mindset that God can continue to work on them, not realizing that God is not able to work on someone's heart that does not belong to him. God is not working on someone's heart that has rejected Christ before the foundation of the world. That person may be in the church, may be in ministry in the church, and may even be in ministry. In retrospect, if the individual's heart is circumcised there is a great chance according to the Word that the individual can change for the better if they participate in that journey. Both are truths.

Hebrews 12:6 God disciplines those who he loves. A lot of times people are getting away with much is because they simply don't belong to God. You could be married to this person. It seems like everything they do they get away with, but let you so much as roll your eyes to someone and you're getting the whooping of your life from God. This is just the truth. There are God's children married to those who are not God's children and God is doing something about it. He is not just going to let you be destroyed. There is too much potential in you and the devil knows it! He knows that if you are delivered from Pharaoh you will be free to worship God and impact others dealing with the same. He would rather hold your mind hostage by thinking it's best to remain in Egypt with Pharaoh. The church has contributed to this stronghold on a number of occasions masking it as trying to save a union, not knowing God's plan for those individuals. Thus such interference could impact lives and hindering Kingdom work to come to past. There is a kingdom work of holding marriages together; at the same time there is much ministry for those who have experienced separation and divorce. The work of the kingdom is diverse and to think that because someone's testimony does not mirror our own that there is something wrong with the person is out of order.

If that man or woman is free and delivered by God to focus on the Kingdom being familiar with deceptive spirits there can be much fruit bearing in the Kingdom, however the enemy knows she or he is no good towards the Kingdom if they have a mindset of remaining just to save face or to be safe from shame and pressure. That person may have a mindset that they are going to stay and remain and fight for their marriage not knowing that, they have been tricked by the enemy to remain in a prison, and that God would have delivered. So by fighting for the kingdom within a life threatening marriage is just the trick the devil wants to do in their lives. They think they have to stay, and must remain all for the fight. The devil knows if they break free he won't be able to weigh both down with one another, because the stronger spouse will be free to fight against Satan. So he'd rather have the stronger spouse remain tied to someone he has easy access to and through, so he can kill two birds with one stone. This is a major strategy of the enemy which attacks many weak marriages. Yes there may be a victorious saint in the marriage but you are only as strong as your weakest link.

Yes it can be very difficult to deal with a person you are married to when you want to live for God and they don't. It can be just as frustrating for a spouse who is not where you are spiritually to deal with you IF they are trying to grow and get to where you are and grow in the things of God.

That is a possibility. The other possibility is that they are frustrated from living with a spirit filled spouse because they don't want to do the things of God or really live a saved life. So looking at both sides, yes the spouse who is less spiritually mature can be frustrated to live with someone spiritually mature, more so if they are trying to grow, hopefully they are, but there are also cases that a less spiritually mature spouse is frustrated just as much as the spirit filled spouse because there are ongoing convictions of right living when they know they will never live a Christian life. They may wear the uniform, but the playbook may not be the Lord's. We cannot assume that a spouse is frustrated with their spiritually mature wife or husband because they are simply trying to do better and are not being acknowledge, but that there is a possibility that the frustration comes because their spouse may not be in approval or participate in unrighteous living with them. The possibility that the less mature spouse may never desire or want to live right, not just today, but every day! That is a truth and a possibility.

This is one of the enemy's best strategies! To have a spouse get away with so much, and there is not a lot of proof. This is exactly how Satan himself is, and he knows this works. Those who have the gift of the discernment of spirits may be well aware of spirits that you have had to deal with at school, on your job, in relationships and so forth. You know that when God showed you the underlying cause of what was taking place behind the veil and in the spirit realm and it may have become difficult to confront the person or bring the issue up at all, because the person is so masked in deception appearing to have all their ducks lined up in a row. There may not always be a lot of proof to demonstrate exactly what you have seen or what your intuition or the Holy Spirit is telling you, yet stay faithful in prayer and watch God expose in ways you'd never imagine. The same thing happens in marriages where there is a deceptive spirit working. The enemy wants to have a spouse appear they are following God's playbook by wearing the uniform of righteousness over the body suit of unrighteousness. This is like being married to someone you know is doing things they should not even though you can't prove it initially. They are smart enough to not get caught yet unwilling to follow the rules for the public eye. Revelation 3:15-17 is where God says I know all the things you do, that you are neither hot nor cold. I wish that you were one or the other! But since you are like lukewarm water, neither hot nor cold, I will spit you out of my mouth. This is the same thing when a spouse in a marriage is lukewarm in the things of God. There is not enough proof on one side, as the other side, and it drives the other spouse crazy, because it's exactly what the devil uses to harass the believing spouse. Not everyone can relate to this, and praise God if you can't, but some can. Please do not mistake me referring to someone that is new in Christ or a baby in Christ because they may just be in a growing phase. We all are at different levels with our walk with Christ and the Word clearly tells us that we must mature and grow up at some point in the things of God. I am referring to the type of spouse and spirit that has been under good, sound preaching and teaching where the Holy Spirit is manifested long enough as an adult particularly, and none of it seems to be taking affect on the individual, and no serious change or fruit is evident by the individual. There is a difference, and sometimes religious people will advise someone to return to a spouse like this because it makes the ministry look good, it makes the witness look good, not knowing that there is a difference between being patient with someone such as a spouse who may be growing in the things of God, and then there is the other side of someone who will never grow in the things of God because they have made their forever choice to reject living a real life in Christ, having a form of godliness, but denying the power within (2 Timothy 3:5). Individuals as such are attributed to those individuals that have rejected God before the foundation of the world to receive Christ as his only begotten son and Lord of their lives. What occurs is that people are able to name the name of Jesus Christ confirming to be a follower of Christ with intentions in their heart to only follow Him the way they desire. Their actions state things like, I'm only doing the Jesus thing to a certain point, only just enough to save face, and I'll do whatever I want to do behind closed doors. They continue to say things like I'm not perfect to give the message that one doesn't even have to try. Yes! There is some truth to believers not being perfect and trying to get better in their walk through the power of the Holy Spirit, but there is a difference from those who truly mean this and strive with their entire being especially their words and actions. Then you have those who are deceiving others as if this applies to them, when in fact it's just a façade.

What happens in the body of Christ when divorce occurs sometimes is that you have a hot believer married to someone who is just wearing a uniform of the Christian faith. They may be in ministry, leadership, or just members, but the one that is tied to this deceiver is being weighed down so much, after a while there won't be any energy left to fight for their life in terms of that which is spiritual, their marriage, and certainly not the kingdom of God. The enemy will have you guilty and condemned if you even think about divorcing, even if you are entitled to a biblical release. It is because the strongholds in society that bring approval or disapproval based upon status quo. People tend to think that when divorce is contemplated it's done so in a way that says, oh well, this didn't work, I'm out of this thing! It is so easy to assume such if one does not know what it's like to be a real believer who is contemplating divorce. No my friend, it doesn't happen like that. You have no idea what trauma, guilt, remorse, and regret that a real believer experiences when they contemplate divorce, actually file for a divorce, go through a divorce, and face life after a divorce. If you have never had to put on these shoes, you may want to have more empathy when you are laying it on divorcees as if you believe they made their decision at the flip of a hat. Do you know what it's like to have to come before the body of Christ once married, now divorced? Do you know what it's like to fail in the institution that is to represent Christ and his church? Do you know what it's like to have to face people who once thought the world of you because of your marriage status and things they hoped for you to do, not know what was going on in your home? Do you know what it's like to have to start all over in life in this area, when you bear the name of Christ? If you don't know what it's like to be a hot believer who loves God and desires to be free to serve God with your life which is being hindered by someone that you chose to marry, then my friend, I don't think you have a right to put your mouth on anyone who has, because frankly had it been you in their shoes, perhaps you may not have made it like they did. It's so easy to evaluate others, and their testimonies, without knowing one cent of what they have gone through. No it is not easy to just get a divorce when one truly loves God. In fact it takes an inner strength of God for a real believer to get through divorce. God knows who can handle it and who can't. God knows who can handle the opposition, the dirty looks, the shunning faces, and the whispering comments, all of it. He knows who can bear it. It may often appear that a believer who is a divorcee was weak in faith and wasn't able to stand in the area of marriage, but you have no idea that in some circumstances it takes more strength, courage, and guts to leave knowing all that is waiting for you on the other side. So you, yes you, the wife or husband who chose to stay, not because you love Jesus but because you didn't have the strength, courage, guts to leave an unhealthy situation God may have opened the door for you to, stop being so hard on those who made the opposite decision as you. It's easy to make yourself look like the hero of the story because you went back or you stayed in the marriage when someone else didn't and had a biblical legitimate testimony to do so according to the word of God. This often happens when those who didn't have a backbone to take a stand, or walk out on faith is viewed stronger or more Christ like, compared to someone who did. There is another side to this truth, that in some, not all, but some situations it may have been harder to remain and stay, it may have taken more courage, energy, and fight to remain in a marriage, whether there was one believer in the marriage, or perhaps both spouses were believers. This too is truth, but it should not be compared or hung over another's head that doesn't have the same testimony. As a scholar we look at both sides of the totem pole. In some cases it may be more difficult to leave, and in some cases it may be more difficult to stay. We don't always know which one applies to the couple we are judging, neither should we do comparisons as if we do know what happened, or what the couple or one of the spouse's should have did. We should not be comparing other's overcoming and testimonies to our own, because they are all different. Anytime you belittle someone's experience as a believer in Christ is the day you may want to think about who you stand for. Christ never belittled anyone's experiences, neither did he turn people away, and even when he did with the Syrophoenician woman in Mark 7:25-30, it was a set up that he had to do in order to keep the peace with religious people that couldn't stand the fact of this woman undeserving of Christ could get blessed, in the end of this testimony, it demonstrates the only argument in the New Testament that Jesus lost, but it was his will and plan all along to lose this argument with her because he wanted to bless her in spite of who thought what. What an awesome God who laid his reputation aside in front of the big wigs to bless a consistent, strong woman who called yes, even Jesus out on front street! Sometimes when we speak up and speak, take a stand and fight even against those in authority (Jesus), it's so that someone else if not many will be saved or set free. It could have been so easy for her to accept his first response and go home, but she fought, regardless of who was there, and probably in spite her own fears. Ecclesiastes chapter three talks about that there is a time for everything, there is a time to speak up and a time to shut up, and that moment with Jesus, was not the time to shut up, it was the time to speak up. So is it with my assignment. Yes, many times a closed mouth must be the response to much opposition, ridicules, accusations, abuses, and persecutions, as even Christ exemplified in Acts 8:32 where he was led like a sheep to the slaughter and he didn't open his mouth. There are times in our lives where this is necessary and it's not always fun, but there are other times when we need to speak up and fight as Christ did when he cleared the temple in John 2:13-22.

Divorce should be the last option, pray, get help, separate and reconcile as many times needed before either you choose to divorce, or before God delivers you either through the death of you, or your spouse, or a release from the marriage occurs by God opening a door if it be His will. There are many successful testimonies of couples remarrying and that is beautiful! I thank God for those who faced divorce, yet there was a turnaround in their marriage for the better!

If you are a victim of sexual immorality know you are not forced to remain in the marriage, neither do you have to leave. The choice is yours, not your family's choice, nor the people you go to church with, although these can be influencing factors. God will show you which route to take. The church should not be telling anybody to go back to someone who has violated them in any of the areas: abuse, adultery, or abandonment. When someone is encouraged to go back to someone who has offended in this way, understand that what is taking place is a form of church abuse because the impact that church has in the lives of people, is powerful. Pray for the person you are encouraging to go back but don't give any of your feedback if you don't have details or know where the person may stand and why. People sometimes do this so the person can feel guilty or bad because of the choice that is being made, and why someone who claims to know God would want to do that to their brother and sister in Christ is beyond me. The person knows what impact is being made, and if they really love God, the believer is going through more in taking upon a divorce status than it could ever be imagined. Don't kick people while their down and stop adding insult to injury. Christ didn't kick you down, when you were down, and yes it may hard to believe, but you were indeed down at some point my friend, therefore we shouldn't do this to others (Ezekiel 16:6 says that God passed us and saw us squirming in our blood, but He said to us LIVE!) Today there are believers that think because they have been married to the same person all of the lives, that they are doing God's word, when that just reflects one area. There could be many areas of the individual's life that do not mirror God's Word. After going through a divorce I became more aware of an arrogance that is projected forth by those who have never experienced divorce. This arrogance gives the nonverbal message that because I have never experienced divorce, I am better than you, or love God more than you, or am more of a doer of the Word. This is making nonverbal statement that one's works determine their doing of the Word when in fact the only way we can do the word of God is because Jesus came and died that we may be reconciled to God in addition to being filled with the Spirit of God.

Many people will make a decision, just because the influence came from a leader. Do you know how powerful this is? Do you know how influential this is? Influence is something that is used to win souls and destroy souls. Influence from the right person is powerful, just as influence from the wrong person is just as powerful. The enemy knows this, so if he can get someone powerful in influence to advise you to do something that will kill, steal, or destroy you and your destiny, do you think he won't? This is why it is important to know God for yourself, to have discernment and know his voice so that he may order your steps. This is not to say that there are leaders who will keep it real with you and advise you well. I know my leaders look out for me, and I am grateful for that.

One may really heed the instruction to go back to a dangerous unhealthy situation out of fear of not being accepted, or fear of being shunned, or having to alter their life with changes to come. Telling someone to go back to a place where God has delivered them from is a form of abuse. We have to stop acting as if we know why people are divorced when in-fact we have no idea of why there was a parting, other than the fact that it makes a ministry look bad and it doesn't line up with Mark 10:9, which was a response to people trying to trap Jesus, and not him answering to address abuse and abandonment, or any other treatment that God would weigh the heart on.

If you feel that you did not marry the right person, and if one or both parties are saved there is much hope for your marriage. There are marriages all over the world that have been arranged, especially in the eastern part of the world, and love was the last thing that determined if the couple was to get or stay married. You don't need to be in love with someone to have a successful marriage, but I am witness that it sure does make a difference in many areas.

Post-traumatic stress disorder after experiencing divorce is real. One person may experience it, and another may not. It depends on their experiences and who they are as a person and what they are released from or what they left. Everyone processes loss and grief differently. Grief recovery is a setting where individuals can group up and review and deal with various losses and grief over one's life. In grief recovery classes one of the rules is that no one should ever tell you that they understand what someone else has been through, even if you faced something similar, the reason being is because you are not that person and that person is not you, therefore your experiences and how you handle and process loss and grief is not the same. A person who just lost their mother may be in tears for months based on the relationship that was there, another person may not have cried at all due to the lack of relationship with their mother. The same is with divorce, one may mope and grope for years after losing a spouse due to divorce and never really heal or recover, others are ready to move on the day after the papers are signed, not that that is encouraged, but each relationship is different and has a different history. You cannot expect all divorced people to be in counseling for years after their divorce because it seems appropriate to you. Yes there should be some grief due to the loss and the failed expectations, plans and dreams, but that time frame is different for people, it is not the same across the board. Look at Abigail's testimony? How long did she go through the church's counseling classes before she married King David?

Church and religion sometimes can say in so many words to forget what Jesus said in respect to someone being able to move on in the case of sexual immorality. In so many words what is being said is, we will tell you and show you what's approved not approved regardless of what Jesus said.

Let us review the beginning. Adam and Eve was created by God, and couples that joined together after them came together in the form of a ceremony of some kind, after the fall. In the beginning it was not meant for husband and wife to part, after the fall there has been a number of results from the fall, some include homosexuality, pedophilia, murder, cruelty of various types and kinds, selfishness, and divorce. As believers we often seem to understand the other results of the fall but when it comes to divorce it's almost as if divorce could never be a result of the fall the way many are surprised that it continues to occur. There are programs that help with a number of results of the fall such as rehab for drug addicts, AA for alcoholics, recovery groups for prostitutes and those struggling with abuse. My question is why are the divorce recovery and grief recovery groups newer to the church compared to past generations? The rate is increasing and having an effect on the church, however there have always been people in the church who have faced this. It makes me wonder if they were just left by the wayside. Nevertheless I believe it's great to see programs being adopted by churches who desire to include everyone in their congregation which promotes health. Eventually man made vows were written after Christ came to earth and spoke on the matter in Mark 10:9. The written man made marriage vows were settled approximately four hundred years after Christ's ascension to heaven. The vows that are said in weddings all over the world were written centuries after what God joined together in the beginning. In the book John 1, we see where nothing came into being that was not made by Christ who was in the beginning because he is the Word of God himself. Therefore that includes marriage, the joining together of man and woman. These manmade vows were later used in wedding ceremonies centuries later after the first man and woman were joined together by God before the fall of man. In reality, before the manmade vows were created, there were several unions made without them. The vows were to be an addition or confirmation of being joined together in marriage according to God joining man and wife together. When the vows were eventually made, by men, they reflected these words: I, (name), take you (name), to be my (wife/husband), to have and to hold from this day forward, for better or for worse, for richer, for poorer, in sickness and in health, to love and to cherish; from this day forward until death do us part. The beginning of recording marriages started with the Roman Empire in the time of the Roman Empire (17 BC - 476 AD). The manmade marriage vows originated from the "Book of Common Prayer" which originated in 1549 included the vows used in weddings, which were not created by God or found anywhere in the bible. We have taken manmade vows and made them the standard for people living in a fallen state, particularly when it comes to adultery, in today's world, the manmade vows are holding more weight than what Jesus Christ himself has proclaimed about sexual immorality, also in addition to abuse and abandonment which the Word of God does not approve of. This has been passed down generation to generation and it has become a stronghold just like slavery was passed down with the mindset of it being right in God's perspective. We often pass down what was passed down to us, especially in regards to how we were taught. Just ask a young lady, "Why do you bake that pound cake the way that you do"? She will often answer, because this is how my mom did it, and her mother, and her mother before her. Throughout the ages, after the fall, divorce was permitted because of the hardness of hearts seen in Matthew 19:8 which was a result of the fall. Christ advised that there is something past the word "worst" referring to the manmade vows.

This is nothing to take light, because the condition of the heart will determine much. God understood what a hard heart is capable of. Hard hearts were never created by God or intended for people to have from the beginning, but because of the fall, they are present. God understands what the results of a hard heart looks like. It was not that God approved of divorce because of people having a hard heart, but I believe that God used divorce in the Old Testament as he does today to set free those tied to people with hard hearts. It is clear to see in the Old Testament that God would kill or cut off a people with a certain type of spirit or blood to prevent it from being passed down or continued. If God would so much kill a tribe, a nation, or group of men, women and children for the sake of his name, holiness, and people, how much more will God deliver one of his children from one with the heart of Pharaoh?

Men were primarily the ones who initiated divorce ages ago because if they were not pleased with their wife they had the option to write her a certificate of divorce, which was biblical in those days. It was a simple as that. She could be abandoned and put away and not have any say in the matter at all. If you look throughout the ages you will see that there were not many divorces in certain eras compared to others. Women just did not have a voice in most of the early eras. Anything that was going on in the marriage was disclosed and kept behind closed doors, and only God's eye was able to witness a lot that occurred. If you were being abused emotionally, mentally, and or physically, a victim of adultery or abandonment, many times there was not legal aid that could help you at all being a woman. As a woman you submitted to men, period, including those with hard hearts. Submitting to men is something that God has caused us to do as a result of the fall, however God never intended for women from the beginning to submit to any man that is abusing her mentally, physically, and emotionally, neither do I believe it's something that he wants anyone to do, whether man or woman if they are receiving wrong treatment from their spouse. In the beginning Adam and Eve were created equal with different roles. The introduction of marital submission never came into play until the fall. Let us review Matthew 19. We see some Pharisees who came and tried to trap him with this question: "Should a man be allowed to divorce his wife for just any reason?"

"Haven't you read the Scriptures?" Jesus replied. "They record that from the beginning 'God made them male and female. And he said, 'This explains why a man leaves his father and mother and is joined to his wife, and the two are united into one. Since they are no longer two but one, let no one split apart what God has joined together."

"Then why did Moses say in the law that a man could give his wife a written notice of divorce and send her away?" they asked.

Jesus replied, "Moses permitted divorce only as a concession to your hard hearts, but it was not what God had originally intended. And I tell you this; whoever divorces his wife and marries someone else commits adultery—unless his wife has been unfaithful"

Jesus' disciples then said to him, "If this is the case, it is better not to marry!" If Jesus told you in Matthew 19: 9 that if your spouse has been unfaithful to you then you are free from the covenant because it has been broken. As we have just reviewed, in 1549 men came along with manmade vows from the Book of Common Prayer that state specifically for one to take their spouse **for better or**

for worst. Man will act as if there is absolutely nothing past worst under the sun, including abuse, adultery and abandonment. Basically what they are saying is, no matter what happens or occurs or what it looks like, even if these things did occur and take place, you agreed to stay for better or for worst. This is an ideology passed down throughout generations and people will be quick to throw this ideology they have adopted because they believe this is right in God's eyes, not knowing where it originated from or how this compares to God's word when Jesus clearly stated that there is something past worst in Matthew 5:32 and Matthew 19:9. Don't hear me wrong that a couple should not try to make it past worst; they should, as I have been there. Just like slave owners thought slavery was right and passed this ideology down to their children, so this has been passed down for people to accept this notion that God never supported, yet has been passed down as a stronghold in the minds of society which keeps people in many different types of bondages.

If Jesus Christ simply stated that there is apparently something beyond worse and that is sexual immorality why then does the church tell you forget what Jesus said, do what we tell you to do. A stronghold has been set up in with the manmade vows of for better or for worse. Jesus knew that even though that God did not intend for any separation before the fall that there would be issues due to the fall that would cause a separation and that which is clearly permissible is what he said: unless it's for sexual immorality: anyone claiming that their spouse has been unfaithful to them should have proof of this, usually this comes in the form of another child being born outside the marriage, or some type of disease that is contracted, or the spouse admitting this openly, or the spouse being caught. These are some examples of evidence, however many times there are affairs that occur in marriages, and it goes with the spouse to their grave. The affair may have never been shared, neither is there any evidence until the funeral that is, when unexpected guest arrive and end up hysterically crying over the casket.

So Jesus clearly states what happens with sexual immorality, but he does not directly mention anything about abandonment or abuse because it was addressed to answer specifically if one should divorce their spouse for any cause or reason at all, to people that were trying to trap him. Jesus knew that many would divorce for no reason at all and then there would be believers who would divorce for a specific reason or cause that his words clearly justifies regarding wrong treatments that God does not approve throughout his word.

The enemy knows that if sexual immorality has happened, abuse, or abandonment that this releases the spouse as a result after the fall, therefore if a child of God that has potential to grow, equip, and be advantageous against Satan and his kingdom, this won't be beneficial for the kingdom of darkness. He has set up strongholds in the minds of religious people to make others feel beyond shame if they do divorce even if it is for a permissible justifiable reason according to God's Word. If Jesus said you are free why then do you not feel free? Because of ideologies of judgments passed down from generation to generation those stereotypes those who divorce to be disqualified by religious people who are not even aware of what they adopted or what they are passing on. Religious people shun you and condemn you, Christians do not. Christians love you and pray for you, and understand that they themselves are not without sin. This has been a demonic stronghold set up in the minds of people that have been transferred down into congregations and it makes one scared to death to actually leave their spouse who has caused them to be victim to any of the three. It should not be forced upon you to stay if you are released to leave biblically, and your decision should be respected as biblical, regardless of how the relationship began. Jesus does not address how the relationship started whether it was wrong or right. If it did not start right perhaps there can be more grace towards the offender and maybe you can clean the slate and start over.

Jesus knew there would be cases where sexual immorality would be encountered and answered their question in the area of where it was asked and that was for the topic "for any reason at all", he knew they would be quoting him here on marriage for years to come and thought it necessary to include that instruction even though there would be more issues such as abuse and abandonment, along with the wheat and tares being joined together. All of this was too complex, and Jesus was not going over all of that with children of darkness who didn't accept what he was saying and doing anyway. Why share your wisdom with people who don't fear God and who are only trying to trap you? Why give a perverse generation a sign when they won't believe anyway. Jesus dealt with those things that were necessary to deal with as he is God and knows all and sees all, therefore whatever needs to be dealt with in the life of his child will be, as he is God and he is greater than his Word. Jesus has a way of communicating to the believer personally that if you are in him he has you covered, you have to trust him, it may not be in the outcome you expect, but he has your back and is watching every abuser in your life whether that is behind closed doors at your home, or on Sunday morning from a pulpit, or in a ministry you are serving in. Jesus knew that if you were in him he would take care of anything that rises up against you anyway.

There is no deliverer like God Almighty! You could look up and be carried away by angels, before you know it you were somewhere in one reality, and God will flip the page in your life, and you will look up somewhere else safe and intact. Look at Peter's release from prison. He didn't even believe he was being delivered when it was occurring because it felt like a daze or dream to him, but it was real! If Paul and Silas wanted to remain in chains after they began praising and worshipping they couldn't. This is what a lot of people don't understand about those who have experienced divorce. Even if you wanted to stay in some cases when a chain is broken off of you, you can't put it back on even if you tried. Just ask Paul and Silas who were singing praises to God when their chains fell off. Do you think chains stop breaking when they were set free from prison? Too many supernatural doors opened for me, to walk back into a jail cell to put broken chains back around my wrists and ankles. Jesus said do not dwell on the past and he makes all things new. God will shut doors no man can shut, and open doors no man can open. We often hear this a lot without the revelation of it, but I am a witness it's real. There will be people who will try and tell you what you qualify for or what you don't. Nevertheless, listen to God's voice and walk in peace, for you were called to it (1 Corinthians 7:15). There are many other books that are geared towards helping married couples and those who have reconciled. This book is for those who have witnessed that there is not a lot of help or books to address where they are biblically with regards to divorce. It is for those who are separated and are not reconciling, divorcees, and those who will be ministering to divorced people within the church, or even church members who encounter divorcees regularly, believe it or not whether you want to or not they are in the world, and they matter, God loves them, and has assignments for their lives just as those who have not experienced divorce. I speak by faith that after I have been married for twenty or thirty years, I'll write another book specifically for successful married couples, and perhaps you may like that book a lot better.

Things can get difficult when choices regarding the future affect health and safety as well in marriage. For example, if you choose to sleep with someone that you know has HIV even though you may be married to them, don't be surprised if you get it and don't be surprised if it takes you to your death bed sooner than you could have gone. You have to be wise and discern the direction. I am grateful to God that I never contracted any type of STD; however others may not have been as fortunate in this area. I know a woman who has gone on to glory from contracting HIV from her husband due to an affair. The sad part about her testimony is that she had several opportunities to distance herself, however she wanted to remain and fight for the marriage.

A companion of a fool will suffer harm. Proverbs 13:20 and Proverbs 26:4 states there is no reasoning with a fool and a companion of a fool will suffer harm. So is it possible to be married to a fool and not suffer harm? A fool is a fool and there is no understanding a fool has, therefore how do I remain married to someone who is demonstrating foolish behavior. You may say, you should have never married a fool to begin with. Ideally that is correct, yet what about after the fact? This is what the majority faces, and every situation does not end the same, and just because you can't relate or perhaps don't care, doesn't mean God doesn't care. He does, because he loves people. A good book to read concerning this subject is called Foolproofing your life by Jan Silvious. This is a read that will encourage those dealing with difficult people you have to deal with, ranging from a spouse, a supervisor, a co-worker, a family member and more. Someone very influential in my life advised me how to listen and interact with a fool. He told me, when you are dealing with this type of a person, always imagine that you are listening and talking to that person, and to imagine a wheelchair strapped to the side of their head, because if you don't see the wheel chair, you will allow their blindness and sickness to invade your peace and your assurance in God.

Let's look at David's wives. Abigail was the only one that God specifically chose as well as David, Michal was the people's choice, Bathsheba was his oops mistake, and Ahinoam was one David chose to take as his. But Abigail was sent to him by God according to 1 Samuel 25:32. He found her as she was sent to him.

Whatever happened to Michal? After he cursed her where did she go, did she remain with David, did she go back to the man that Saul had married her off to while she was married to David still, and what about those encounters with her second husband being taken back by David to be united to him. Did she just stay with him in the palace not to give birth to any offspring or did he send her away to be with someone else? We don't know.

If issues aren't corrected they can be repeated in another marriage, this is a possibility, there is also the possibility for a successful marriage in the grace of God to be established and maintained. I would include that if a person has a special call on their life nothing including a bad marriage and or divorce can stop their assignment even if that includes them being married to someone others may deem them unqualified…let's look at Moses. Of all the babies killed by Pharaoh's order he was the one who survived. He was the 1% out of 99% who lived and made it through the dangerous journey of the Nile River right into the home of his enemy.

Had David been anybody else perhaps things wouldn't have gone well for that person. Because it was David, a man after God's own heart, things were unique. Look at Sarah in the King's palace, had it been anyone else taken in the King's palace, perhaps the story would have ended differently, but she was Abraham's wife. I speak to your life, that God is covering you just the same. When you belong to God, he will ensure that what would have typically taken you over, will not!

Throughout the word there are several scriptures that pertain to how God does not support abuse and abandonment. Again, Jesus was replying to Pharisees and didn't see fit to give them more on the subject because they were trying to trap him. If they would have asked with a pure intent to really care about the answer for themselves and others instead of trying to trap him, perhaps Jesus would have answered differently, the responses that Jesus gave usually addressed the heart and motive it was being asked for. Example: Mark 12:17, give to Caesar what is Caesar's and give to God what is God's. His responses were directed toward their intents.

It is important to know the origin of where something came from and why it was said because that could make all the difference. Paul gives some instructions regarding marriage. They address some things, but they don't address many other hypothetical examples. He gives some of his perspectives and advice, and he also gives instructions from the Lord. Paul was a single person during his time of ministry yet he may have been married when he was a part of the Sanhedrin council, as it was a requirement. Paul's assignment may be different from yours. Paul had the assignment to be a trailblazer in the gospel and to plant the early churches. There are high callings today to do similar things for those with a similar call, however Paul's assignment was unique. Paul says it's better to be single as he. In the beginning singleness was not meant to be good, just as separation was not meant at all, however there are some benefits of remaining single as Paul sees, just as there may be a beneficial purpose in separation due to circumstances God acknowledges, even though man may not. Paul says it's better to be alone. In Ecclesiastes 4:9 it says that two are better than one because they have a good return on their labor, if either of them falls down, one can help the other up, but pity anyone who falls and has no one to help them up. Also if two lie down together they will keep warm, but how can one keep warm alone? Though one can be overpowered, two can defend themselves. A cord of three strands is not easily broken. God also says it is not good for man to be alone in Genesis 2:18.

In the beginning it was not good for man to be alone but due to the fall Paul says it is better to be single, but it was not so in the beginning when God said it wasn't good for man to be alone. There are many results from the fall that were not intended from the beginning as we have discussed.

I find it interesting that all the women in the genealogy of Christ were pregnant when God saw fit for them to be. Ruth didn't get pregnant by her first husband; Tamar didn't get pregnant by her first husband or his brother. Did Bathsheba have children with Uriah? The Bible doesn't say, if she didn't, did God know that she would carry King Solomon? Did God know that David would sin in adultery before he even did it? If so, could it be possible that God chose the woman that David would have adultery with? Of course this sounds absolutely silly, however if God did know, and David was God's anointed wouldn't he be involved with even his wrong decisions? Absolutely God didn't cause the affair, but after a while he was involved with how things panned out with taking the first child by death that was conceived and later He loved the second child and gave Solomon an assignment.

Mary of course were not like the others, it wasn't that she conceived and gave birth as the others, but she conceived earlier in life but it too was a suddenly surprise that was a serious dilemma. Mary was found to be with child prior to getting married to her espoused husband Joseph. A man who desired honor his entire life. Can you imagine being hungry for honor your entire life come to a point where you are now the laughing stock of the town. Humiliation was not honor! Joseph was going to put her away silently, but he too didn't understand God's plan. God's plan was to honor Joseph with the Lord's honor that would be tracked from generation to generation. You may be looking for something to come to you in one way, and even push away the very blessing you have been waiting on and living for, because of how radical you have to be in order to obtain it. Yet, God gave Joseph a dream not to fear taking Mary as his wife, and he indeed received honor in a way he'd never imagine!

Luke 13:34 is where God talks about gathering his children like a hen (female) gathering her young. Why did God use a feminine example? Because he knows that women have a way of reaching him. Women are soft, caring, and sensitive. Not to say that men are not, and not to say that all woman are. But God will often call for the wailing "women" when the expression of emotion is necessary.

150

Do men wail? In my opinion, not like women. We women feel! It was given to us by God, and it is not something to categorize with "the flesh". God called for the wailing women in Jeremiah 9:17. All throughout the bible you see where God and his people had emotions and expressed them. This is a very fine line, because when it comes to the things of the Spirit God does not have emotions like us in the flesh, yet he is passionate and experiences different feelings. God gets jealous, angry, and He can even be grieved. He can be joyous and sing and dance which derives from celebration.

Look at David who was expressive in his depressions and his joys! Women are designed to tap into feelings a little differently than men. Women are designed to care and nurture naturally. Our cultures impact how we view feeling as well. The people of the bible were Mediterranean people who respond to their feelings and emotions much differently than Americans who are taught to suppress their feelings which manifests even in our dry worship. It is not common to go to other countries to see them pour themselves out before God in praise and worship because it's how they have been conditioned and hardwired. In America we hardwire our children to feel nothing and to suppress emotion, we even call it godly. No wonder his presence isn't always ushered into a place. God says to enter his gates with thanksgiving and his courts with praise. The closer we get to God, the more expression sometimes ought to take place. God said let everything that has breath praise the Lord. That means noise is an indication that we are alive and have breath, however in certain cultures noise is discouraged. This is not to say that there are not riches in silence, there are, however when dealing with our relationships with God there is a time for everything. In the bible, when someone passed away they literally mourned for weeks and months. It was not custom to teach someone to suppress feelings and emotions all their lives to finally come to a funeral with dry eyes. God said no, bring wailers, people who feel. In order to cry you have to feel a little something, but in order to wail you have to get expressions out my friend. John 11:35 is where we see Christ weeping.

A man and a woman sat and heard the same sermon, at the same church, on the same day. When walking out after service was over, the man was asked what did the preacher teach today. The man answered and said, Jesus said if you love me you will keep my commandments. The same question was asked to the woman who was sitting two seats beside this same man. The woman answered and said, the pastor taught on Jesus praying for people who knew not what they were doing. A logical response verses a heartfelt one. Are both right? Yes both are right. The pastor did preach on this, but the way it's interpreted derives from the lens, heart, and emotion that one has.

Whatever was inside of Adam that he originally had was taken out of him before Eve was fashioned. Was it care and sensitivity? We don't know, but we do know that a woman has things inside her men can't seem to get in touch with. We see this in Matthew 26:6-13 where a woman broke an expensive perfume jar to express her love and feelings for Jesus in the presence of many men who didn't get it. Luke 7:37-38 says and she wiped the feet of Jesus with her hair and tears.

There are other passages where the opposite is shown. Look at David's wife Michal in 2 Samuel 6:16. Michal despised that David danced out of his robe as he was praising God. What was the condition of her heart? We also see where men cried unto God such as David and the prophets. The difference in all is the weighing of the hearts. When the heart weighs just right, worship always is to follow.

Studies show that remarriages fail however there is a small percentage that is successful. If God has a plan for your life if you are divorced and that does involve remarriage, don't be discouraged by the statistics. Remember that Moses was 1% out of 99 babies who not only lived after Pharaoh's decree, but survived through the Nile River, and even past this, he survived in the house of his enemy for years without his identity being revealed, until the appointed time set by God.

What happens in the area of sex that contributes to the breakdown of marriages that end in divorce? The connection of sex in a marriage is so important and critical and yet there are so many couples who are not healthy sexually. There are many women who struggle in this area. Women are driven by affection and love and when that is not received it is not easy to freely give themselves when they don't feel valued by their husbands. When his physical need becomes greater than the commandment to love her, the heart is penetrated in that his love for her may be no love at all. In loving someone, you consider and listen to them. When his need to gratify his flesh is more important than her heart walls begin to rise up. When you know she may not be in the mood and you take it anyway, what you have just said is I heard your heart; however I don't care because my flesh is more important than you and your heart. This damages a woman and makes her feel as if there is only one thing she's desired for and that is to be used physically to gratify her spouse's sexual need.

A wife is not commandment to love her husband but respect him. When she refuses her body she is saying I don't respect you, but it can be difficult to respect someone who does not love you and you're designed to receive love. A husband is expected to love to his wife like Christ loved the church and gave himself up for her. Women are expected to just accept the fact that their husbands are not willing to die, but meeting the need of their flesh regardless how she may feel, and it doesn't make sense if the husband who does this wants to act spiritual after communicating to his wife that he doesn't care about her heart because his flesh is more important. This is sad, because intimacy is supposed to be beautiful and not selfish.

He begins to love her out of his definition of love and not by what the Word of God says. The mindset is eventually built that says, I'll love her my way and I won't be convicted by the fact that I really didn't love her the way I was commanded by God. When this happens it makes women not want to be connected to someone who is supposed to love them but just demonstrated the opposite.

The same goes for the wife in respecting the husband in a way she feels is acceptable, knowing it does not reflect biblical respect and honor. Men need to be built up and we as women can tear them down with our words that pierce their esteem. We as women give birth not only give birth naturally but spiritually as well. There are many negative things that can be birthed from how we use our words and if we are building up men instead of tearing them down. It takes effort to keep the bedroom hot and interesting. What is done in the beginning can't be slacked later on. We as women have to keep it right, and keep it tight. We have to keep the tutifruity fruity! There are books you can look into getting that will show you precisely how to keep those muscles tight and right! Do your research! Men are also visual creatures. I admit, I even slacked in this area after all I was carrying as a young wife. I didn't always wear things I knew my spouse at the time would go bonkers to see and experience. Men you too have to keep it tight and switch up the attire as well. The pressure is usually placed on the woman, however we like something to look at and experience as well.

Sometimes when sex is being withheld it's a silent cry that screams show me you love me, prove to me you love me by listening and caring for my heart more than your forever hungry penis. However it is viewed as withholding because men can be more analytical instead of emotional so instead of recognizing the woman's emotions he immediately classifies her behavior according to what Paul says in 1 Corinthians 7:5. You can say with your mouth you love me but when it's time to show that love, prayerfully the actions back it up. I do believe there is something in the hearts of many wives that want to know how much their husband's love them outside of lip service and the one thing men seem to need and want so much other than respect is sex. When the man blows up or throws a temper tantrum if the woman doesn't have a mutual desire, or he begins to react in a way that says my flesh is more important than you or your heart, then that is when there are thoughts planted in the wife's mind to make her feel as if she is not truly loved. There are many women who don't struggle in this area, but I believe many do, however they don't want to admit it. If you are not one that does praise God for you, you are not able to empathize with those who do. It is true that when a man takes on a wife there are marital rights such as sex, just as a man is to provide for his wife. Rights are real, and no one should have to be denied their rights. Yet, rights have nothing to do with the heart. If you want your wife to give you sex because it's your right and you're not considering her mind, heart, and emotions at all, I'd ask if you are obeying the instruction to love your wife and give yourself up for her (Ephesians 5:25).

As a wife, if you receive the provision your husband sustains you with out of mere rights, but you are not considering his efforts or acknowledge how hard he works to provide, or demonstrate gratefulness, I'd ask if you are really respecting, honoring, and cherishing him. It's not always easy, especially when there are so many unresolved issues. We as women can get stuck with issues and are not able to move on, when I have learned, men tend to just move on, even on top of issues that are not discussed or resolved. It doesn't always mean they don't care; it's just how many are programmed. We as women are more detailed and have a need to address many things, when men just move forward. This is a good thing I have learned because it keeps you on the move in the relationship; however it's not to say that certain things should be ignored. What happens a lot of the time is that rights are exercised in marriage without love. It's called going through the motions. When couples operate out of obligation and duty verses an authentic love, breakdown is soon to occur. Regardless of position or roles the word calls for believers to honor each other, submit to one another, and love one another. We all are to be clothed in humility according to 2 Peter, not arrogance, pride, or harshness. This applies to those in leadership when dealing with those who are not. There is a particular honor and reverence that is due to those in authority and at the same time they are also called to honor, love, and submit to other believers as well. 2 Peter 1:5-9 demonstrates what we are to look like as we mature and grow in God. He or she whom has authority and has not grown in the things listed here are said in verse 9, that but those who fail to develop in this way or lack any of these things are shortsighted or blind, forgetting that they themselves have been cleansed from their old sins.

It is easy to say to another to stay with a spouse if there is physical abuse going on, and you are not living in that person's shoes. This is the issue with many things. We are looking at people's situations on the outside looking in; we have not walked in their shoes. Jesus knew this. That is why he said in Luke 23:34, Father forgive them, for they know now what they do. If he took sin upon himself who had no sin, then he knew fully the ignorance that sin brings. The Word says he who knows God obeys him, and you can't love God unless you obey his commandments however when sin is involved, this brings separation from God. There also comes a lack of knowledge and this brings destruction: Hosea 4:6. Let's face it Jesus is the most understanding person in the world. He says not to judge any many before the end time because only he knows who the saved and unsaved are. No matter how hard we fruit inspect and no matter how much we discern someone being in or out of Christ, we are never to judge. The instruction is not to judge anyone before the last day. This does not mean you can't make wise decisions about interacting with someone specific. The Word says a companion of fools will suffer harm. I am not to judge you, even though all your actions say that you belong to the devil, it is not my job to know if you are saved or to judge you but it is important to know if there are any threats to harmful situations that could directly influence my life. I can either position myself to remain in a life threatening relationship or take measures to enhance health and safety. Couples who do not face such extreme measures may not be able to relate in this area. Abuse is so real and it can damage your entire being if you allow it to continue for a while. There are people who remained in relationships to later discover they have a life threatening sickness or disease, some have died from causes not known. I believe it is a truth that the enemy doesn't have to flat out kill you in a split second by a bullet, and life threatening murder scene, or ill-gotten fate, but that he can kill you silently over a lifetime in a toxic relationship that is soiling your organs alive moment by moment over years.

All the work you put in is in vain if both are not in agreement. Perhaps the spouse may be won, perhaps they won't. The scripture gives light to the truth, and the truth is **either a possibility,** not just the one side that is primarily displayed, nor the side you'd prefer. We know what to do with the one scenario in the church of a spouse being won to Christ which is great! All your perseverance seemed to have worked, and to God be the glory, but in the church we don't do well with the other possibility if the spouse is not brought to Christ even over a lifetime. This is also a reality. The church is to be a place for sick people who are getting better and growing into the likeness of Christ, and for sinners to be convicted to give their lives to Christ and change for the better. It is not a museum for perfect people to be put on display.

Your prayer is variable as God will not violate the will of another person. Pray without ceasing, but know that God is a gentleman and He is not interrupting one's will if they choose to reject him, and biblically speaking has already rejected him before the foundation of the world. God is not forceful. That is not one of his characteristics and it shouldn't be anyone who represents him either. Because one rejects Christ does not mean they are a mean person, in fact they could have lovely characteristics, and be kind, and rich, and handsome, beautiful, ugly, or fat. They could be intelligent, and wise, and smile a lot, and they could even be a philanthropist. But in one area of life, if they have chosen to reject Christ as Lord and savior of their lives, it is written that they will not be with Christ after this life on earth. Those that reject Christ does not always look and sound like Satan. Many do, but there are others who don't, they actually seem like great people. Being great, nice, kind, or a good person does not save you. It is only believing in Christ Jesus, that He is the way, the truth, and the life, and that no one comes before God unless by way of Him!

Yes, it is certainly evident that people are not preparing well for marriages in today's time, but that is not stopping them from marrying. So when ministering it's not supporting to say it's not our responsibility that you choose to marry who you did. This is very true, yet if one is called to ministry it will be their responsibility by the time the ministry is affected by those marriages in one form or another, which will be many, of different situations and circumstances. We have to stand and fight in the face of what's going on in the world, but you don't leave your brother or sister out there saying fend for yourself, you got yourself in that mess, get yourself out, all the while believing to be the good Samaritan who stopped alongside of the road to help. We are to bare one another's burdens, not say, well I'm happy, too bad for you and your life, I got mines, you go get yours. Ministry is messy, and sometimes you have to get in the mud. As I mention "ministry", know that formally it's nice to have a license to minister and ordination if your particular church requires that, however any person that you discern by God that is able to help you with where you are, don't let a lack of credentials from man keep you from your deliverance, your healing, or your breakthrough. The titles, licensing, and positions are what man uses to affirm what God has already done in one's life, not the other way around. Be mindful, that God will and can use anyone. What a license or ordination says is that **man** has approved or affirmed the call of God on your life. Every prophet and priest in the Bible we read about did not have a piece of paper from man that qualified them to do what God called them to do. There were those who were anointed formally as priest or confirmed by God to be a prophet among the people, yet in today's generation you have many who hold a title or position yet have no real anointing from God or call from God, even though man has confirmed them. Nevertheless, it's nice to have those things, yet you don't need them to be who God has called you to be. If it be His will, and if it's important enough to God for your assignment, then those things will occur in the timing it's supposed to.

In marriages today, people are geared up to enter into a covenant that is totally self-seeking and self-gratifying. My spiritual father always asks couples two questions when they come for counseling. The first question is what did you expect to get when you got married. People go on and on pouring out their long wish list of things they wanted to get and expected to get. Then the second question he asks after they have exhausted themselves of their desires is, and what did you expect to give? This is usually when there is silence. The silence indicates that the person didn't expect to give that much, and if so, not as much as they desired to get. It goes to show that society has trained people to write their wish list and not to settle for anything less until you receive just that, when that is not biblical. When did Eve have to pass the bar exam to qualify for Adam? Did they have a wish list? I am not saying don't go for what you desire, but when you have all these things on your list being very picky you are failing to realize that marriage is not about you sulking up your desires, but it's also for you to give without measure as well.

Measuring Different Shades of Blue

Marriages are like snowflakes. All come from the same source and are made by the same principles having begun alike in origin and a destination aimed for but different.

There can be similarities among marriages, however not one of them are the same. So it is with your finger prints. However we don't understand this, and we operate as if all marriages are to look exactly alike. We all come from different home of origins that may look similar, but due to the idiosyncrasies of individuals, and life's circumstances we are not all the same. So it is with marriages that are different. For example, in one marriage the husband may be the more spirit filled believer than his wife. In another marriage, the wife may be the more spirit filled believer. I have often heard the question, how is it that two Spirit filled believers can get a divorce? I'd ask the question back, why is it that you assume both people are Spirit filled believers? I agree, if both are Spirit filled, divorce should never occur, yet the truth of the matter is that because both participate in church functions and wear the believer uniform doesn't mean that both are believers and both are Spirit filled. This is why divorce usually happens in the body of Christ, someone who is professing is not filled with the Spirit of God. Then there are other reasons divorce could happen between believers as selfishness sets in and abuse, abandonment, and adultery occur. Yes even believers are subject to these. You might ask, well, if you are a Spirit filled believer why would anyone filled with the Spirit of God do any of those things. Someone apparently gave in to a temptation, a selfish motive, or chose not to walk in the will and Spirit of God even after a filling occurred. Marriages that exist with two believers who are Spirit filled will never understand what it is like to face certain challenges others may face who are joined to one who is not a believer or is not Spirit filled. The ideal marriage is for both spouses to be Spirit filled prior to the marriage, yet we can see this is not occurring as the majority. The question is what now? What do we do? If you have been married as a believer who is filled with the spirit of God to another who is as well, hats off to you, I thank God for your life, struggle, and testimony as it will serve as a major witness, yet do not believe in anyway shape or form that you are somehow better than another, or that God loves you more, or even act as if you have kept the law more than another who is divorced.

In another marriage, both may be spirit filled. In another, both may be spirit filled but they both were filled at different seasons in their marriage. Perhaps one speaks in tongues and the other does not. In another both could be spirit filled and they were already spirit filled before they joined in marriage. The last example is the ideal one, but it is not the reality of most marriages in the church, which is that both spouses are supposed to be filled with God's spirit and power. Is the power within the church missing because the power within marriages is missing? The church is only as strong as those that make it up. Is the enemy not clever to attack marriages knowing that there is more power in evenly yoked marriages than those that are not? This tearing apart is not the same as God separating the wheat from tares within marriage. This is the enemy wanting to destroy both people in the marriage, but if he can get in through one and destroy one he will. He has more of an advantage if the stronger is tied down by the weaker. The longer the better. The longer, the less time he has to worry about the strong one in spirit breaking out to come against his kingdom. One strong believer is much more effective than ten cold or lukewarm believers. If the strong, hot believer does separate or move on, the enemy has a lot more to worry about than if that believer was still tied down to dead weight. The enemy has a lot to worry about if the weaker believer in the marriage is strengthened in spirit. This is the goal and this is what should be desired and aimed for, nevertheless it is a possibility not a guarantee. My spiritual father has always taught that when one disciples another, not only the good characteristics are passed down to the mentee, **but also the bad ones**. He is very honest and transparent about his shortcomings so that you know what they are, so you don't pick them up. You don't always find that everywhere. Therefore if someone is strong in the area of faith, those characteristics can be modeled and taught to the one being discipled, however there are some things that could be passed down that are not beneficial to that individual's life. That's why it is wise to find out what negative characteristics are present in someone that is equipping you. Learn this so that you don't unknowingly pick this up during your time with them and pass it on to someone else. That is a good tip for discipling others and being discipled. We all have imperfections and God isn't done with us yet until He calls us home, so be patient with one another, yet be aware of what not to pick up, and what not to pass on.

Yet, you may ask, why would anyone want to be hopeless? Aren't we to always have hope? The answer is, figuratively yes, depending on what the issue is, it may be best to give up hope with regards to life being threatened. For example, if a man is beating his wife, she can have all the hope and faith she wants to have, but it may be wise of her to have faith and hope from a far to ensure her safety and any children involved in that situation is safe. The book by Henry Cloud called Boundaries is a great read to teach our hopeful culture to get hopeless about some things. We hold on to hope so much that in situations where someone needs to let all hope die so they can move on or a new cycle can be birthed, the old one has to die first. This can be controversial as we learn to always keep hope alive. If your husband or wife has been beating you for the past thirty or forty years, I am sorry to say that you need to get hopeless about them not beating you anymore. This is not to say that one day they may actually change, however for you to experience a new cycle the old one has to die, the old has to go away so the new can come. I am not saying not to hope for better, because we should. I did. I am saying in some cases, depending on those variables, we may not need to preach keep hope alive depending on what's at stake. There was no hope for Satan from God. When dealing with the demonic you either have to cast the spirit out or disconnect totally. You cannot counsel a demon; a lot of people think they can. I assure you, you are wasting your time. Daniel 12:10 says clearly that the wicked will continue to be wicked. Why? Because they are wicked. This is something God clearly understands. If somebody gets taken out or eliminated, more than likely there were many times for that person to get right, but due to pride, all were refused. We see this in 1 Corinthians 5:5 and in Exodus we see Pharaoh having multiple chances to get things right, however his choice was to refuse God. Hell is a real place and it is for people who have had time to get things correct but instead have refused Christ over and over again. Time has an expiration date and so does our decisions.

People don't understand there is no having patience with the devil. There is no negotiating or counseling with a demonic spirit. Yes it may appear for a moment there may be peace, or all is well with subtle smiles and hugs, but if it is a demon you can always rest assure that at the end of the day the true nature of the spirit will always manifest and be revealed. You cannot wait for Pharaoh to get it together because he is not. It's like petting a wild lion. He looks friendly but actually he is dangerous. This is why it's not good to fellowship with darkness because of the aftermath. It's easy to tell someone this who has suffered from consequences that reflect this, than it is to go through this yourself. If you haven't had this experience you shouldn't be so quick to pride-fully tell this to others.

So what happens when you have a congregation with all these types of marriages mixed up? Small groups are formed. In one group you have it mixed with wives who are spirit filled with wives who are not, some of the husbands are spirit filled and others are not. Some may not even really be saved. Who helps who? The wives who are not spirit filled just don't get the wives who are? Why does she shout like that? Why can't she just be still and shut up and be silent as the bible says, she must not have a quiet, meek, and gentle spirit that the Word of God clearly states a woman should have because we always hear her praising God out loud. This is a contradiction and many contradictions are seen like this in the Word that may be confusing to one trying to understand opposing points within it. How can a meek and quiet woman break forth in praise and worship at any given moment? I'd ask how could she not? Women have the spirit of man inside of her. The same spirit that was breathed into Adam was breathed into Eve. One thing about real praise is for sure, which is that real praise cannot be structured or constricted to only being lifted up at certain points in a service or throughout life. Real praise breaks forth and out no matter how meek and quiet a woman or a man is for that matter. Real praise will interrupt and come out when the well of living water is struck. Anything that has God's spirit eventually makes noise. Psalm 150: 6 says let everything that has breath, praise the Lord! Heaven itself is not quiet. Therefore a woman who praises God externally may also have a meek and quiet spirit, to believe the opposite is far from the truth. Sometimes it is necessary to cry loud and spare not. Real praise does not allow you to hold your peace, although recognizing when it's necessary to be silent is vital to walking in God's spirit as well. They just don't have the revelation that the woman or wife is filled with the Spirit of God and when something is filled it begins to overflow. Intellectually this may be understood but perhaps not experientially. There could be husbands who are Spirit filled in the same group with those who are not. All he wants to do is play basketball? Really? All he wants to do is play video games. He's so loud when we are watching the game and full of vigor and excitement, but I can't understand why he is as quiet as a mouse during praise and worship at church. What is not being understood is that he is just not there yet. Where is there? To a mature point in Christ where he is filled with God's Spirit and praise and worship happens as naturally as rooting for the ball game. He may not be saved at all, only God knows. Then you may have the husband who isn't Spirit filled talking to the one who is Spirit filled thinking, "why does he always have to bring his bible to our fellowships, why is everything so spiritual, why is he trying so hard, it's making me look bad". This man doesn't realize that Jesus is his life, not just a jersey he puts on at church. What evolves is a group of people who belong to the same church and look to be on the same page, but all are on different pages and perhaps speaking different languages. Miscommunications occur, rejection soon follows, and then cliques form. What usually happens without understanding is judgment sets in, preconceived notions are maintained, and people are put in boxes and labeled. What we should be doing is putting it all in God's hands allowing him to judge as he sees and knows all things. In the mean time, those who are filled with the spirit of God should intercede for those who are not filled or far in their walks. This design reflects yoking together for the kingdom, instead of separation due to differentiation. The enemy already has the people of God separated by denominations; better yet even within those denominations there is an even greater divide among God's people as we don't understand anyone whose testimony doesn't mirror ours.

Why do we suffer and struggle so much on earth? According to a biblical study by my spiritual father it is because struggle started in the Godhead. The Father, the Son and the Holy Spirit struggled in the beginning of time when someone had to volunteer to be a sacrifice for people that were yet to be created in-case they messed up. Jesus signed up to go after free will was extended and mankind fell. You even see it in the garden of Gethsemane in Matthew 26:39. Jesus struggles with God about his letting the cup pass from him if possible. God clearly struggled with reminding Jesus of their initial agreement and he was strengthened by the Holy Spirit and prayed for the Lord's will to be done, not His own. You see another struggle in the Godhead when Christ was dying on the cross and cried out to his Father asking why have you forsaken me. If struggle was in the Godhead, we certainly will face struggle. If you look at creation and life itself it all is a struggle. From vegetation coming forth from the ground, to a baby being born out of womb, from crawling to walking, to maintaining on cane. The idea of "struggle" may be more godly than we think. To know that He is with us in the struggle makes all the difference! It may not be that of human struggle but if struggle began in the Godhead, struggle may not necessarily be a result of the fall, but perhaps it increased after the fall. The world has a name for how the universe evolved. It is called the big bang theory. This theory states that the universe came into being by a cosmic explosion and different parts of the world broke apart. When we look at God it is always evident that when something major is about to happen chaos is usually close. The chaos in a sense brings divine order in the end. Not all trouble is bad. The chaos of the big bang could have been divinely ordained by God to bring the planets into orbit. The chaos of the flood in Noah's day was to deal with what needed to be dealt with and to bring order. The chaos down in Egypt was going on to bring the Israelites up out of Egypt. Anytime there is a deliverance about to take place all hell breaks loose and chaos is happening. Anytime a major kingdom assignment is at hand chaos occurs! When the right man of God meets the right woman of God to join in a holy marriage and both people are Spirit filled, you better believe all kind of chaos and opposition is occurring. Chaos is not always a bad thing. It could be an indication that things are being ordered.

Just like within the church there are different marriages. There are different types of marriages that deal with divorce. Those who separate and reconcile, those who divorce and later remarry again after reconciliation, and those who divorce and move on whether they are single for the remainder of their lives, or whether they remarry someone different. Factors that could impact this could be age, children involved, and much more. It is not our job to tell people what they should and should not do when they reach this point. People have to hear from God themselves. If one is not to marry again in God's eye sight perhaps you shouldn't be telling them to get married. I personally believe that it is not good for people to be alone and God is relational and desires for us to be relational.

Then you have someone who is divorced and who has moved on and desires to remarry after their time of counseling, healing, and restoration has taken place to the extent necessary. You should absolutely let the dust settle at the same time be wise about where you may be in life, and everyone's situation is not the same. For example, if you don't have children and you desire to have children, it's nice to hear about other women giving birth to their first child at forty or fifty, but that may not mean you desire to or that is God's timing for you to give birth that late in life. There is a time to have your children, and it's not always at a ripe age for most. You shouldn't be telling this person God does not want you to marry again; perhaps he has some special for that person. Perhaps all that man or woman went through in their first marriage can be used for the glory of God in God's eye sight for another marriage assignment. Life must go on. The point is we have to stop "playing God" in people's lives and telling people what their testimony should be after experiencing divorce.

Everyone may not be single for ten or twenty years, and the Word says in 1 Corinthians 7:28 that it is not sin to marry. And 1 Corinthians 7:8-9 explains that it is better to marry than to burn with lust. Everyone cannot attest to being sexually active within a marriage and cutting that off due to death or divorce. That is a real process and God can do some awesome things in your spirit during that time. You can encourage, give your opinion, and pray for people but you are not God or the Holy Spirit in their lives. The Word of God references many scriptures where there is wisdom in a multitude of counselors, but be aware that everyone is not a counselor and every counselor may not be a God assigned counselor to you.

This is why in addition to seeking wise counsel you have to hear from God yourself! You have to be able to make decisions being led by the Spirit of God. What God may share with you, may not be for everyone else to know or hear. It may not make sense to others, but God wants us to fully trust him just like Abraham who went to a land he knew not. If you are married then this may be a bit different as the man is the head of the marriage and typically should have the final say in the matter with the consideration of his wife of course, nevertheless if he is wrong then she has to be willing to go down with him in the matter because he leads. She leads too but in different areas as designed by God. The woman is the chief operational officer of the matters of the atmosphere of her home, it is nice to be the director of your department, or the fortune five woman of the month, but to be in leadership in your home in the vein God created you to be, whether male or female. This does not mean you are controlling and running everything at home, but it does mean you know everything you need to know and are aware of everything you need to be aware of when it comes to your home and your family. Yes, thus says the woman who is divorced with no children. A wise first lady once said when someone gives you change, you take the pieces of change you need, and if there are not pieces you don't need, lay it back on the table, put what you received in your pocket, walk away and have a nice day. Similar to eating the meat and spitting out the bones. Because one can preach on the matter or subject does not mean that the person is always getting an A in that area. It is often where you see a man of God preach a great sermon to end it by treating his wife rudely in public, or a mother who publically appears to be sweet and generous but abuses her children. We are to practice what we preach; however there are things being taught by people, and they are still working in that area having yet mastered it. Be patient with one another.

This is not to be likened to a hard hearted spouse saying I am working on it, be patient with me, this could be the farthest thing from the truth, it could mean just what they said, or it could just be something to say and in reality, he or she is not working on anything. Like Pharaoh, his heart and mind was already made up when he put on a front and had Moses pray for him so the plagues would cease. The moment when they did cease, he went right back to being his satanic self.

The point here is that there must be action that follows. You are working on it? But does it take 20 years to finally get something simple like watching what you say, not hitting below the belt with words, not cheating on your spouse any longer? Still spending money any way you want and refusing to budget. These are some of the things I am referencing.

God only makes originals and never copies. This includes our callings, purposes, and our relationships with him. Yes they are similar in the fact that we are producing the same goal. They may be very different in other areas that God may only see and know. Look at Moses and Joseph. There are a lot of similarities. Joseph helped Israel (his family before they grew into a large nation) get to Egypt to save them from famine. There could be more to this than what is written. Perhaps God saw a need for Israel to become slaves. Perhaps God saw a need for one to be placed in a temporary bondage. Maybe there were things they needed to learn or grasp in spirit and character.

Moses helped Israel get out of Egypt to save them from Pharaoh and to freely worship God. What we have a tendency to do is judge another's assignment as if we know how it should be going, or judging a married couple's assignment as if it should be the same as another's. Yes the work is similar as the rules are the same in terms of the universal rules of marriage. The authority of the man over the woman, and the woman submitting to her husband as he loves and honors her back. Marriage should represent the same message, and that is the relationship of Christ to the church. Yet the many marriages we see have the same rules to it, yet the assignments are different. One couple may be called to minister to others who have never experienced divorce with children from the same house hold. Another couple may be called to minister to blended families such as theirs. Another couple may have faced adultery, abuse, abandonment and reconciled anyway.

If you cease from judging you will see that there is such a diverse work in the Kingdom of God. There are young, old, middle aged, married, divorced or widowed, sick, healthy, different ethnicities; different home of origins, different gifts, and my point is we all need to be ministered to. There is something for everyone to do and just because my work is different from your work does not mean that something is wrong with me. Perhaps there should be an evaluation of self-centeredness and a re-evaluation if you think everything is supposed to look, sound, and operate like you, your church, and your marriage. Yes churches should follow God's standards, but they all have different personalities usually that of the founding or operating leader.

I recall one moment in my life where I boiled with rage upon learning what was behind the fake presentations that were displayed with some married couples I had grown to admire. I had often wondered in my mind were my husband and I the only ones going through such difficulty. No one else ever seemed to be facing challenges like us. All the other couples seem to be so happy and problem free all the time. I remember wanting and trying to uphold a standard with my marriage to some I later learned was unrealistic. After being around couples who had been married thirty and forty years who seemed to have it all together I was determined to be just like them, and if they could make it, then so could we. I'd often receive advice and testimonies of how wonderful their relationships were and that we were just doing things wrong, until later when I discovered that the same couples I was looking up to, to try and meet the standard of overcoming, were the very same couples that had faced, and were presently facing adultery and abuse, but was never exposed or shared. I was a young lady learning this marriage thing and I had never experienced a more raging moment in my life as I discovered the very standard I was being held to in regards to being successfully married and a great wife were the very same standards they were not upholding themselves. I encourage you if you are mentoring or helping someone younger than you are, or another couple or believer who has not been where you have been, please be very transparent with them because people will almost kill themselves trying to uphold and meet some unrealistic standard that you yourself have not met, or are struggling with. This can be compared to a leader preaching something so critical in regards to walking with Christ but not upholding the standard him or herself. They are not practicing what they preach, or they are insane enough to believe they are yet while everyone else can clearly see they are not. For example you may have a leader who teaches on honoring and respecting one's husband yet while she seems to disrespect her husband behind closed doors or when no one is looking. Or you could have a husband who teaches on all the wonderful things of being strong in the Lord, and five minutes after teaching something this great, run home to pornography. This is dangerous because in the minds of people they are actually believing what is being projected is real, when in fact it is a goal that the person teaching it is also trying to arrive to as well. Then when one begins struggling in those areas they take on the mindset that they are unworthy or just can't do it when in reality the one teaching it is barely meeting the mark. It is so important to be transparent, and today we often have a serious lack of transparency among those who are the standard. Christ is so many wonderful things and we are to be just as he is yet everything about Christ's walk was not sunny days and tulips and smiles. There was much oppression, accusation, slanders, suffering, and persecution. Be mindful if you are as he is then there should be all the characteristics that reflect him in his being and not just the delightful powerful ones you choose to take on.

Let's look at this example: you have two married women. The first has been married over 30 years to her loving husband. Her husband had an affair during their marriage and fathered a child outside of their marriage. He does not have a heart of pharaoh; he had a weak moment of disobedience that has brought long lasting consequences and affects upon his life and those close to him. Let's say he stepped out again on his wife. Does he have the heart of pharaoh? He may not. He treats his wife like a queen and he speaks well to her and loves her and provides and protects, he just had some issues with is his flesh and yielded to temptation. His wife starts a ministry for women who have dealt with the same issue in their marriages and to help women struggling with what occurred. Let's call her Mrs. Smith.

Let's look at another woman. She has been married over 10 years and her husband continues to have affairs by yielding to temptation, however her husband is different. Her husband physically abuses her, does not love her and barely provides for her and their children, he is verbally abusive and is never really sorry for having outside children from their marriage. Let's call her Mrs. Jones. Mrs. Jones has decided to leave her husband after years of trying to make things work but receiving the same result (which by the way is insanity, when one does the same thing over and over again, expecting a different result). Regardless of how the marriage began she has a right to leave the marriage, not a right to not forgive, but she has a right to leave that marriage biblically. She decides to forgive Mr. Jones from a distance with boundaries in place this time. It is not Mrs. Smith's job to then come over to Mrs. Jones to tell her she shouldn't be leaving her husband and that she can stay and fight for her marriage just like she did. Mrs. Smith has no idea that Mrs. Jones husband is nothing like hers, he is not kind to her, he does not love or provide for her, he is not repentant about his affairs and neither is he willing to stop. Mrs. Smith now looks like the hero of marriage and Mrs. Jones now looks like the failure in marriage because she did not stay and remain in the marriage, even though she was biblically released. It could be the enemy who would want Mrs. Jones to remain with someone like that. Yes she could stay and suffer harm as that's what she said I do to, however if she has a biblical reason to leave per the words of Jesus Christ, it is **her choice** not Mrs. Smith's not the church, not family members, or anyone else's decision.

Let's look at Mrs. Lot. Mrs. Lot is married to a different man than Mrs. Jones but her husband has the exact same heart and behaviors as Mr. Jones. Mrs. Lot has experienced the same things in her marriage as Mrs. Jones. Mrs. Lot however decided to take Mrs. Smith's advice and remain in her marriage unlike Mrs. Jones who left hers. We have a tendency in the church to praise Mrs. Lot because she stayed and we make her more honorable than Mrs. Jones. We say things like, it is harder to stay in a bad marriage and more respected if you choose to stay even though you biblically could have left, we honor you Mrs. Lot, job well done, way to suffer for the Kingdom and way to not let the devil win. We say to Mrs. Jones, she took the easy way out; she let the devil win. Mrs. Smith looks to be more noble and solid in character as she remained with her spouse compared to the other woman that left her husband, even though Christ released her. Marriage is a covenant not a contract. Covenants are serious and God understood this along with the fact that a covenant can be broken as he faced this with Israel. We often reprimand the person that decided to walk away from the marriage even when they were not the one responsible for breaking the covenant. One may break the covenant they made and desire to remain in the marriage; however the reality is that the other spouse can either choose to remain or choose to go even if they are not responsible for breaking the covenant. We all know how David had no fear as he ran towards Goliath to slay the giant of the Philistines. It is very true that there are fears in life we must face and run towards just like David did as he overcame the giant of the Philistines; however the same David that ran towards Goliath is the same David that ran from Saul and his own son Absalom. In Psalm 3:6 we see David stating he will not fear ten thousands of his enemies that rise up against him, so why would the same man who killed a giant be running from Saul when he was supposed to be at his dinner table in 1 Samuel. It is because the anointed man of God had **the wisdom** at a very young age to understand that there are things in life you run towards with all your might as you are to overcome them, and there are things in life it would not be wise for you to run toward, in fact it may be best for you to move in the opposite direction depending on the dimension that is involved, particularly if life is being threatened. There is a time to hold on, and there is a time to let go. David knew when to hold it, and when to fold it, regardless of who thought what of him. When you hold onto truth and the Word of God putting God first in your life this may bring your circumstances to where you are as you put the demand on how those circumstances are to be as a believer calling those things that are not even though as they were, yet it is also wise to know that when you hold on to the stability of Christ and his Word, sometimes the people in your life may not come in the alignment that you are hoping for, sometimes those very people will end up breaking and falling off your life. It may appear as if you have given up on them or quit trying to make things work, when in reality it is not understood that the person or things supernaturally fell off of your life and with the direction you are going they couldn't be glued or tied to you again even if you tried to make it work again. When Christ sets the captive's free bondages are broken and chains that are broken can't be refastened. The point I'd like to make is that many people today are trying to tell you what your Goliath is and what your Saul is. Many church people will tell a separated or divorced spouse to return to a Saul or Absalom because in their perspective that should be your Goliath you should be running to in order to overcome what they believe is your fear, to stay in that marriage or relationship, even though they don't know two cents about your experiences and all the variables involved. It is not anyone's place to assume they know what occurred in someone else's marriage if they were not personally there as Jehovah Shammah was and is. As a divorcee one thing I have learned is the very people who claim they don't stereotype or judge are the same people putting all divorcees in the same box or category that is labeled quitters. Sure you will hear things like, oh I understand everyone has a different story, but the actions towards everyone they have put in this category are the same across the board. Everyone separated or divorced is not separated or divorced for the same reasons or causes. Many reflect similar testimonies however there are no two testimonies alike as people are idiosyncratic.

Here is the truth of the matter: Mrs. Lot has every right to leave or stay in her marriage and if she stays that's great and honorable for her. That gives her husband 10 more years to put the disclaimer out there of how his wife just puts up with him and how grateful he is for that, but by no means should that be compared to Mrs. Jones's situation. It can seem stronger to stay in a life threatening marriage, but it could honestly take more guts to leave that kind of marriage knowing what you will have to face on the other side if you remain in the faith, better yet, I should say church. Knowing that people are about to judge you left and right, knowing that your life is going to change, knowing that you may be leaving financial comfort, sexual comfort, ministry comfort, social acceptance, status quo, and so much more. The woman who always had her husband to identify with regardless if he played out his part right in the marriage or not, was seen with her throughout society and played a key role in her protection and safety. This may have been a sign to other men not to approach her in the grocery store, in the shopping mall, and at church. Now she has to go into church herself, to the grocery store herself, to the car dealership herself with no one to act as a covering for her. I say act because just because it looks like he is there to protect does not actually mean he may be, trust me I am a witness, even though the reality can be different than the picture I am painting, it is still nice to have a man with you to keep others off of you. Yes! I know it takes more courage and guts to go through all of this instead of sitting in the life threatening marriage another 10 years because you are afraid to step out on faith and trust God in every area in spite of what you will face, if your situation calls for biblical release. In fact your refusal to step out on faith demonstrates a lack of faith in God and your perspective of yourself worth. When you really get in tuned with knowing God you will know yourself well, and what you are worth and what treatment is acceptable and what is not acceptable. If you continue to communicate to your spouse that yes it's okay for you to treat me any way you wish, then you are being an enabler and you are communicating something to your spouse that is dangerous! You may think you love them unconditionally but you really are telling them with your actions or lack thereof that you can do anything you want to do and stand before God on your judgment day and all will be well. People tend to think God's unconditional love means that he does not have boundaries. You can have unconditional love and still value yourself and not allow others to cross certain lines. Even God who loves unconditionally, he allows consequences for those who break their fellowship with Him. In fact the woman who chooses to allow her spouse to treat her in this manner doesn't love herself or her spouse because if she loved her spouse she'd love his soul and would care about his relationship and fellowship with God, even if that means putting the divorce papers in his face as a wakeup call that you will one day have to give an account for your actions and you cannot do anything you want to do and think all will be well, especially live forever in heaven, but in reality, living a life full of unrepentant sin. The same goes for husbands who experience the same with a wayward wife. I believe the wife who sucks it up and does the latter is wiser, stronger, honorable, and more courageous that Mrs. Lot. I believe God loves Mrs. Lot just as much and there could be a purpose in her staying, but I don't believe the church should lift Mrs. Lot on a pedestal because even though it looks honorable and even though Mrs. Jones doesn't look honorable it could be the opposite and it can communicate to children who are watching what they should do in those circumstances once they arrive there as well, thus allowing history to repeat itself if not corrected because a wrong mindset was passed down.

After reading about Mrs. Smith, Mrs. Jones, and Mrs. Lot I want you to know that nobody is better than the other they are all God's daughters, and all their marriages have different testimonies. Because there is differentiation does not mean there has to be separation. This is what you often see, because your story is different from mine I cannot associate with you and this is not Kingdom that is carnal.

There seems to be a secret club in churches today where the message is being communicated that if you're husband doesn't have at least one affair on you then you really haven't been through anything serious, or you really are not a woman yet.

My message to these women is that you can keep the cheater's club pin, I don't want it. You want me to put the pin on and shut up, however forgive me if I decline and use my story for his glory, because there are thousands of young broken women being raised such as myself who will wake up in a self-inflicted hell and will be told things like you knew what you did and perhaps to an extent you did know, however depending on where you were spiritually there is a likelihood that you knew not what you were doing. There will be people of influence in your church that will come to you and tell you what you should do and because they hold a title or position you may operate in fear resulting in you losing your way of escape provided by God. The enemy knows the way of escape can be denied. If you are reading this book ten years from now, twenty years from now, or fifty years from now and this is you, know that I have been where you are right now. If you are involved with ministry and you can't imagine the emotional trauma of going through a divorce bearing the name of Christ, know that He is with you and He understands everything you are dealing with that others may not see or know about. You are not alone.

One thing I noticed after faithfully attending a marriage Sunday school class for three years with approximately thirty to forty different couples, many who were mature is that many comparisons were often made between marriages. I'd often hear people trying to measure someone else's pain and experiences through their own, even if their marriage looked nothing like another's. For example, the Matthews have been married for over thirty years. Over the years it is clear to see that it was not easy for them to remain standing in their marriage. There were many challenges they faced, and trials and tribulations just like any other couple, however Mr. Matthews had never laid his hands on his wife, he never called her out of her name, to her face that is, he never disrespected her in public. Mr. Matthews always thought it was his responsibilities to provide for his family regardless of how things were going in the marriage. Mrs. Matthews never had to experience any of that during the thirty years she has been married to Mr. Matthews.

Then you have the Riley's. This is a young couple that has struggled for the first ten years of their marriage. Mr. Riley doesn't come home at night. He has had at least three major affairs where children have been birthed outside of the marriage. Mr. Riley occasionally hits his wife, and he provides for his family if he is in a good mood only.

The Riley's have only been married ten years compared to the Matthews thirty years of marriage. One day, Mrs. Riley decides she is leaving her husband. Mrs. Matthews then begins spreading her comments around church about how these young girls just don't hang in there like they did in her day. Mrs. Matthew's can only reflect on her marriage and how their struggles have been, never realizing that she has not had to face the same struggles that Mrs. Riley has. Yes. Mrs. Riley may be younger than Mrs. Matthews and that's not to say that there are not things Mrs. Matthews cannot teach Mrs. Riley, however Mrs. Matthews does not have a clue on what it is like to be married to someone like she is. Mrs. Matthews has never had to experience emotional and physical abuse, or wonder how their bills were going to be paid depending on how her husband feels. Mrs. Matthews has never had to worry about many things that Mrs. Riley has had to endure in her young marriage. One might say, well, Mrs. Riley shouldn't have chosen to marry Mr. Riley. What if Mr. Riley was in good character when they were married, what if he wasn't. Those details are important for much, however the details are not important when it comes to Mrs. Matthews comparing her pain, endurance, and marriage with that of someone else's that does not and has not looked like hers in regards to encounters and experiences.

Mrs. Matthew's has no right to make it appear that because she has been with her spouse for thirty years it makes her better than one who has been married only ten years. Mrs. Riley's ten years could have been more enduring than Mrs. Matthew's thirty years of marriage. Perhaps Mrs. Matthews would not have lasted two years in the marriage that Mrs. Riley was in, as she judges her and makes her feel weaker than her.

This is what typically happens within the church setting, whether it's said or unsaid. People are comparing their testimonies and often times making others look weaker as they play the hero of their story. It is often assumed that if one has been married over thirty or forty years then they have a greater endurance or strength than those who have divorced do not have, when that is not the case. Yes there was endurance over those years and that is absolutely commendable, but what actually was endured may not be anything compared to someone married for even as little as one or two years who perhaps abandoned their family, or brought an incurable life threatening disease to the relationship. God knows this and he sees all and he knows all, everything is laid naked before God. He sees things that we as humans cannot see. If you have been known to act as Mrs. Matthews, I highly encourage you to pray for those you are judging as you may understand what it's like to suffer in your marriage, but you don't know what others may face in theirs no matter how short or long another has been married compared to you. This is sometimes done in a way for one to look better than another. If you have to make yourself look good to make someone else look bad, I'd encourage you to lay your walk before God almighty. You don't know the plans, purpose, or destiny for the one you could be putting your mouth on or spreading rumors about.

This situation is just like someone judging another's job duties. For example, a lawyer looks at a doctor and says I could do his job, that's easy. When that Lawyer has no idea the work put in to obtain credentials, to deal with sick people on a constant basis, and to have the knowledge and skill set to be able to deliver effective services. Then you may have a teacher judging a janitor within a school. Oh wow, how easy it is to swing a mop around. This teacher has no idea that the janitor has three other jobs he attends before he comes to mop a floor being provided materials that are not adequate for the football stadium sized facility he has to clean. This is not right; however this is what happens, and sadly by mature saints. It's to show even the wisest, ripest, most mature saints of God are capable of UN Christ like behaviors, attitudes, thoughts, and actions. We all need Jesus! The point is, that you have absolutely no idea what people go through and for you to belittle their experiences as if you know all about them, as if you were there. When we belittle others pain and testimonies it mirrors Satan. Christ never turned anyone away in the end or belittled them, including the little children. So who are you to belittle God's children if Christ didn't and doesn't?

Be careful who you judge, because the one you're judging could be the one God uses to win your children or family members to Christ, to help in another form down the line in life, such as helping with employment, housing, food, clothes, references, and so forth. It's sad when someone has to cover another person's light, gifts, and significance in order that others don't notice it, with the intent of trying to make one's self look better. This is a spirit of competition which is not of God. 2 Corinthians 10:12 indicates it is not wise to compare one to another, particularly those in leadership. Labeling and comments are made so that others will see the "bad" things about the person so the one being childish doing this can look much better. It is important to remember that God is love and the things of God must be revealed, just as God must be revealed, love too must be revealed. Many people believe they understand and know love and it has not been revealed to them in a deeper dynamic than what they are familiar with. The enemy knows if he can keep that husband or that wife from receiving the revelation of love then there is no way that person could ever love their spouse the way God intended because one cannot love another if he or she does not know love, it has to be revealed. Today we have many marriages where spouses that are doing all the right things and following the Word of God, yet there is a lack of real revelation of love, and because that deterioration occurs. Women don't just want love, women need love. We were built by God to feed off of it. Men also need love but not as much as they need honor and respect for he was built by God to need this significantly.

Encouragement

There is nothing new under the sun. You are not the first that God may be bringing out, and you won't be the last, just know what you are going through is not new and there is hope. You may choose to undergo what I call a death and resurrection season of your life, where everything about you has to die and be buried, your reputation, your dreams of your marriage, your ministry, rearrangements will be all over the place and the only one who will carry you through is God Almighty. God will reshape and mold you into someone you never imagined you could be. If you go through the process right and do not interrupt what God will do in you, he will restore you and you will be a powerhouse in the Kingdom of God to break the chains of the devil's bondages. This is not for every married woman or man encountering issues. It is only for those who have the mindset of Esther who said if I perish I perish, who thought like Naomi: what else is there to lose, I am as good as dead anyway, (not knowing there is so much blessings and peace on the other side of where you are). If this is God's will for your life. There is something about being willing to die and just yielding all of who you are and walking through that regardless of what's to come. God can use you in territories and take you before spiritual giants to accomplish a great work in the Kingdom.

God's great works are not always broadcasted in the pulpit; they sometimes are done behind the veil where he will send a David or a Davidess to a Goliath or Goliathess when no one even knows about it. Why would God use little old you? Because **He will be the only one who gets the glory.** Yes you may show up to a new church as the foreign divorcee and you may be broken and in need of ministry yourself, but depending on what God will do with your story don't be surprised if God puts you on assignment in a setting such as this, notice I said God not people. I am talking about God giving you an assignment in the midst of where you are, you may think you need to take all the rational steps to your healing of dealing with this and dealing with that in a step by step format, but God may say you are the one I am sending to usher in a new kingdom work. I encourage you if you do choose to leave a marriage as a woman or man, or stay at your current church, or go to another if God orders your steps, don't sit in the back! Find a front row seat and praise God in the presence of everyone as the church is a house for all of God's people, not just those who seem to have it all together. Don't do this to prove a point, but to take your place as a child of God who reigns in heavenly places with Christ Jesus where there is now no condemnation for those who are in Christ Jesus, Romans 8:1.

John 10:28 says I give them eternal life and they shall never perish, no one can snatch them from my hand. They may manipulate some things to show you are not worthy of ministering so to speak, but God has a way of dealing with people and silencing every mouth raised against a child of God, and bringing down everything that rises against you. If you belong to God, you are marked and no matter if people can see it or not, doesn't matter, they will know in the end, that you are covered and honored by God. Remember God sometimes will use the least likely candidate to accomplish his assignments, I know beyond a shadow of doubt that could be you, because it was me. I was given an assignment I never would have chosen personally after I left my home church. I wanted the assignment of being married to the same man all of my life, to minster to God's people, have a home and a white picket fence (which I did get the home and white picket fence), however, there was hell in it. I wanted the perfect patty ministry, and sadly I would have been great at it. God had different plans for my life, and it has everything to do with the times I was born in and am living in. I believe God saw this assignment on my life before I was born, and the day I got married to the wrong person.

Do you remember Tameka's testimony? God knew she needed to be in a boundary so that she would not be harmed. The same is with giving the same message to a spouse. If Tameka didn't get in a boundary she could be dead, perhaps only God could see this. So yes she may have self-inflicted her position, but God will use it because she belongs to Him. It is likened to a child who wants to jump in a deep swimming pool. They may cry and throw a tantrum because they were not able to jump in the pool and you will hurt their feelings because you don't let them, but you saved them from harm. God does this in some of our circumstances. He hurts you so you won't be harmed later. He says no that man is not the one for you, no she is not the one for you. Yes you may be hurt now, but you won't be harmed later. He says no that job is not the one for you, that ministry or church is not the one for you. No you don't need a title in the church or be in forefront. You may be hurt now, but you will see how much God saved you from later. So it is when a spouse communicates this by leaving for biblical reasons if he or she is unrepentant and is demonstrating the heart of pharaoh. What message, the message of yes I will leave you, and it may hurt you now, but it will keep you from harm later. Love sometimes is tough. 1 Corinthians 5:5 says that someone should be turned over to Satan due to their actions that have not been corrected so their soul won't enter hell. Why is that? So that his spirit may be saved in the day of the Lord. A lot of what we see is chaos happening and disconnect so that the soul and spirit of a person may get it right before it is everlasting too late. I believe this is why the divorce rate is increasing in the church as well, in addition to some of the more discussed factors. If someone is to encourage a wife to return to a husband as such, not only is her life affected, perhaps children too. The man or woman's soul or spirit may not make it into eternity if this separation doesn't occur, and Christ knows that, this is why scriptures like 1 Corinthians 5:5 were written. However religious people in trying to keep the image of that marriage together may end up influencing the man or woman's soul further toward damnation if they are not turned over to the devil for the destruction of their flesh so their soul may be saved on the day of the Lord. This is a reality that is clearly in the bible that is rarely depicted. It's always go back, try it again, it's not easy, you're not overcoming. The reality could be if I don't leave this man or woman, he or she won't ever change and they will be on their way to hell. That could be the case if he or she stays with a spouse as such, but there is a better possibility of one getting their act together when the smoke has cleared and they are left alone surrendered into the hands of almighty God alone. It's during that time, when they cannot lean on their spouse's spirituality and walk with God. Here is where many can find God for the first time themselves.

We have this rationality as if things have to be either A or B or it has to be black or white when there are many shades of gray. This is not to be compared with being hot or cold or lukewarm. In life there are absolutes. Is God real? Absolutely. Is Barak Obama the president? Absolutely. Is Mrs. Jones's husband saved? Perhaps. Is he not saved? Perhaps. Was it necessary for you to go through what you went through? Perhaps and perhaps not. It is beautiful when couples make it in spite of the odds and the challenges they face **but it is also beautiful when Jesus delivers his son or daughter from a bondage with as many obstacles and odds that would keep that person enslaved**

to someone that could eventually harmed them long-term. Our church society approves the one side, but not necessarily the other, as they don't know what to do with separation. Psalm 12:5-8 says, The Lord replies, I have seen violence done to the helpless, and I have heard the groans of the poor. Now I will rise up to rescue them, as they have longed for me to do. The Lord's promises are pure like silver refined in a furnace, purified seven times over, Therefore, Lord we know you will protect the oppressed, preserving them forever from this lying generation, even though the wicked strut about, and evil is praised throughout the land. There are scriptures throughout God's word where it is evident that God hears the cries of the oppressed and he delivers his people. Some church people do not always know what to do when a child or daughter is delivered from a harmful marriage. Even though God hates divorce because of what it represents and the consequences it brings, his love for his children is greater than allowing them to be harmed, therefore in order to preserve life deliverance is essential for some situations.

The necessary is determined by God and not man. None of the things we go through are necessary when it comes to consequences to sin, yet when mankind fell, every person born after that was born into a sin present world with a sin nature. Therefore, the age of accountability is different for all human beings that give their lives to Christ. People will often tell you that it wasn't necessary for certain things in your life to happen, and there is truth to this, however God knows what things were necessary to occur in the life of a child he is bringing back to Him from the world. It is easy to judge what we believe was or was not necessary, however God knows all about a person including the very number of hairs on our heads. He knows more about what we need or needed a lot more than people who may know little about you. This is viewed in God's eye sight not man's perspective. Man may say it wasn't necessary, but it could have been in order for salvation. The man that was delivered over to Satan for the destruction of his flesh was delivered over because it was necessary for his spirit to have a chance at being saved on the last day. Some extremes are necessary in order for a positive change to occur.

One great example of seeing done what is necessary is in the movie called Betty and Coretta. The wife of Malcolm X and Dr. Martin Luther King Jr is great! It shows the challenges they faced behind closed doors. It was clear to see that Farrakhan had something to do with the death of Coretta's husband Martin Luther King Jr, and she knew this in her heart. When Coretta's daughter had gotten into trouble with the law, Farrakhan had money to bail her daughter out of jail. How can you accept money from someone to help you when you know they had your husband killed? What a strong woman. The only way he would present the money to her was if she was publically seen shaking his hands with him for a photo shoot, as the rumor was going around that he had something to do with Dr. King killed. In the movie, the gesture wasn't from the heart; it was just for the public eye to get the message that he would never do such a thing to Dr. King, as he was helping his wife and child. That was the message for the public. The message for Coretta was I killed your husband and now you need me to help your child. That was the truth, but the public eye didn't see the truth. What manipulation! This was the silent message. Messages like this are happening all over in the gospel. It is not honest when people are claiming to be under well-known authority for the public eye, yet in private doing whatever they want to fulfill self agenda. Many people appear to be working together in the media, on television, on the radio, when in reality it's far from the truth, it's a front, and it usually has to do with money, sadly.

The Shift Has Occurred

Right before Miles Monroe passed away on November 9, 2014 along with his wife due to a fatal plane crash, he gave a prophetic word from a dream he had. In his prophetic dream he noted how an athlete was clutching a baton. He said the baton was not being passed on to those it should have been passed on to. It is clear to see that there is a fight going on in the spirit realm for the kingdom baton to be passed to the remnant of believers it should be passed to. Much of this has to do with authority and how it has been handled over the years and how it will be in the future for centuries to come.

How are our churches set up? Do we usher in ministry soon enough for the next generations by releasing it? Do we hoard ministry and get behind over the years never including our youth but instead allow our ministries to die off so everyone who's anyone can feel significant?

What is hoarding ministry? Hoarding ministry versus releasing ministry: Moses was to release ministry to Joshua. As I have witnessed with saints that have been over ministries for years, it's hard to face that a particular assignment completed or concluded. This is not to say that God is through with the person or there won't be other areas that God is calling them to, however it seems as if sometimes everyone else sees that their assignment has been fulfilled and completed but them. No, God is not done with you yet, and the best is always yet to come, but sometimes with the church we fail to discern when to release ministry and pass the torch. It gets real when you're walking into ministries where people are shouting to you silently that this is their territory, and there is no room for you.

There is a work to be done with the older teaching the younger so that the younger can step into place when the time is rightly appointed by God for them to be that Joshua generation that springs up. It is sad to say that sometimes this is hard for some mature saints who have had the ministries for years and don't wish to release ministry because of how significant it has made their lives. The older generations of the church hold much wisdom and experience, and we cannot make it without them! This is not to say that youth have nothing to offer. Maturity does not always come with age. Just because one is young doesn't mean they have little to offer either. God will use the young and the old to accomplish his plans. We must work together. There are many things affecting church membership today. Just because a ministry is large in numbers does not mean that God is responsible for the increase of church membership. The Word says wide is the gate to hell, and narrow is the path to eternal life. Therefore, we should not be judging if God is moving within a ministry based upon church membership. So it is with a church that has very few members. This does not always mean that the membership is low because the members of this smaller church are holier than those in the large church. That could be a possibility, however people leave church for many reasons. People choose not to come to church for many reasons. It is not always due to a lack of witnessing or compelling, sometimes some people have just made up in their minds they don't want to go no matter how many times you try and persuade them.

We are living in the last days where our churches are being heavily infiltrated and new believers are being trained in a way to oppose traditional teachings of God's word for a more convenient entertaining style of the gospel being presented. Yes we must remain relevant but one thing that will always be relevant is a burning hell that awaits those who reject Christ Jesus. Throughout God's word the instruction to hold on to the Lord's ways are very clear. We are living in a generation where the liberality of religion states that one can be a good person with good intentions and a good reputation and still have eternal life. I hate to disrupt any perspectives that have adopted this idea that one can be admitted into heaven and eternal life after life on earth from just being a good person, however, the only way to eternal life is through Jesus Christ. There is no other way according to Acts 4:12 which state there is no other name under heaven where by men must be saved other than the name of Jesus. No one can come before the Father unless by way of Jesus Christ. John 14:6 is where Jesus says I am the way the truth and the life. A lot of people are in relationships with others who hold this perspective. As long as they are a "good" person, they actually believe they are in good standing with their spouses, family, employer, other relationships, and with God, because they do good deeds. Your doing will flow out of your being. One does good deeds as a believer because it flows from who they are. Wicked people can also do good deeds as well. This is where a lot of deception occurs. The point is that there are many people who believe they are a good person however they are rejecting Jesus Christ as Lord of their lives by their repetitious actions. This is another way that man looks at the outward appearance. Yes, someone may be employee of the year for ten years in a row, and give to charity; they may even appear to be blessed beyond measure materially; however that does not mean they are saved. God looks at, and weighs the hearts of a person.

I received a revelation when watching a program on Reelz TV called Bomb Girls.

Women were making atomic bombs in 3rd world countries to receive income for their families but had no idea what they were creating. They just knew they were putting something together and it was meeting their present need of income and giving instant gratification for their physical needs. They had no idea they were creating monsters, weapons of mass destruction that the enemy would use for destruction to take the lives of people. This is what's going on in some modern day churches where deception and the Word of God is being diluted and adulterated. People who have never been "churched" or come from traditional church settings are being set up like an army of demons being bred and trained to oppose Spirit filled believers of God that may be more traditional in the things of God. They think what they are doing and agreeing with is correct because of the entertainment, the laughter and jokes, the sense that is being made from the pictures that are selectively being portrayed, all the while being completely dumbfound that they are helping to create a monster that the enemy will use to deceive even more people, or utilize to keep saints spiritually dull. If someone is being introduced to Christ by one that is not of God but a deceptive spirit is working at hand, that new believer will never know that the one leading them to what they believe is Christ is a counterfeit. So much trust and approval will be extended toward these individuals and an allegiance and commitment is usually made to the counterfeit. Everyone supports their pastor and would die for their pastor as it is sensitive to ever talk about one's pastor (even though you often find more pastors talking about one another instead of lifting one another up), but the truth of the matter is, if one's pastor is a counterfeit and the members don't know it or want to accept the truth, then this proves this argument. The bible states there will be counterfeits, so please don't act as if I've stated something false. We all know that if the devil can just get you to agree with him, and commit to him, then you end up working for him and building his kingdom. Look at the Apostle Paul before his conversion. The devil had him sold on what he thought was the right thing to do, which was killing Christians. Saul was totally deceived and fighting for the absolute wrong side, but no one could tell him anything because of the Sanhedrin Council he came from and all the things he thought he knew from those who taught him, which we are not to blame him, because a person only knows what they are taught. The same applies today. We often beat people up because they only know what they were taught, and because it may not mirror better teaching, expectations, behaviors, or actions, we received; we often crucify them for doing what they were taught. Paul didn't get it right the first time around, but he sure did the second time around. The same is with many people today, if the man who used to kill followers of Christ can make a turn around, my friend you can make a turnaround no matter what you have done. This is a major reason God selected Paul, to demonstrate that if Paul could be forgiven, then so can you. This is why Jesus prayed to the father for those who were killing him. They surely did not know what they were doing, and this is due to what they were taught, and because of what was ingrained in their minds. I can reflect on this with regards to my first marriage. My spouse and I were doing what we were taught in a number of respects; however the breaking point comes when new behavior has been taught over great periods of time, and is not being implemented. Bad habits are hardwired, but God is greater to bring about change if one is willing. God will never force you to change for the better or force you to do anything for that matter. I'm always cautious of forceful people. If God doesn't force, then for one to think they can make someone do something is beyond my understanding.

Looking back over my young life I can see where God opened doors for me and gave me keys and access to places and people I had no business being around if you measure on the basis of qualifying. I didn't qualify with my age, gender, ethnicity, education, or other determining factors. I'd always walk right into a place and be placed right at the top. People may have been there longer or had more qualifying characteristics but for whatever reason I was always headed for the top including organizations, clubs, and ministries, that are not open to just anyone. It doesn't matter what people deem you as, if God sees fit for you to be there for whatever purpose believe me my friend you can be the last qualifying candidate and you will still be granted access because of what God wants to do through you. Many times God is looking for an available vessel, someone who will go into territory where things need to be shaken up and aligned in order, or where your destiny will manifest, and he will use someone no one ever expected for a many reasons. The main reason is you're the last one anyone would suspect to do what God has assigned you to do. No one will ever suspect that you are the one sent by God because of your life's testimonies. Plus, our God doesn't like to share credit with anyone. Usually when he does a thing it's done in a way that nobody can get the glory for it but Him. He has a sense of humor and will shock the world with what he was working on all along.

What happens when you hear about a believer's life being ripped and torn apart as they go through various trials and tribulations? There used to be a time when saints realized that when serious chaos was occurring in the life of the believer it could be due to that believer being a serious threat to the kingdom of hell. Today we equate a problem free life with being saved and being Spirit filled, when that's far from biblical truth. The devil is not thinking about you until you get lined up with God's will, purpose, and destiny for your life. It's not until you get serious about the Kingdom, he finally comes to wreak havoc in your life at another level. Job 14:1 says that the days of man are short and full of trouble. Everyone in trouble is not in trouble in life because they did something wrong. Some are in trouble because that is just what occurs with being born on this earth, in addition to naming the name of Christ. Don't get me wrong, the enemy still hates you, and will try and bring havoc into your life, but not the way he attacks believers on a mission. These particular believers he wants to destroy, kill, delay, and stop from reaching their purposes. This is why you will see an entire operation shut down on behalf of the one God chooses. What am I saying here? Look at Joseph's story in Luke chapter 2: And it came to pass in those days *that* a decree went out from Caesar Augustus that all the world should be registered. This census first took place while Quirinius was governing Syria. So all went to be registered, everyone to his own city.

Joseph also went up from Galilee, out of the city of Nazareth, into Judea, to the city of David, which is called Bethlehem, because he was of the house and lineage of David, to be registered with Mary, his betrothed wife, who was with child. So it was, that while they were there, the days were completed for her to be delivered. And she brought forth her firstborn Son, and wrapped Him in swaddling cloths, and laid Him in a manger, because there was no room for them in the inn.

What happened here? An entire operation was put in place to try and shut down the coming Messiah that was prophesied about. The census was put forth by the devil not God. See the enemy will shut down a company, start new rules and regulations imposed by law and other measures just to take out one entity that has an assignment to save many. So you mean to tell me that all the men had to return to their homes for the census put in place by Caesar? All for one little child? Absolutely! We see this in Exodus when Pharaoh ordered for all the male children to be killed to stop the deliverer from arising. Many babies were killed all to find one. The enemy will take down and out what ever and whoever necessary to get to the main target and that target is the one that God has chosen for major assignments. After all if he goes for the big one, he can take down many in addition to.

I often wonder how we have believers who don't go through anything. Their home is right, money tight, family in order, kids cleaner than a whistle, so it seems. Where is the modern day Job, Moses, Joseph, Naomi, Jacob, and Naomi? This isn't to paint a picture that God wants us to always suffer, however Christ learned through the things he suffered, and so will we. Ecclesiastes 7:3 says sorrow is better than laughter, (at certain times in life). There is a work done in the spirit in regards to suffering, this is not to lift suffering up on a pedestal, but many things are accomplished, and birthed through the suffering of saints. As a young lady I often saw my peers full of vigor and laughter and youth, and when I look at my life, it's not that I don't obtain the same, however it is written that sorrow is better than laughter. Not that I am always sorrowful, because I am filled with Joy continuously, however wisdom is better than being naïve. The issue arises when saints start going overboard with the suffering message. This is not to say that there aren't blessings and prosperity in God, as son and daughters of God, however Christ didn't promise that the road would be easy, but that he would be with us. Signs of disaster, loss, setbacks, and a good name or reputation well established that becomes torn down or lost for a season, are labeled today as one not having enough faith, or they must not be walking with God, or there must be serious sin going on. It is not always attributed to the believer being recommended by God to the devil in order for God to show Himself greater in the life of that believer.

Truth is that the enemy is not really worried about lukewarm believers or those who have no real impact against him. He will enable an organization to flourish financially and in every area as long as he can control it. If there is no threat, he doesn't mind the success for such people. On the other hand he works overtime and double time and a half for those hot believers who will give up their very lives let alone reputation, money, time, and more.

We know that God is bringing up a remnant to carry on the real church of Jesus Christ. What kind of mantles and spiritual batons will be handed off? Those that are toxic filled with stress, pressure, and burdens? Or will they be healthy, refined, and restored? Scales of the Heart was written to address issues that are not often discussed within ministries, yet the issues are affecting the church. This was written from the perspective of a sheep, servant, child of God, and church member. Not one that has arrived at the top, but a grass root movement that the Lord has burdened my heart in anguish with. You don't have to leave from under authority in order for your voice to be heard. I thank God for my leaders and their openness to help me with this assignment and directing me in a safe path to share the input the Holy Spirit has given to me to share with the body of Christ. I have often heard that those in leadership are there to serve the sheep and to minister to the sheep. If this is the case, my prayer is that if that applies to you, that you would take the voice of a sheep in perspective when leading in the manner that you do.

Ask yourself this? Is my ministry more focused around God's sheep that he advised should be fed and taken care of, or is it more centered business matters? Does it say business first is valued? If it's the business of loving and tending to people and sheep, then that's different, however in reality it's not always so. What are some steps you intend to take to genuinely restructure areas in need of restoration? Are there any you recognize? Are you in a position to help? If not, how can you help? Seek out those the Lord will advise you to in referencing to what healthy insight God gives you to bring restoration and wholeness to your walk with Christ, your home, your ministry, or your organization. Perhaps you think your ministry is perfect? None are, so if this is what you believe, chances are you may be in denial. Just because none are perfect, it doesn't mean allow things to remain in dysfunction, instead why not aim for the highest capacity of excellence and health? This is a great place to begin coming out of denial, and decide how progression will be made moving forward as God guides you. Many may not be able to accept the advice, or insight from a young black lady who is no high clergy official, however real Pioneers for the kingdom don't discriminate on where sound advice is coming from, as long as it's helping others and bringing positive change, they will roll with it. It's not always about the multitude of people being changed as it is the right person(s) being impacted. The right person will impact the multitude.

I thought it was interesting to learn that every church has its life and death peak moments of thriving and surviving especially after hitting the twenty five year mark. As we have all encountered our church's offerings and membership declining in one season or another, it is not always due to the economic climate. Sometimes people have been so abused or drowned in silenced that they don't want to come back to the house of God, simultaneously many financial and spiritual factors do apply.

How are women used within the churches today? God has often used women to usher in great Kingdom works and many are never recognized. Take Mary Jane Featherstone. She was the wife of Smith Wigglesworth who taught her husband how to read the bible he later mastered and led others to Christ with. Her investment alone was the tool God used to usher in the man of God's ministry. Myles Monroe discusses how the spirit of "man", mankind that is, lives inside of females: women. Therefore a woman also can be filled with God's spirit and according to Joel 2:28 and Acts 2:17. God said he will pour out of his spirit on all flesh, which includes, women and children. Not that God began pouring his spirit out on women in the last days; however it is imperative to note that God may use one wearing hair bowties instead of a neck bowties. It is not common to see a pastor with a long line of young men that are being mentored and groomed for leadership, as this is important as men are the head, nevertheless you may be missing an anointed servant of the Lord by placing all women in a category of limitations. Our god who has no limits put his unlimited spirit in men **and women** yet we turn around and limit women. This is not to direct a woman away from their

God given responsibilities of the home, however do not believe that the same unlimited spirit that is in a man is not in a woman, she too can lead people to Christ, teach and preach God's Word, help to Sheppard God's flock, and give biblical wisdom and advice. If you are not able to receive a word from the Lord from a woman, as Myles Monroe indicated, close your eyes so you are not looking at her gender and listen to the spirit of "man" inside of her.

The same spirit God breathed into Adam was breathed into Eve. Monroe elaborates on God calling women to certain leadership roles to help vast majorities. God said in Micah 6:4 that the leaders he gave to Israel himself were Moses, Aaron, and **Miriam**. One of them was a woman. I am not condoning her later actions and attitude of rebellion against Moses, but I am pointing out that **God selected her** to help lead beside the men, who were also her brothers.

Always remember that church is a place for sick people, not a place to view perfect people in glass cases. If you were once sick as I was, and Christ came and changed your life and carried you, then share your testimony for the glory of God. The enemy will always try to disqualify you before you grasp hands with destiny. His desire is that your failures will keep your mouth closed when it comes to taking your place in the Kingdom of God. Make the devil out as the liar he is. Tell him, no failure, no mistake, no setback, no divorce; no shortcoming, etc. will keep your mouth shut on what your assignment from God may be for the kingdom of God. Many may not like it, I'm sorry, let me rephrase, many will not like it, or like you, and the enemy will always bring up your past to demonstrate you should keep quiet, but when the time comes to speak up, cry loud and spare not. It's a must, others will experience what you have, and if they don't find help in the place they are looking for help, perhaps they will find it in you. In a vision I saw my testimony playing out in the lives of thousands of young ladies and gentlemen who are probably getting their diapers changed right now, and they were all traumatized with a deep hunger and thirst for God and to do his will, yet sowing seeds in ignorance. It is my prayer that no religious person will be successful in dealing with you in church settings the way I have witnessed, and if so, Scales of the Heart is to encourage you that God knows what you are going through and every mouth raised in judgment against you, shall be silent. Allow your righteousness to speak up for you. God has a way of making a table for you in the presence of your enemies and pulling down to the ground anything that tries to shame you.

John 14:12 is where Jesus said anyone who has faith in me shall do what I have been doing; he or she will do even greater works than these! Anyone is not limited to men only, it doesn't say people over the age of 40, married people only, rich people only, or people who have been ministering for several years, but he said ANYONE! I dare you to step out on destiny as you align yourself with God's timing.

When it comes to manipulation God says he catches the wise in their craftiness (Job 5:13). There are silent manipulations within many types of organizations, and God sees them all. For example, if Sister Carrot is over a ministry and she is withholding meeting times and locations and pertinent information from people within her ministry because she is trying to shoo away specific people from the ministry that she doesn't want to be a part of it. Is this a form of manipulation? Sadly childish things like this occur. Information that everyone is supposed to have is not given appropriately if at all to create confusion, anxiety, pressure, and stress, which we know is a work of the enemy. Situations like this are difficult to prove and no one wants to voice up and makes Sister Carrot look bad or create tension, but the reality is that things like this happen all the time, and it creates so much unnecessary discourse when leadership and influence is placed in the wrong hands.

I was watching television one day and noticed a program where the pastor had asked for a specific dollar amount for an offering which was rather high. Those that were able to give the exact amount were asked to come on stage with him as he applauded them before the congregation. Those that were not able to give that exact dollar amount were not deemed as faithful. I thought about the woman who gave all she had in Mark 12. What if some of the people on stage gave out of their wealth and it was no sacrifice at all. What if some people who were not on stage gave all they had and really made the actual sacrifice? This wasn't right. So those who were able to be recognized publically may not have truly been like the woman who gave all she had compared to those in the pews. What message is being communicated with this example? Is this Christ like? What is the focal point here? Jesus? People receive recognition for following certain rules. If you don't follow their rules, then the message is clear, you won't be recognized, and perhaps the trick of the enemy will work to make you feel insignificant, and cause you to conform to requests as such.

Another example would be to say the scheduler for a particular ministry is scheduling mandatory meetings for that ministry during times she knows for a fact someone specific in that ministry won't be able to make it. Yes it can't be proven that there is manipulation occurring with the scheduling, but it's happening to boot someone out a ministry. Perhaps the one being booted out is competition, perhaps he or she has an anointing that threatens the scheduler, perhaps there is jealousy involved, perhaps the one being manipulated was sent by God to a deceptive ministry and they are trying to get rid of that person all together so that the kingdom work can be blocked. These are just some hypothetical examples. Call it what you wish or view it as you wish, but things like this occur within churches and the only one affected or who generally cares is the one being manipulated. Of course, no one wants to create chaos or disclose something that looks terrible, yet if not, many others can suffer the same. Somebody has to die and be the sacrifice for change to come.

Of course the issue of deception in modern day churches is primarily where the enemy is gaining ground. It wouldn't be relevant to discuss everything else occurring except another obvious. Church has become a place to be entertained on Sunday mornings. The sanctuary is no longer a holy place where God's sprit is reverenced; instead it's turned into a Sunday morning comedy club where the spiritual intelligence is being offended behind jokes and humor. While the enemy is appealing to the senses of people to relate they are being won over deceitfully for motives other than truly presenting Jesus Christ. The spiritual senses are being dulled down tremendously. People are now being taught that if they don't belong to a certain church then they are not saved. As I recall and reflect when an alter call is done it should be an invitation to come to Jesus as your Lord and savior not only to become a member of a local congregation. People are being taught erroneously in many areas. What will happen if present and future generations are not taught the right way to operate in God's house? The remnant will become even more few and in between. A people is being raised to despise the real things of God, the traditional things of God, and not that tradition has always been right as practices have been passed down that are not godly, however in God's Word it instructs the church to operate in a particular way or pattern which is found in 1 Corinthians 12. People who do not know the things of God or God himself are being led astray as they are taught what they sense to be godly having no prior knowledge or experience of God. This is why you have to experience God for yourself, because if you don't you could adopt anything just by going off of another's testimony.

Just like we discussed those women who were building atomic bombs and had no idea what they were building, so it is with ministries being built today. People are building atomic bombs in the form of deceptive ministry and have no idea what their hands are contributing to as they believe they are doing the right thing from what they have been taught. Sadly this has everything to do with money. Merchandising is replacing the unadulterated Word of God. There is all kind of dirty money in the world. Prostitution, drug deals, unethical business deals, and it all can be turned into the offering plate at church, to advance the kingdom agenda, however I believe the worst kind of money on the face of the earth is that of which has come into existence by way of spiritual manipulation. If someone's spirit or soul was manipulated in order for the dollar to be accrued, that's the last dollar I'd desire to feed me or take care of me in any way. That money comes with major spirits and chains even the most anointed cannot always break off. Is this even important anymore? Anyone operating in this manner doesn't necessarily start off to manipulate, it was something that happened along the way as a door was opened to the enemy. The ministry could have begun on fire for God, and somewhere along the way it was infiltrated by major demonic spirits who were placed over sensitive ministries that gave the enemy access to the gates that were not guarded. 2 Peter precisely talks about what occurs in deceptive ministries. Please take the time if you are not familiar with this chapter of the bible and thoroughly go through it to become familiar with what is clearly laid out as warnings for you, your ministry, or organization.

The devil knows that the anointing breaks the yoke, so if he can get you to trade yours in eventually for his packages it will stop you from taking your place in the remnant of believers that will overcome his territory, and plans. There may be great entertainment going on in a church but if there is no anointing what do you have? Many have gone to places as such and have traded in their God given anointing for a golden handcuff the devil has passed out. Give me your anointing for this package he says, and I'll give you this or that. It is disheartening to see a saint that was once filled with the spirit of God trade in their anointing for materials. It gets real, I'm sure as elevation and promotion occurs, temptation increases. There is still a spiritual battle going on whether we acknowledge it or not. To keep people dumb founded in being lukewarm is exactly what will destroy our foundations. Have you ever heard a message from someone who said all the right things and made all the right points but something about it was not right? That something is the source it came from. The enemy can tell you all the right things, whisper sweet nothings in your ear, but there is just one problem, it's the devil talking! When the crowd is wound up and you're the only one sitting down as you recognize the deceit will make you appear as if you're not in on the grand message that's being delivered however I would rather have a billion people sitting down on me as I declare the unadulterated Word and Jesus Christ being the only one standing up in heaven as he did with Stephen in Acts Chapter 7, than to have a billion people encouraging and agreeing with me as Christ is sitting down in heaven in disapproval.

If people are taught wrong that's all the enemy needs. We are certainly experiencing the transference of the wealth of the wicked in addition to kingdom keys being transferred to the next generations. God is even eliminating people who have proven over time that they will not follow the kingdom agenda with a pure heart and love for God's people; he is replacing them with those who will.

Obedience is a key factor in determining spiritual success no doubt; nevertheless there are case by case situations in our idiosyncratic lives that the Word of God demonstrates biblical principles on how to live and handle life. The narratives in the Bible are not really for you to learn about the people of the Bible as it is for one to learn about who God is. The narratives are written so the reader can learn understand and grown into a better intimate fellowship with Almighty God. For example, the book of Daniel it shows what the Hebrew boys went through in the Babylonian context nevertheless the underlying principle of the book is that when you stand, trust, and obey God Almighty, in the face of opposition and persecution to the end, the Lord is mighty to save. Yes we learned about Daniel and the Hebrew boys and some great characteristics to adopt and live out in our faith, but **the meat of every chapter of the Bible is how Awesome God is and what he wants you to know from the narrative in retrospect to our personal relationships with him**, knowing him all the more. Every person depicted in the Bible has died physically and gone away to either heaven or Hades, yet the one who is depicted in the Bible that still lives on in every dynamic is the Great I AM who forever lives in the present. He is the one left with the believer to walk, talk, lead, direct, and guide unto all truth, not Abraham, Daniel, John the Baptist, and Mary the mother of Jesus. The lesson is of course to learn the Word of God and bind it to your head, hearts, hands, and door posts, but the real lesson is what did you learn about God? Are you getting to know who He is better? Are you able to recognize Him in your life? When things are occurring around you are you able to discern the hand of the Lord? The Voice of the Lord? Have you come to know his character, what about the Person of God the Father? The son? The Holy Spirit? Are you able to engage in a sermon and as many would say eat the meat and spit out the bones? Recognizing the wisdom of God for your life compared to what a man or woman is telling you that you should do, especially in the situation of them knowing nothing about you, your past, what you've encountered, and the assignments God has given you.

In church we often are taught never quit, never give up. When in life there are things we need to quit and give up on. Such things are quitting to allow other's opinions to validate our decisions, quitting to people please, quitting trying to fit in when you don't, giving up on trying to make everyone think you're alright as you seem to have it all together, but you really don't. Geri Scazzero wrote a book called the emotionally healthy woman which was birthed from the book emotionally healthy spirituality. These are great reads to encourage you to quit what needs to stop in your life so that you may be healthy. You won't often hear these sermons in church as the message is always don't give up, don't quit and keep hope alive, which we are motivated to do in the area of our faith! Yet this strong faith determiner and goal achieving of not quitting has paralyzed people in situations they don't know how to let go and let God in because they don't want to be deemed a "quitter". Wisdom will teach you when to hold it and when to fold it.

What are some of the key ingredients of your home? Your marriage? Your church? Your ministry? Today you hear some of the vaguest basics. It is no longer reflective of the instructions of God. The key components of your life as a believer and especially a leader should be to bind the Word of God to your forehead, to your door posts, seek ye first the kingdom of God and his righteousness and all other things will be added to you, buy the truth and do not sell it, and stand firm against the enemy even if you are the only one standing or sitting for that matter. A real believer should be able to monitor when their spiritual senses are dull. Iron sharpens iron as one man sharpens another. The goal of the enemy is to have the church so spiritually dull that it has no power against him. This is being done through the avenues of entertainment and agendas of the flesh. As long as the flesh is appeased the spirit is weakened. What appeals to the flesh? Humor, jokes, food, drink, performances, all kinds of things that are not bad, however they can be when being used to spiritually manipulate. The goal is to create an atmosphere where it is easy to manipulate because it appeals to your fleshly nature, weakening the spiritual nature, for it is by the Spirit of God that we overcome the enemy, and we cannot overcome him in any other way. I have been blessed to be under amazing shepherds who leave no room for the atmosphere to be tainted. As a young girl growing up I watched my shepherd. He exemplified the essence of a real shepherd to me. One of the things that ministered to my soul about him is that he worships with his flock.

He worships with his congregation and he is there overseeing the operation from start to finish. He sees what is going on the moment service begins and he is there to see what occurs throughout the service until it is well and over. That speaks volumes that he truly is overseeing the souls of those God sent to him.

We have a human make up and a divine make up. Christ is a great example how to live among people loving them and ministering to them yet knowing when to draw away to be strengthened in prayer and alone time with God. Mature believers can shift in the spirit at any time necessary. We could be at the mall, the store, at the game and deal with people all around us yet drawing away at the same time as the Holy Spirit directs. That is why you can listen to lecture or be in a service and move immediately into your spiritual language. It becomes who you are.

Today we live in an era of Christian celebrities. Usually these are people with a natural talent or God given gift and ability. We all know the young handsome gifted young man who gets all the ladies attention in the church. Knowing he will not commit to all of the young ladies he gives time and attention to, yet it's always worth playing with their emotions just to see if he could get them if he wanted. It all has to do with his ego and pride to confirm to himself that she too is interested in him. Eventually the broken hearted young ladies understand that he never interacted for a serious commitment, but only to paint a picture and message to himself that he's the bomb. The same goes for young ladies who are gifted knowing she won't offer her hand in marriage to the many admirers she has, but it's worth getting the attention anyway even if that means disappointed guys at the end of the day. Beware of such, and if you see any of these things, take it to the Lord only in prayer, and trust that God will take care of the rest.

Why would anyone spiritually manipulate in the church you may ask? Because we are fighting principalities, spiritual wickedness in high places according to Ephesians 6:10-18. The very thing that is to be strengthened according to God's Word is our Spirit. There are churches today that have tried to eliminate the spiritual all together. You rarely hear anyone speak in a spiritual language and if so, many are frightened or offended. Ephesians 6:18 says to pray in the Spirit at all times. Being filled with God's Spirit is essential to living a victorious life in Christ. If Christ had to be filled with the Spirit of God, why is it that modern day believers think they don't have to be? If you are saved but not filled with God's Spirit with the evidence of speaking in other tongues, pray to God and ask that he will fill you with his Spirit. You may have necessary steps to go through in your sanctification process depending on where you are with your walk with Christ, yet open your mouth and allow your spirit to pray and practice praying in the spirit every single day for thirty minutes to an hour until you are praying not from your head or mind but from your Spirit. Church should be the last place we are apologizing for being "too spiritual".

Today many traditional preachers are being mocked and made fun of by modern day relevant teachers. Many people are being taught that churches that are not full are not full because of country preachers who can't feel where you are. There is a reality to preachers not being able to relate to our lives in certain areas if they have not experienced those areas yet. God still chooses the man or woman of God he desires to use for the kingdom of God and whether that person is deemed country or not is irrelevant in the perspective of the twenty first century preachers is no concern of God's. If God is using someone to usher in souls to the kingdom of God, I am not understanding why one would think it is okay to put that servant of God down in the presence of people who have no idea of what that servant of God has faced to take a stand as such for God. It certainly belittles another servant of God and brings a comparison with a message that one is better than another. 2 Corinthians 10:12 says those leaders that compare themselves are not wise, yet this is exactly what is being done. No matter how boldly you go to the throne of grace, it will always be mistaken by arrogance by those who don't like you, regardless how arrogant they may go, and label themselves as bold.

Nevertheless, erroneous teachings are turning many people (especially young people and new believers) who do not know the things of God, away from the very teachings and source of power that will save their souls, strengthen their walks with Christ, and defeat Satan's works in the earth. Because one may be excellent at speaking, teaching, and motivating doesn't mean they are spiritual, however these things are mistaken as being spiritual with people who are not familiar with God, such as new believers, particularly those who have been ensconced in the world deeply prior to coming to Christ. God can use those things to edify the body of Christ, but remember the enemy is a mocker, he doesn't create anything, but always copies what God does. Therefore if he can use the same thing to manipulate people in thinking what is going on is spiritual, he will. A trust and approval will come into play with the people being led astray where the enemy desires to use that influence for the agenda he has. Because one can speak well or paint a nice picture does not mean they know God or have spiritual revelation.

There is nothing cool about mocking and making fun of preachers who are standing on godly principles. If God called someone to do an assignment that is different from yours do not talk about him or her, encourage them. You will have people thinking that what he is doing is silly but it could be god's assignment on his life, so who are you to call God's assigned child country or irrelevant because it doesn't mirror yours? According to 1 Corinthians 1: 18-23 the message of the cross is foolish to those who are headed for destruction! But we who are being saved know it is the very power of God. As the Scriptures says in 1 Corinthians 1:19,

> "I will destroy the wisdom of the wise
> and discard the intelligence of the intelligent."

So where does this leave the philosophers, the scholars, and the world's brilliant debaters? God has made the wisdom of this world look foolish. Since God in his wisdom saw to it that the world would never know him through human wisdom, he has used our foolish preaching to save those who believe. It is foolish to the Jews, who ask for signs from heaven. And it is foolish to the Greeks, who seek human wisdom. So when we preach that Christ was crucified, the Jews are offended and the Gentiles say it is all nonsense.

To me that sounds like your soul is saved by the foolishness of preachers. There is an element of humility that is necessary in order to represent God by totally losing your reputation and getting out of your comfort zone. In Africa, you will see how people will literally roll around on the ground to worship God demonstrating that God is everything to them, and that he is more than worthy for them to be humbled as low to the ground. If that type of worship were present in modern day American churches, security would probably be assigned to carry someone as such out. Modern day Christians are not always equipped to lead others to Christ. If your first lady or leaders can't go down to the bus station to witness and win souls to Christ, why are they positioned where they are? If your armor bearer can't go to the street corner and effectively lead someone to Jesus Christ right there confidently, then what are we doing?

Church is no longer a special place we gather bringing our best before God as it has become a casual entity to come before God any type of way. This does not negate the fact that we can come boldly before the throne of grace at all. This is to point out the way we approach God must be valued and understood. Our clothes could be very nice and our hearts could be a hot mess, this is true as it is not about what one puts on but what is in the heart and the spirit. Yet, if you'd dress up to see the President of the United States how much more should you dress well and present your best in the house of God. The house of God is where the saints of the Most High God meet for corporate worship. It is paramount to be able to relate to those who are un-churched or who are coming out of the world, but we do not have to compromise the high calling of God on your life to do so.

You often hear that it is not about clothes but it is about souls. This may be hard to accept when you have on jeans and a t shirt which appears down to earth and humble, but your jeans, t-shirt shoes, and watch costs more than the average church member's mortgage. One may be dressed in a suit and tie that they bought from the goodwill, and they could be judged for trying too hard and not coming as they are, when it could be that the person wanted to honor God and reverence him with their best.

At the same time if someone comes in church with jeans and a t-shirt that could very well be their best and they could have a heartfelt relationship with God. We are not to judge.

The point is we need to stop worrying about what someone has on or don't have on and worry about what is in their heart and the condition of their heart and soul. Young ladies who may not dress appropriate to church need to have a mind and spiritual makeover before they have an actual dress make over. Give them time and prayerfully they will learn. My opinion is that one should wear their best to God's house, whether that is a suit and tie, or jeans if that is their best. I don't think we should be casual with God and informal with Him as we approach his house. Not that we worship the building, but it is his presence that is being honored. That is not to say that every time you go to church, even if it's to drop something off, pick something up, going in for prayer, or something like this, that you have to be dressed to the nines.

A construction worker may have had it approved for him to leave his job for an hour to come and pray with the congregation. He may not have time to go home and change as he may have to go back to work from church. Does this mean he does not honor God because of how he came dressed? Absolutely not, it shows how much he honors to put God first that he'd leave work to come and pray with the saints on his break. The take away is, let God do the judging as he sees and knows all things.

I would think as much as God is grieved by divorce; he is grieved by his church not being in a healthy state, or by believers condemning one another. Let's not just assume that our lives, marriages, relationships, churches, jobs, and families are healthy, effective, and keeping the mission, vision, and values that have been put in place by God's Word. Take it a step further and monitor these areas and contribute where and as the Holy Spirit guides you. Let each man examine himself and sharpen one another in love as iron sharpens iron. The church will be judged first according to 1 Peter 4:17, before the world. What are you and I going to do together to make sure we weight out on the scales as we are the living, breathing, alive church of Jesus Christ! If you have taken the time to read this book, I want to applaud you for reading the entire way through this controversial perspective. Prayerfully you received something out if beneficial for your own calling and purpose no matter if you've mastered ministry and have arrived, or if you have just answered God's call on your life. Perhaps it has given you some things to contemplate for your ministry, small group, friendship, marriage, or ministry. I pray it has. This book was not insight to tell anyone what to do as much as it was designed to be a tool for you to think outside of familiarity within your ministry operations. It is to challenge where you are, in examining any area of the kingdom God has called you to be responsible for. If you are a part of the remnant of believers that God is ushering into the next dimension keep in mind God will instruct you on things we are to do and keep traditionally, at the same time, he will teach you what things not to do, and when the shift or new move of God is occurring. Take note of your spiritual surroundings and be flexible to adjust anything necessary to align with healthy practices and follow Godly leadership submitted under authority that follows Christ. If you were convicted about any manipulations perhaps you have done to another, I want you to know that God is a forgiving God and with a pure authentic repentance he will weigh your new heart. If you have acknowledged areas where you have taken advantage of people due to delegated authority given to you, I applaud you. That is one of the hardest things to do. The fact that you would even admit it, exposes it, and deal with it, says that I am able to commit to a better future than my past. I certainly have had to confess in areas as such. So how do we implement Christ and a perfect Kingdom in a fallen broken world? Religion will tell you that with mistakes made your life is not representing the Word of God, you don't qualify, or that you have to go through a million steps and works to reflect God or be honorable in his sight, yet remember that Christ didn't wait until we got everything together until he died for us, he died for us yet while we were sinners as stated in Romans 5:8. I know there will be haters, who know they have read a great book, but just because I wrote it will downplay it. Nevertheless, my prayer is that you have been sharpened, even if you choose not to share it with others.

I strongly encourage each individual reading this to take responsibility for your own relationship with God and not depend upon your anointed husband, or anointed wife's, or anointed pastor's, family member's, or friend's relationship with God only. You are not granted Salvation only because someone connected to you is saved, each person must accept the Lord Jesus in their heart, believe he is the Son of God in their heart, and confess with their mouth their sins and that Jesus is Lord. I encourage all readers to implement the discerning reflections in this book to enhance health in areas necessary for people to be liberated and ministries to be restored where needed, which will manifest in the healed and ready bride of Jesus Christ. The multitudes will begin flocking to your ministry as there is a hunger and thirst for liberated worship with pure authority that keeps us all safe. You may say that I am crazy to write, publish, and promote such a book. You are right. I am crazy about Jesus, the church, and loving people! If that means an attacked reputation, so be it, been there, done that, I have let go to let God.

Always remember that God is always watching and reading the scales of the hearts of men. Psalm 139:23 is where David cried to the Lord saying, search me Oh God, and know my heart, try me, and know my anxious thoughts, and see if there be any wicked way in me, and lead me in the everlasting way. Let's plan to weight out in God's favor! To God be all the glory!

Printed in the United States
By Bookmasters